ELON
UNIVERSITY

**Compliments of the Office of Leadership
and Professional Development**

**Check out our website
www.elon.edu/olpd
for programs and trainings.**

A GOOD JOB

René Jackson

A GOOD JOB

Campus Employment as a
High-Impact Practice

George S. McClellan, Kristina Creager,
and Marianna Savoca

Foreword by George D. Kuh

STERLING, VIRGINIA

Published by Stylus Publishing, LLC.
22883 Quicksilver Drive
Sterling, Virginia 20166-2102

Library of Congress Cataloging-in-Publication Data
Names: McClellan, George S., author. |
Creager, Kristina, 1984- author. |
Savoca, Marianna, 1968- author.
Title: A good job : campus employment as a high-impact practice /
George S. McClellan, Kristina Creager, and Marianna Savoca; foreword
by George D. Kuh.
Description: First edition. |
Sterling, Virginia : Stylus Publishing, LLC, [2018] |
Includes bibliographical references and index.
Identifiers: LCCN 2017039357 (print) |
LCCN 2017060671 (ebook) |
ISBN 9781620364734 (Library networkable e-edition) |
ISBN 9781620364741 (Consumer e-edition) |
ISBN 9781620364727 (paperback : acid free paper) |
ISBN 9781620364710 (cloth : acid free paper) |
ISBN 9781620364741 (consumer e-edition)
Subjects: LCSH: College student development programs--United
States. |
College students--Employment--United States. |
Universities and colleges--United States--Employees. |
Education, Cooperative--United States. |
College dropouts--United States--Prevention.
Classification: LCC LB2343.4 (ebook) |
LCC LB2343.4 .M44 2018 (print) |
DDC 378.1/98--dc23
LC record available at https://lccn.loc.gov/2017039357

13-digit ISBN: 978-1-62036-471-0 (cloth)
13-digit ISBN: 978-1-62036-472-7 (paperback)
13-digit ISBN: 978-1-62036-473-4 (library networkable e-edition)
13-digit ISBN: 978-1-62036-474-1 (consumer e-edition)

Printed in the United States of America

All first editions printed on acid-free paper
that meets the American National Standards Institute
Z39-48 Standard.

Bulk Purchases
Quantity discounts are available for use in workshops and for
staff development.
Call 1-800-232-0223

First Edition, 2018

CONTENTS

FIGURES AND TABLES

Figures

Tables

FOREWORD

Why and How We Can Increase the Educational Value of Working During College

When I was in college, a handful of my classmates worked off campus. Paul was one of these off-campus workers. His junior and senior years, Paul was on the dock at the local United Parcel Service depot from 4:30 a.m. to 7:30 a.m. three or more days a week, depending on the time of year. We were in the same social fraternity, so I occasionally caught a glimpse of him when he returned to the house after work to take a well-earned quick shower and sprint to class. Like me, Paul was the first in his family to go to college, and he needed the money to augment his financial aid package in order to make ends meet.

Paul was somewhat of an anomaly, given the nature of the times and my alma mater, a rural Phi Beta Kappa residential liberal arts college on the fringe of a town with 8,000 people. Most of my peers relied on family contributions, summer jobs, and occasional weekend labor to cover beer money and other incidentals.

I did not know then that since colonial times many college students had combined work and their studies, as explained in chapter 1. Moreover, as the authors of this volume make plain in various places, working while going to school is the norm today. Indeed, about half of undergraduates self-identify as students working to meet their expenses; another quarter describe themselves as employees who are taking classes. Almost 25% of students at baccalaureate-granting institutions, and 41% at 2-year colleges work at least 35 hours per week (McCormick, Moore, & Kuh, 2010). With so many students working, and such large numbers devoting a considerable amount of time to one or more jobs, work is—after going to class—the most common activity in which undergraduates engage.

At the same time, many employers are concerned that too many college graduates are not prepared to function effectively in the workplace (Hart Research Associates, 2015). Among employer worries is that while students generally know a good deal about the subjects they studied, they are not able to readily transfer what they know to the unstructured problems and circumstances they encounter on the job. This is a major reason employers much prefer to hire college graduates who have had an internship or a similar kind of experience, such as a co-op.

Yet, as noted in this book the effects of work and college success are mixed. Yes, the money students receive in turn for their labor can be the difference between going to and staying in college or dropping out. There can be other benefits as well, such as an opportunity to acquire and hone practical competencies (e.g., time management) that employers value.

At the same time, some studies show the number of hours students work may have a deleterious influence on persistence and time to degree (King, 2003; Tuttle, McKinney, & Rago, 2005). Working many hours a week also makes it difficult if not impossible for students to participate in activities linked to such desirable learning outcomes as service-learning, research with a faculty or staff member, study away, and other high-impact practices (Kuh, 2008; Kuh, O'Donnell, & Reed, 2013). The term *high-impact practices* (HIPs) refers to institutionally structured student experiences inside or outside the classroom that are associated with elevated performance across multiple engagement activities and desired outcomes, such as deep learning, persistence, and satisfaction with college. More about HIPs later.

Too often overlooked in discussions about working in college is recognizing that the job often puts students in situations where they can apply what they are learning from their studies. This allows students to demonstrate—for better or worse—how well they deal with messy, unstructured situations and interact with other people.

Another aspect related to the interplay between college-going and work with nontrivial implications is goal realization, which is an early college predictor of persistence (Kuh, Kinzie, Buckley, Bridges, & Hayek, 2007). Goal realization is a state of awareness whereby students are able to find personal meaning and relevance in at least some aspects of what they are studying. In this sense, goal realization is represented by being able to recognize and appreciate how to use the knowledge and proficiencies one is acquiring in some areas of life that are considered important. Students who exhibit this disposition are more likely to persist and be satisfied with their college experience.

Most faculty and staff are not aware of the importance of goal realization to student success or how to foster it. One promising approach toward this end is to use the work experience as a vehicle to help students see and realize the tangible applications of their studies to common, practical situations through connecting to their work what they are learning inside and outside of class. But making such connections is not a simple matter.

One reason why transferring classroom learning to the work setting is challenging is that many students—especially but not only 18- and 19-year olds—are mired in the dualistic stage of intellectual and cognitive development. That is, they tend to see information as either right or wrong; ambiguity and complexity, along with abstract concepts—the main diet of the general education course packed into the first two years of college—tend to be beyond their grasp. Thus, dualistic students tend to become frustrated with or avoid ideas that are very difficult to comprehend, preferring fairly uncomplicated, straightforward explanations and activities that have concrete applications to practical, real-time problems or situations.

In large part, this is why most first-year students taking, for example, a lecture-oriented eighteenth-century literature course have trouble finding anything in the readings or class discussions that might be germane to their intended major or realizing how to use the information in their part-time job at, say, the campus recreation center. These kinds of academic offerings, including other large, lecture-heavy general psychology and science classes—staple general education offerings in most undergraduate programs—are perceived as uninteresting, confusing, or irrelevant to their pressing priorities. Such a circumstance leads many students to wonder whether college—an increasingly costly endeavor—is worth it.

Imagine, however, if there were a purposeful and thoughtful effort to connect campus employment to curricular content. For example, imagine that a featured component of the part-time campus recreation center job included periodic structured, focused conversations with the work supervisor in the company of some peer coworkers about what they are learning from one or more of their classes that they are using in their recreation center job and vice versa. Initial conversations of this nature can be brutally awkward and paralyzed by silence; indeed, most students have difficulty saying anything material. Most often, they have not before thought about the prospect that there *should be links between work and classroom learning*, or even that they *could* think deeply about such matters. Over time, between and during such discussions, students begin to pay attention and bring into awareness in real time how some experiences from the job make classroom learning less abstract and more practical.

Of course, not everything introduced in every course will be applicable to every job, nor will every day on any job present opportunities to draw on something from the courses a student is taking. But only a few examples are needed to demonstrate the relevance of one's studies to matters that students consider personally important and meaningful.

These kinds of interactions also can stimulate and further the development of a capacity for thinking about one's own thinking in terms of the value of what one is learning and its concrete, real-world applications. This form of intrapersonal interrogation is a kind of metacognitive transformer through which one learns how to connect various experiences inside and outside class with other aspects of life. By discussing these reflections and related activities with work supervisors and their peers, students are able to construct and practice describing key components of their learning and what they can do with it, which will be invaluable later when interviewing for other jobs on campus and after college.

The benefits of connecting work with learning are multiplied if students are building an ePortfolio at the same time and integrating key features of their job into the process. Briefly, an ePortfolio is far more than a record-keeping system. When implemented with a high degree of integrity, it is a comprehensive pedagogical approach that provides a framework for organizing learning. Building the ever-evolving repository requires active learner engagement and reflection about the relevance of the learning artifacts that populate the ePortfolio as well as the process of learning that contributed to the desired outcomes (Eynon & Gambino, 2017). Also important is that faculty and other educational professionals are involved in guiding student reflection and discussion about the meaning of the curated evidence of authentic student learning. Such artifacts may take the form of papers, demonstrations, project reports, and—apropos of the topic of this volume—supervisor evaluations and the student's own valuation of the work experience in relation to the intended outcomes of one's major or institutional learning goals. When the ePortfolio is integrated into the emerging comprehensive educational record that augments the traditional academic transcript by documenting the proficiencies students have acquired beyond the classroom (Matthews, Zanville, & Duncan, 2016), what students have learned and can do will become more transparent, understandable, and meaningful to faculty, staff, employers, and students themselves.

From this brief discussion, two points stand out. First, work has a non-trivial yet often underestimated influence on students in terms of their making meaning of the value of what they are learning and being satisfied with the college experience. Second, the times compel colleges and universities to ensure that working during college adds educational value rather than competes with or distracts from the academic program.

Indeed, I am persuaded that employment during college—especially but not only campus jobs—can be structured in ways to mimic the attributes of and outcomes associated with such HIPs as learning communities, service-learning courses, and first-year seminars (Kuh, 2008). There is fairly strong evidence that participating in 1 or more of the now 11 HIPs (Watson, Kuh, Rhodes, Penny Light, & Chen, 2016)—when implemented well—is positively associated with persistence and desired learning outcomes, valued by the academy as well as employers (Kuh, 2008; Kuh, O'Donnell, & Reed,

2013). That is, students who participate in these programs are more engaged overall in the college experience and gain more from their studies. Moreover, while all students benefit from participating in HIPs, they seem to have a compensatory effect for students who are less well prepared academically or who are members of historically underserved groups; the performance of these students seems to be stronger than what might be otherwise expected (Finley & McNair, 2013; Kuh, 2008).

I have briefly described not merely an abstract depiction of what *could happen* if we intentionally tried to link work with learning during college; rather, it is the premise on which the seven federally designated "work colleges" (Work Colleges Consortium, 2015) are grounded and also sparked the development of the University of Iowa's Guided Reflection on Work (GROW) initiative (University of Iowa, 2016). GROW is one of the more advanced, comprehensive efforts that can inform and be adapted to other institutions. Other approaches are described in the chapters that follow.

Final Words

The contemporary college student experience differs in many ways from that of many current faculty members and administrators. With so many undergraduates today working while pursuing their studies, it is incumbent on college and university leaders, faculty, academic advisers, student affairs professionals, and others committed to helping students to become more informed about how to harness the benefits of employment and both student engagement and educational outcomes.

Granted, finding ways to connect academics and employment is only one of the many practices that institutions must have in place to enrich student learning and help more students survive and thrive in college (Kuh, Kinzie, Schuh, & Whitt, 2010). Even so, promoting greater levels of deep learning and goal realization through the work experience is one of the few promising approaches that does not require additional resources to implement. This timely book can help us better understand how to make working during college more educationally purposeful to the benefit of students, institutions, and employers.

George D. Kuh
Senior Scholar, National Institute for
Learning Outcomes Assessment
Chancellor's Professor of Higher Education
Emeritus, Indiana University

ACKNOWLEDGMENTS

George is thankful to students for whom he has served and with whom he has learned and to the staff and faculty with whom he has served for 35 years as a student affairs professional, particularly those who are members of the Indiana University–Purdue University Fort Wayne (IPFW) community that he proudly called home for nearly a third of those years. He also appreciates the students with whom he has discussed this project for sharing their experiences and insights, including the students of Mimi Benjamin's SAHE 781 course at Indiana University of Pennsylvania. Special thanks to Chancellor Vicky Carwein for her support of his involvement in professional associations and scholarly activities and to Danita Lehman, who has been the keeper of time, space, and sanity in the office. George has been blessed to have benefitted from fabulous teachers and mentors throughout his life, among them Margaret (Peggy) Barr, Jim Carlton, Dale Breckel, Robert Menges, Saunie Taylor, and Doug Woodard. He is grateful to his parents, who made it clear from the beginning that going to college was the goal, even though neither of them had that opportunity themselves. It probably never entered their minds that he might never leave once he got there. George is also grateful to his friends for their support and steadying influence, particularly Steve Grud, Shelly Lowe, Jason Laker, Joe Minonne, Chad Richmond, Jeff Sun, and the Practical Theater Company /Rockme Foundation nation. He professes his love for Chicago and all its sports teams, the blues, Mick Foley and the Undertaker, Cajun/Creole culture and food, and fried bologna sandwiches. In regard to this book, thanks to George D. Kuh for a great dinner conversation that helped crystalize the project and strengthen the resolve to undertake it. Special thanks to Krissy Creager and Marianna Savoca, who accepted the invitation to get involved and who have been thoroughly enjoyable and truly remarkable partners throughout the process of bringing this book forward.

Krissy thanks her students at IPFW, both past and present, for being the reason she happily comes into work every day. She equally extends gratitude to her incredible team in Student Success and Transitions (SST) and to an extraordinary group of colleagues and friends throughout the campus beside whom it is a privilege and a blessing to serve. Particular thanks to Kim Wagner, Ken Christmon, James Velez, Carl Drummond, Julie Yoder, and Lynette

Coughlin for their support. She is indebted to her parents and family for a lifetime of unending support and love. Additionally, she owes much appreciation to David Forgues, Michele Murray, and Jeremy Stringer, who lit the student development flame many years ago and continue to fan it regularly. Krissy's goal is to positively impact lives the way they did hers. Likewise, she wishes to extend love and thanks to her Manicur 2016 faculty mentors and cohort for modeling leadership, collegiality, and student service! Thanks to Marianna Savoca, a newfound friend and partner in this process, for the constant support and insight. Finally, Krissy wishes to thank George McClellan, who brought her to IPFW eight years ago and who entrusted her with the concept and confidence within this book as well as his Student Affairs Division throughout his incredible tenure.

Marianna is grateful to Rich Feller, Jackie Peila-Shuster, Gene Gloeckner, Mary King, and Linda Kuk for mentoring her as a scholar. She is also grateful to her family for their steadfast support of her professional involvement. She is thankful to George D. Kuh for introducing her to the project, and to George McClellan and Krissy Creager for giving her the opportunity to work with them. She has learned so much from all of them!

George, Krissy, and Marianna thank the students and colleagues who have helped inform this project. Thanks to the scholars and scholar-practitioners whose work has informed the discussion and to the reviewers whose comments have helped strengthen it. Last, but by no means least, tremendous gratitude to David Brightman and the team at Stylus Publishing for their willingness to give this book a home and for their support throughout in bringing it to the readers.

I

STUDENT EMPLOYMENT ON CAMPUS

An Overview

Collge students in American universities from colonial times to the contemporary period have encountered opportunities and obstacles when it comes to achieving their academic goals. Among the opportunities are the diversity of institutional types and academic programs available; the quality of the curriculum and faculty; the financial support available through family, philanthropy, and financial aid; and the freedom of inquiry and expression. Over the years, students interested in pursuing a college education have confronted limited higher education opportunities based on development of the higher education system, geography, or discriminatory law or policy. They have also faced disruption of studies as a result of economic downturn or military conflict at home or abroad. Of course, throughout the history of American higher education, students have also encountered the challenges of life circumstances and personal finances that make study more difficult if not impossible. Like those who came before them, current students face a broad and unique set of challenges as they pursue their higher education goals. As Tuttle, McKinney, and Rago (2005) observe

> Today's college students face a complex set of dilemmas about whether to attend college, where to attend, how to pay, how much to work, how many jobs to take, how to pay credit card bills and car payments, how to juggle family and children, and how to balance these competing priorities while in school. (2005, para. 2)

Working during their college years is nothing new for students in American higher education (Kincaid, 1996; McCormick, Moore, & Kuh, 2010; Tuttle et al., 2005), but the proportion of students working and the number of hours students are working have grown markedly over the course of our nation's history (Tuttle et al., 2005). These changes reflect shifts in the diversity of students enrolled and in public policy with regard to the financing of postsecondary education (Pusser, 2010). Students enrolled in college during the earliest days of American higher education were almost exclusively young able-bodied men born into relative affluence. Thankfully, over time, student bodies grew to include women, people of color, people with disabilities, adult learners, and people of varied socioeconomic statuses (Ortiz & Waterman, 2016; Schuh, 2016; Washington, 1996). The American people, including students themselves, have supported students in higher education through direct payment of tuition and fees, philanthropic giving for scholarships, and through the use of government funds to support state and federal financial aid programs (Johnstone, 1999). Government aid typically takes the form of either grants or loans. Federal aid is by far the largest single component of these government aid programs, and loans have been part of the federal aid mix since the late 1950s. However, beginning in the mid-1970s, there has been a marked shift upward in loan programs as a proportion of federal aid (Washington, 1996), reflecting a shift in the view of higher education from largely that of being a public good to an increasing perception of it as a private good.

Not surprisingly, these shifts in who is attending college and how they are funding their education are reflected in fundamental ways in the student experience. Not terribly long ago, staff and faculty discouraged entering students from working during the freshman year (Noel, 1996). Today "work is a fundamental part of life for many undergraduate students. The average college student is now not only employed but also working a substantial number of hours" (Perna, 2010, p. xiii). Working while in college is a defining characteristic of today's student experience. Indeed, Kincaid (1996) observes, "Student employment is, after class, the most universal experience of college students" (p. 3).

In this book we explore college student employment, specifically undergraduate student employment on campus. This chapter provides context for that exploration, offering a broad overview of college student employment. Subsequent chapters focus on frameworks for considering campus employment: student development, career development, learning, retention and student success, management and supervision, and legal issues. Building on the preceding chapters, in the concluding chapter we argue for a campus environment in which college student employment as a high-impact practice is a purposeful and powerful component of student and institutional success.

We open this chapter with a brief history of college student employment and highlight the nexus between college student employment and the origins of the student affairs profession. Next, we present information regarding how many students work, where they work, and a bit about why they work. *Work* is defined, drawing attention to various dimensions of its social construction. The important constructs of students who work and workers who study are also introduced and described. This sets the table for an invitation to consider various dimensions or facets of student employment before moving into discussion of the student work experience on campus—what it is and what it could be. The subsequent chapters in this book focus on the latter consideration.

History

Just as American college students have always faced opportunities and challenges in pursuing their college aspirations, so too have they always worked. Tuttle and colleagues (2005) state, "Historically, working through college has been part of the college experience for much of American history" (para. 5). McCormick, Moore, and Kuh (2010) similarly observe, "College students have combined work and schooling since the earliest colleges were established in the United States" (p. 179).

Given this long tradition of hardworking students, that there is not more in the literature on this history is somewhat surprising. Individual biographies or autobiographies as well as institutional histories may contain snippets here and there, but an authoritative single source seems lacking. Rick Kincaid's (n.d.) informal history stands out as the lone resource for those interested in this subject, and the information in the remainder of this section is drawn exclusively and substantially from his work.

Very little information is available on the earliest student workers. Zecharia Brigden, a student at Harvard University who graduated in the late 1650s, is noted as the first student mentioned as having worked his way through college. One suspects this mention might have lapsed from public attention were it not for the fact that Brigden went on to be an astronomer of note in the mid-1600s. Student work in colonial times often took the form of students hiring themselves out as tutors for the children of local families as well as serving as apprentices in local businesses. There was no organized program for student employment, but faculty members would help students in need identify opportunities, including small jobs on campus. As colleges grew, institutions like Harvard, Yale, and Princeton developed more organized student employment programs to assist students.

The passage of the Morrill Acts of 1862 and 1890 helped spur the growth of student employment on campus. These pieces of legislation provided resources to create public universities designed to spur economic development and scientific discovery, particularly in the areas of agriculture and the mechanical arts. Meeting this development mission required creating on-campus facilities that served as practical learning environments as well as hubs of campus employment. Given their focus, these institutions were often located in what were at the time more rural areas of the state. Students moved to those campuses, and those students needed housing. The residential and dining facilities that grew up in response also became centers of student employment. Many of the students attracted to these institutions were from middle-class families where a strong work ethic was the norm, so it seemed entirely appropriate to students and parents alike that students would work to help pay their way through school—not only as a matter of need but also a matter of appropriate conduct. Meanwhile, students at universities on the East Coast were showing an entrepreneurial spirit by developing businesses to sell goods and services to their fellow students. Also during this period between the American Civil War and the onset of the Great Depression cooperative education programs were developed, and students began to arrange with faculty members and local businesses for learning employment opportunities.

The Depression and the New Deal saw the federal government once again play a role in expanding student employment. The National Youth Administration Student Work Program, a forerunner of the College Work Study Program, was founded in 1935 to support work for high school and college students. It ran for about eight years. A 1937 study from Columbia University noted that 65% of undergraduate and graduate students in the 1920s and 1930s were working (Tuttle et al., 2005).

Following World War II and with the passage of the GI Bill, there was an influx of adult students into higher education, students who differed significantly from their traditional counterparts. One difference was that the adult students tended to be working people who were taking courses to pursue a degree as opposed to students who worked to support or extend their education. This distinction is important when considering student employment and is discussed in greater detail later in this chapter. The growth in community colleges during the 1960s saw more workers who study moving into American higher education.

Also in the 1960s, the College Work Study program (hereafter referred to by its contemporary name of the Federal Work Study [FWS] program) was born. A part of the federal government's War on Poverty, this program provides funding for a substantial portion of student wages where employment is awarded by the institution as part of financial aid packaging. It is intended to provide support for part-time positions for undergraduate or graduate students with financial need (Federal Student Aid, n.d.b). The Middle Income Assistance Act in the 1970s established the Job Location and Development (JLD) program as part of the broader FWS program. JLD locates and develops off-campus job opportunities for students who are currently enrolled in eligible institutions of higher education and who want jobs regardless of financial need. This means that jobs may be located and developed under the JLD Program for FWS and non-FWS eligible students. (Federal Student Aid, n.d.a, pp. 6–47)

Funding was stable for FWS during the 1980s, which meant there was a relative decline in support given the growth in enrollments and costs of living and education. In the 1990s the government added a requirement that 5% (then increased to 7%) of FWS funds be used to support community service positions off campus (Baum, 2010).

It is clear from Kincaid's (n.d.) account of college student employment that national economic conditions and federal economic and education policy have played important roles in the development of college student employment, particularly campus employment. Another factor has been the growth of the higher education sector. The American higher education landscape has grown from Harvard, the original colonial university, to over 4,000 institutions, and enrollment has grown to more than 16 million students (C. Kaufman, n.d.; Thelin, Edwards, & Moyen, n.d.). The growth of American higher education extends beyond the number of institutions or the number of students enrolled in those institutions. Growth has taken place in curricular and cocurricular programs as well. Examples include the growth in libraries, research and research facilities, recreational facilities, information technology infrastructure, residence halls, and student success support programs. Each and every one of these growth areas provides additional opportunities for student employment on campus.

One interesting historical development in higher education and student employment in college is the emergence of work colleges. At these institutions, students fund a significant portion, if not all, of their tuition and fees through work at the institution. The Work Colleges Consortium's member institutions, some as old as 100 years, offer students an opportunity to both earn a degree and have a rich learning experience through a service-learning program on campus (Work Colleges Consortium, 2014a). The seven member institutions are Alice Lloyd College, Berea College, Blackburn College, College of the Ozarks, Ecclesia College, Sterling College, and Warren Wilson College. All are liberal arts institutions, and several feature a curricular focus on issues of the environment and sustainability (Work Colleges Consortium, 2014b).

Another historical note is the relationship between college student employment and the development of the student affairs profession. This nexus has at least two strands. First, student affairs has substantial roots in the area of employment. Coomes and Gerda (2016) point out that Walter Scott, one of the early important figures in what is now known as *student affairs*, had an interest in using psychology and testing to match people to positions. The interest of Scott and others was a precursor to what Coomes and Gerda describe as an era of vocationalism early in the profession. In fact, the origins of the American College Personnel Association (ACPA), one of two large generalist professional associations in student affairs, are in the National Association of Appointment Secretaries, a group representing the university staff members we know today as *career services professionals.* The second strand of the nexus is the rise of student affairs programs in colleges and universities across the country. As student bodies grew and diversified along with student expectations of their universities, student affairs units developed programs to serve the changing population and meet emerging needs. Programs for orientation, diversity, health education, residential learning, recreation, and more were introduced, and student workers have performed much of the work done in these programs and others like them. The growth of the student affairs profession and the growth of campus employment for students are most certainly correlated.

Current Employment Statistics

Having offered a brief history of college student employment, we turn our attention to information about current employment of students. A good deal of such information is available from a variety of sources. Studies show that the percentage of American college students working grew from 40% in 1961 to 80% in 2000 (Tuttle et al., 2005).

> In 2003–2004, about 75% of dependent undergraduates and 80% of independent undergraduates worked while enrolled (Perna, Cooper, & Li, 2007). Working dependent undergraduates averaged 24 hours of employment per week while enrolled, and working independent undergraduates averaged 34.5 hours per work (Perna et al., 2007). (Perna, 2010, p. xiii)

Data from the National Center for Education Statistics in 2009 show that 79% of undergraduates work at least one hour per week (Perozzi, 2009). A 2010 Noel-Levitz report indicates 21% of entering first-year students intended to work 1 to 10 hours per week; 29%, 11 to 20 hours per week; and 26%, 20 or more hours per week (Rowh, 2014).

The work of McCormick and colleagues (2010), drawing on data from the 2008 National Survey of Student Engagement (NSSE), is particularly rich in describing current student employment (see Table 1.1). The NSSE is administered to a substantial number of first-year students and seniors across a wide variety of institutional types around the country.

TABLE 1.1
Current Student Employment

	Full-time first year	Part-time first-year	Full-time senior	Part-time senior
% Working	46.5	76.3	73.9	84.2
% Not working	53.5	23.7	26.1	15.8
% Working on campus	20.7	11.5	30.4	13.2
% Working off campus	30.9	69.4	53.7	76.8

Note. The percentage working on campus and the percentage working off campus do not equal the percentage of students working because some students work both on and off campus.
Source. Adapted from McCormick, Moore, & Kuh (2010).

A relatively small percentage of students reported working both on- and off-campus. For full-time students, about 5% of first-years and 10% of seniors held positions both on- and off-campus.

First-year students attending part-time were more likely to work a greater number of hours than were their full-time counterparts. Almost 14% of part-time first-year students reported working between 21 and 30 hours per week as opposed to only 8.7% of their full-time peers, and 41.8% of part-time first-year students worked 31 or more hours per week while only 5.3% of their full-time counterparts did the same. The pattern for seniors is more mixed. Only 14.2% of part-time seniors said they worked 21 to 30 hours per week, whereas 16.9% of full-time seniors said they worked as much. The most marked distinction is that 51.9% of part-time seniors say they worked 31 or more hours per week, but only 13.8% of full-time seniors put in as many work hours.

Tuttle and colleagues (2005) point out that students of color are likely to work more hours than do White students, with roughly one-third of African American and Latino students working 36-plus hours per week. Kasworm (2010) reported students 25 years of age or older were more likely to work than their younger counterparts. Not surprisingly, students living on campus were more likely to work on campus than students living off campus (McCormick et al., 2010). Baum (2010) found that 10% of students who work do so on their own campus; 68% work at a for-profit firm; 10% work at a not-for-profit entity; 7% work for the government or military; and 6% are self-employed. That same study found that 7% of students in FWS relied solely on work study for employment; 86% of students had employment outside of work study; 7% had both (Baum, 2010).

Work Defined

An interesting word with many meanings, *work* may refer to the product of energy or effort (the final project is the work of a group of students), the result of specific methods (good camera work on film), a place where labor or effort occurs (the steelworks south of Chicago), a fortified structure (earthenwork barricades), and more (Work, 2015). Most commonly, as Mueller (2000) notes, *work* can be defined as "the mental or physical activity of an individual directed towards the production of goods or services that are valued by that individual or others" (p. 3269). In addition, there are ways of further refining our understanding of work within this common definition. Pusser (2010), writing specifically of student work, observes, "Mueller's definition emphasizes productivity, the concept that separates work from leisure. Work is further differentiated as a practice that produces both exchange value (work for remuneration) and use value (work for personal development)" (p. 137). Pusser goes on to cite both Pahl and Arendt in noting social relations (power dynamics) as well as personal motivation (intrinsic or extrinsic) as defining factors in distinguishing labor from work.

The distinction between work for remuneration and work for personal development shapes much of the discussion of student employment throughout this book. It is not a binary condition, a sort of all of one or all of another proposition. Freidson (1990) speaks about a continuum from pure work for wages to pure use values. Pusser (2010), who speaks of students engaging in campus employment as intellectual work for use value, comments, "For students, the challenge in separating the conditions of work from wages from intellectual work raises the possibility that the conditions and processes of student employment will shape the conditions and processes of a student's intellectual work" (p. 138).

Students Who Work and Workers Who Are Students

Having gained a sense of who works and how much, we now turn our attention to an important perspective to consider regarding college student employment. One helpful way of thinking about this large population of students is to recognize two subpopulations—students who work versus workers who are students. Ziskin, Torres, Hossler, and Gross (2010) cite the work of Ewell, Schild, and Paulson, who have referred to workers who are students as *mobile working students;* they move to campus from their places of employment and then back again. The role of student is a much more important factor in the identity of students who work, whereas the role as an employee or worker is much more salient in the identity of workers who are students.

> Given differences in financial resources, family responsibilities, and other circumstances, work is likely to play a different role in the college enrollment of a traditional student who enrolls in college full time in the fall after graduating from high school than it does for adult or non-traditional students. (Perna, 2010, p. xv)

Keith (2007) has identified work as a constraining factor in the use of academic and social services by nontraditional students, though one might well wonder if that negative constraint is mediated for the relatively modest number of adult learners who report working on campus.

Students Employed on Campus

Our focus in this book is on undergraduate students who work on campus. Although they do not make up the majority of students who are employed, they are the population upon whom staff and faculty have the greatest impact, given the role that they play in creating employment opportunities, shaping employment conditions, and providing employment supervision and guidance.

As part of developing our own thinking on the topic, the authors found it helpful to draw on the work of Perozzi and colleagues (2009) in providing a fairly precise description of what we mean when we speak of working on campus:

> Employment is conceptualized as students who are paid by the institution and officially report to a supervisor, as opposed to students who may be in a role where they receive a stipend or other remuneration for their service, time, or leadership role; for example, many of the traditionally volunteer positions on student governments and programming boards. While unpaid positions such as internships, practica, and some undergraduate research roles would not fall within this definition, most of the principles can be extended and applied to these other categories of student workers. (p. x)

Although we largely embrace Perozzi's (2009) description of student employees on campus, it appears to us that it ought to be extended to include those students who are employed by contracted service providers as well. One might expect to find students working in campus food service, residence halls, or copying centers operated by contract partners for the institution.

Towle and Olsen (2009) provide a very useful discussion of ways in which colleges and universities can work with contract vendors to help assure the quality of the student employment experience in those operations.

Students serving in paraprofessional roles are a unique group among student employees on campus. Although the term *paraprofessional* is commonly used, it may not be commonly understood. Of course, it begins with *para*, which has its origins in Ancient Greek and means beside, near, or next to. The second part of the word is *professional*, which is commonly understood to refer to someone performing a role requiring special education focused on unique knowledge and language, serving to benefit others, and acting within an ethical framework. Professionals are typically afforded respect and some degree of autonomy by virtue of their training and selflessness of service (Brint, 1994). Confusion can exist with both parts of being a paraprofessional. Serving alongside and providing assistance for a professional staff member requires a level of training different from that required of students in other sorts of positions, and whether a particular field qualifies as a profession is sometimes the subject of debate in an era in which occupations seem drawn to professionalization (Wilensky, 1964). Still, in a time of professionalization, accountability, and litigation, careful thought should be given to the paraprofessional role of student employees, with particular attention given to training and supervision, particularly relative to ethics, knowledge, and skills required in the role.

Throughout this book, we intentionally refer to *student employees* rather than to student workers. We believe the term better conveys the expectations we have for the student experience in those positions and the expectations that departments ought to have for students filling those positions. The authors also believe the term *student employee* reflects a more appropriate sense of parity for the people and the positions relative to their regular staff counterparts. Finally, we believe *student employee* is more educationally purposeful, in that it helps clearly identify the opportunity for students to see their role on campus as helping them prepare for their future employment.

The term *work study* ought to be used exclusively for positions that are funded through the FWS program and only when discussing the source of funding for the position. To do otherwise is to risk inadvertently conveying a message to students that the expectation we and they should have is that we see their role as a blend of work and study as opposed to being about development, learning, or retention.

The authors also make use throughout this book of the terms *student employment practitioner* and *student employment professional*, referring to people responsible for providing oversight for student employment. The word choice is also intentional here in that it conveys a sense of thoughtfulness, purposefulness, and professionalism in the endeavor. One final note with regard to language: The authors use *we* or *our* in a number of ways that context should make clear. *We* can refer to those, like ourselves, who serve in higher education to support the success of students and institutions. *We* can also refer to the authors, as well as the community of authors, readers, and practitioners that the book encourages. The term *authors* is occasionally used when limiting our remarks to the three of us.

With this understanding in mind, where do students work on campus? In what sorts of places and programs may we expect to find student employees? It turns out the short answer is "almost everywhere." "On college campuses large and small, in administrative offices, libraries, cafeterias, and fitness facilities, student workers have long been part of the fabric of campus life," according to Rowh (2014, p. 2), and Perozzi (2009) observes, "colleges and universities provide myriad types of employment for students. From clerical work to research work to research assistants, an array of opportunities is available to students during their college careers" (p. ix).

Given the ubiquity of students working in various roles on campus, it is not surprising to find contemporary professional literature addressing college student work in specific areas of the university. For example, Rockey and Barcelona (2012) discuss student employment in campus recreation as an arena in which student workers gain professional development. McGlone and Rey (2012) discuss the benefits that students, departments, and the institution reap when students are employed in campus recreation or athletics. McGinniss (2014) offers a thoughtful piece on learning opportunities for student staff in libraries, in which she notes that student employees outnumber librarians by a two-to-one margin. Lipsky (2008) and Newton and Enders (2010) offer works on students as peer educators. Blimling's (2010) book on working with resident assistants is well established, and Foubert (2013) also provides a helpful volume in this area. The recent dissertation by Albaneso (2012) is particularly noteworthy, given its focus on curricular design in training programs for resident assistants.

Student Employment: What It May Be and What It Could Be

Some evidence suggests that employed students are seeking both exchange value and work value. Tuttle and colleagues (2005) cite one study in which students in focus groups describe looking for work with meaning and that was meaningful. These students also indicated that they started with a view of their employment as being focused on remuneration but developed additional appreciation for other factors related to academic, social, and career advantages. Tuttle and colleagues (2005) also cite a study focused on students who consider themselves students who work. In this study 26% of those students said their coursework benefited from the work experience, and 55% saw it as helping with career preparation.

An important and natural question, particularly as it relates to campus employment for students, is, "To what extent are the work opportunities meeting the aspirations and expectations of the students in those positions?" A number of authors have previously spoken to this question. Pusser (2010) opines

> Social theory suggests that what is generally characterized as student work in research in higher education is actually student employment, or "work for wages." It is important to distinguish the different types of employment that students engage in and to develop a clear conceptual distinction to maximize the intellectual and developmental potential of students who are employed. (p. 138)

Lewis (2008) adds, "Many student positions are one-dimensional jobs where the chief criterion for hire is a student's willingness to sit behind a desk for hours on end" (para. 2). In addition, Perozzi (2009) states, "Employment of students, particularly on-campus employment, is relevant and germane for the student experience, yet the academy rarely embraces employment as a means to education and student development" (p. vii). Put another way, campus employment for students may be too often thought of by the institution as, *What do we get?* and not, *What can the students get?*

What could the students get? What might we develop if we in higher education focused our attention on developing truly meaningful student employment opportunities on our campuses? In addition to helping finance their education, student employment on campus can foster student development (Lewis, 2008). It can also be an active learning environment and venue for supporting student success in which students "apply classroom learning in an applied setting . . . strengthen students' bonds with fellow student workers as well as with faculty or staff supervisors . . . [and] broaden and deepen [their] support network . . ." (McCormick et al., 2010, p. 180). Pusser (2010) argues, "Practitioners and other advocates for students in various arenas of higher education can make a significant contribution to the transformation of student employment by remaining mindful of the distinction in higher education between employment and intellectual work" (p. 148) and pursuing the latter, and McCormick and colleagues (2010) suggest, "The goal is to make faculty, advisers, and student life professionals full partners in helping students connect curricular and cocurricular experiences with student employment" (p. 205).

The authors find themselves in agreement with these arguments that campus employment can and should be much more than merely a modest paycheck to cover laundry, pizza, or life essentials. Drawing on the work of Watson, Kuh, Rhodes, Penny Light, and Chen (2016), our purpose in developing and bringing this book forward is to offer encouragement for consideration of student employment as a high-impact educational practice.

Summing Up and Looking Ahead

In this opening chapter we offered an overview of college student employment. The review included a history of student employment as well as information on the current state of college student employment. The meaning of work and how consideration of that meaning might inform further thinking about college student employment was also explored. Next, information was provided about students who work as well as the areas in which students work on campus. Finally, again focusing on students employed on campus, consideration was given to what that work may be today and what it could be in the future. With that notion of what is possible, we offer this book's remaining chapters. They explore campus employment and development, learning, and retention; issues related to supervision and management; legal issues in supervision of student employees; and models for an institutional level focus on campus employment for students.

Readers are likely to recognize the three distinct voices of the authors in the chapters of this book. They reflect our various experiences and strengths in higher education, and we hope that by highlighting rather than homogenizing this diversity of perspectives, our readers find the book more engaging and helpful.

Our goal in these chapters is to introduce readers to the available literature regarding this particular topic and to highlight promising programs and thoughtful models of practice. The chapters are shared to encourage thoughtful consideration of what campus employment looks like on the campuses of our readers and what it could look like with intentional design and leadership. Some of what is presented will be of greater interest to those whose roles find them responsible for broad oversight and supervision of institutional programs. Hopefully all of what is presented will be of particular interest to student employment professionals—those with direct (or next-level) responsibility for working with student employees. Note here the use of the word *with*. It reflects the belief of the authors that everyone working together in higher education has an equal role to play in the success of our students and our institutions.

2

STUDENT DEVELOPMENT
AND CAMPUS EMPLOYMENT

Having presented an overview of campus employment from its beginnings to the present day, we now turn attention to ways in which
we can conceptualize the value and outcomes of a campus job for
students beyond, as stated in chapter 1, simple remuneration. In this chapter
we focus on campus employment and student development. We first present
brief reviews of seminal and emerging psychosocial theories of student identity
development, followed by theories of moral and ethical development. In each
section, we illustrate the relationship of theory and practice through concrete
examples of ways in which these theories may be used with student employees.

Identity Development

The concept of identity may seem obtuse, fluid, and complicated; the authors
concur. For the purpose of this text we focus on the aspects of a person's identity that are commonly understood to be formed, questioned, and re-formed
during the college experience. The ways in which the college years support,
enhance, accelerate, or delay development are also considered. Identity development in college is much more than deciding on a major and a career path.
It is about students developing a sense of their core self, understanding more
deeply what they believe, what they stand for, and who they are. Identity is
about determining an overarching purpose in life.

Universal Identity Theories

The three theories of identity development described in this section may
be considered *big tent* theories—theories that have a wide reach and broad
appeal. The most well known is the seminal work of Arthur Chickering and

Linda Reisser from the scholarship of higher education. However, much of the identity work comes out of the scholarship of psychology, and the authors have chosen to present two representative psychological theories that relate very well to the college student population: James Marcia's identity statuses and Jeffery Arnett's emerging adulthood.

Chickering and Reisser's Seven Vectors of Development

Perhaps the most popular among developmental theories relating to college students is Arthur Chickering's classic work that describes seven aspects, or vectors, of development. He introduced these concepts during the late 1960s and early 1970s, a time in the history of higher education where few considered student development outside the classroom as an important component of a college education. Later he revised and updated the vectors with Linda Reisser (Chickering & Reisser, 1993).

The simplicity of the vectors is what makes this theory accessible and enduring, even 50 years after it was introduced. Each vector follows:

1. *Developing intellectual, physical, and interpersonal competence*—Increasing students' confidence and belief in their own abilities.
2. *Managing emotions*—The ability to acknowledge, express, and work through emotions and emotional reactions, both negative and positive, and the ability to manage gut emotional reactions and impulses without losing self-control. This vector also represents emotional intelligence, which is covered in detail in chapter 5.
3. *Moving through autonomy toward interdependence*—Becoming independent in thinking and relationships, trusting oneself to make decisions, and recognizing connections to others and their autonomy, as well as the interdependence among oneself, one's peers, and one's mentors.
4. *Developing mature interpersonal relationships*—Respect for differences and the ability to create intimacy through healthy, trusting, and open relationships with peers and friends, as well as romantic partners, supervisors, and mentors.
5. *Establishing identity*—Developing a sense of self in cultural and social contexts in relation to others, and a solid sense of personal stability relative to values and beliefs, race, gender, and sexual orientation. We review several theories related to these aspects of identity later in this chapter.
6. *Developing purpose*—A sense of what one will accomplish in the world and the type of life they wish to lead. This vector moves beyond job and career intention; it begs a holistic view, perhaps even vocation as calling and plans for personal and family goals.

7. *Developing integrity*—Clarifying and articulating core values and having the confidence to live them. We discuss theories of moral and ethical development later in this chapter.

Marcia's Identity Statuses

James Marcia is a psychologist who saw identity as emerging from a combination of exploration and commitment, resulting in what he described as four identity statuses (Kroger & Marcia, 2011). The four statuses follows:

1. *Identity diffusion*—A status in which a person has engaged in low levels of exploration and has a low sense of commitment. Students in identity diffusion status may be viewed as wanderers, not quite looking for something and not feeling any sense of urgency to do so. Diffused students may be quite happy in this status, as they experience no crisis or motivation for exploration or self-examination. In other words, students in identity diffusion do not have a strong sense of identity but are not worried about it.

2. *Identity foreclosure*—A status in which a person makes a commitment but has not engaged in much exploration. A common example of foreclosure would be a student who is set on pursuing a law career because at a young age she was told that she would make a good lawyer. Students in foreclosure may never experience a crisis of identity if their commitments are strong and they are satisfied with those choices.

3. *Identity moratorium*—A status in which a person engages in high levels of exploration but has not yet made a commitment. Students in moratorium are likely experiencing some anxiety about their inability to make a commitment. It would be common for a student in moratorium to have a new love interest every month, all while worrying about making the right decision. Students in moratorium are constantly searching for who they are.

4. *Identity achievement*—A status in which a person engages in exploration and makes a commitment. Achievement status does not imply that a person may never again reconsider identity; it is a result of searching and careful reflection, possibly crisis, and most certainly resolution. Theories of racial and lesbian, gay, bisexual, transgender, and questioning (LGBTQ) identity development that demonstrate this process of crisis, reflection, and resolution are presented later.

Arnett's Emerging Adulthood

Psychologist Jeffrey Arnett spent years studying the development of young people between the ages of 18 and 25 in industrialized nations. After conducting hundreds of interviews, he discovered patterns in their self-perceptions, their feelings about personal identities, and their thoughts about the transition from adolescence to adulthood (Arnett, 2000). He proposed a unique stage in life-span development for this age group that he termed *emerging adulthood*. This "age of in-between" (Arnett, 2010, 1:20) occurs when a person leaves adolescence behind but is not quite ready for adulthood. Emerging adulthood is a period of uncertainty, experimentation, and self-examination. It is characterized by instability, exploration of self, and changing relationships, residential status, roles, and purpose. During this stage, people test out identities and possibilities, come to assume responsibilities, and gain independence.

The five aspects of emerging adulthood (Arnett, 2006) are as follows:

1. *Identity exploration*—Individuals explore multiple dimensions of their identity, including gender; race; sexual orientation; relationships with family, friends, and romantic partners; and reaffirmation or changes in values, worldviews, and political and religious beliefs.
2. *Instability*—Individuals may be moving physically, such as among residential communities and rooms, as well as psychologically, as they test out various identities and learn more about themselves.
3. *Self-focus*—Individuals have limited responsibilities to others and thus the freedom and time to self-examine and come to understand who they are at the core.
4. *Feeling in-between*—Individuals know they are no longer adolescents but they also know they are not quite adults and not yet ready to assume full responsibility for their survival and future.
5. *Possibilities*—Individuals have hope and begin to envision a future for themselves that is positive, imagining success in work and personal relationships and not necessarily being in alignment with who they have been or used to be.

Arnett's theory has been subject to scrutiny. Cote (2014) provided a vigorous critique, suggesting that this developmental period may not be universal as it leaves out people from lower socioeconomic strata who may not have the luxury of time or resources to explore and ponder possibilities. Indeed, one might also view the nontraditional student, the adult student, as having already launched into adult thinking and responsibilities. However, this critique notwithstanding, the theory does provide a useful framework through which we can view identity development in the college context (Tanner, 2006). Adults returning to college may also have feelings of instability as they transition roles. They may be faced with questions about their identity that they thought they had already resolved or had perhaps never considered or confronted.

Using These Theories With Student Employees

Thus far we have reviewed three major theories of identity development that have seemingly universal application. Critics of theoretical models may bring to light reasonable arguments against universal applicability. However, student employment practitioners may very well find one or all of the aforementioned theories useful lenses through which to view their student employees.

For example, when considered together, Marcia's identity statuses and Arnett's emerging adulthood both describe a time in life when individuals may feel unsettled about who they are and whom they wish to become. Student employees may feel pressure from family, friends, professors, or advisers to make commitments about their future adult lives they are not ready for, with respect to choice of major or career path, establishment of identity or life purpose, on even finding a partner. Supervisors of student employees may pick up on anxiety related to these pressures. Supervisors can support their students' interest in exploration and reassure their students that the feeling of being in-between is perfectly normal and acceptable. They may encourage their students to pursue experiences, explore identities and relationships, and consider possibilities. Exploration can also take the form of learning new skills or assuming new responsibilities at work. Supervisors may also look for signs of Marcia's identity statuses to help student employees examine ways in which their work responsibilities might inform their identity exploration and commitment.

When considering Chickering and Reisser's vectors, student employment practitioners are uniquely positioned to help student employees understand that stability, competence, mature relationships, and interdependence, as well as life purpose, come only with exploration and deep self-examination. A student employee's development of work-relevant skills, accomplishments on the job, and the confidence to make continuing and higher-level contributions to the organization are all part of emerging competence. We can observe our student employees progressing to higher levels of competence and provide positive, reinforcing feedback that increases confidence. As supervisors, we observe students' capacity to recognize their own emotions at work, which could range from anxiety, frustration, anger, embarrassment, and disappointment to excitement, elation, and pride. Student employees can develop the ability to manage emotions when dealing with others, such as when they engage with difficult customers or clients, face conflict with peers, or receive difficult feedback from supervisors. We can help them develop mature relationships by exposing them to diversity and encouraging them to see other perspectives and value the contributions of their peers. We can model ways to hold healthy, respectful disagreements and mature debates with peers, supervisors, mentors, and other professionals at work.

In addition, we can structure opportunities for student employees to reflect on and integrate their experiences and relationships at work with their academic and extracurricular experiences. The structured reflection process, which we cover in detail in chapter 4, can help student employees develop a heightened awareness of self and contribute to their search for life purpose. Student employees develop integrity as they examine their own sense of right and wrong when confronted by moral and ethical dilemmas at work. Finally, supervisors can help student employees develop a sense of interdependence, in which they gain confidence and trust their own abilities without the need for external validation, while understanding how their role fits into the larger organization. Student employees can learn to negotiate ways of working, project design, and workflow with their peers, supervisors, and other professionals in their department. Invariably as we supervise and mentor our student employees and encourage them to explore their identities and try on a few, we are, indeed, facilitating their identity development.

The authors wish to explicitly acknowledge at this point in the chapter that some supervisors may have concerns about their role in identity development, believing that identity development is something that should be attended to outside of work time. The authors believe the opposite. We believe that students at work have developmental experiences, and through work they are making self-discoveries. Supervisors can be assured that addressing aspects of student identity development can happen within structures already in place to support student employees, such as individual supervision meetings, group trainings, and staff meetings. With a deeper understanding of how students come to understand themselves in the world, supervisors and mentors of student employees can modify these existing structures to support whole student development, which in turn will help student employees make a deeper commitment to their campus jobs.

Identity Considerations

Research in higher education is not limited to generalized conceptualizations of identity development. Scholars have delved deeply into aspects of college student identity related to race, ethnicity, gender, sexual orientation, ability, spirituality, and other dimensions. This text is not meant to serve as a comprehensive primer of all prominent identity theories; it highlights a few and provides applications to student employment. The authors hope that these theory-to-practice examples do not limit the reader's understanding of identity, but serve as a starting point.

Women's Identity

Historically, most empirical research on identity development was conducted on males. Josselson (1996) sought to understand women's perceptions of their own identity; through a longitudinal research project, she interviewed women extensively throughout a 20-year span. These interviews involved personal history, thoughts about occupation, politics, religious views, sexuality, family, and personal growth. "The experience of identity," Josselson (1996) wrote, "is one of meaningful continuity over time and place" (p. 28). Her research revealed that the influences of context, family, personal experiences, and the changes in society's expectations of women over time were previously underestimated. Josselson's investigation opened a new way of thinking about identity as both having an internal feeling about self and as being informed by external context and relationships. Ely (1995) studied women's gender identity at work and found that a woman's sense of identity can be different depending on the representation of women in positions of power in the organization.

Ethnic and Racial Identity

Another aspect of personal identity is our racial and ethnic identity. How do we view our own race and ethnicity? How do we develop a sense of identity relative to our race and ethnicity? Racial identification is a "process by which self is constructed and a basic psychological need is satisfied via the establishment of a sense of belonging and symbol around which a group of similarly affected people may organize for effective collective action" (Sanders Thompson, 2001, p. 164). Several scholars have written about this process, which as Sanders Thompson so eloquently stated, involves a sense of individual self and also self as a member of a group or collective identity (Cross, 1995; De Walt, 2011; Kim, 2001; Porter & Dean, 2015; Tatum, 1992; Zirkel & Johnson, 2016). "An ethnic identity refers to a sense of self. . . . It involves a shared sense of identity with others who belong to the same ethnic group" (Phinney & Ong, 2007, p. 9). Phinney and Ong (2007) described the following four components of ethnic identity:

1. *self-categorization*—how individuals identify themselves
2. *commitment and attachment*—the extent to which individuals feel connected to their ethnic group
3. *exploration*—how individuals strive to understand more about the group's attitudes, beliefs, behaviors, heritage, language, and traditions, and how these characteristics are viewed by others
4. *salience*—the level of importance of ethnic identity to a person's core self

As we review a few examples of racial and ethnic identity, keep these four components in mind.

African American/Black

Cross's model of nigrescence (1995, cited in Allen, Hubain, Hunt, Lucero, & Stewart, 2012) involves five stages of identity development: pre-encounter, encounter, immersion/emmersion, internalization, internalization-commitment. Individuals are theorized to move from a starting point in which they identify with the majority race; then come to see themselves as other; learn more about their racial identity through immersion in the community; develop a deeper understanding of sociopolitical history; and emerge as self-confident, self-identified, internalized racial beings. Zirkel and Johnson (2016) emphasized sociopolitical awareness as part of the process, suggesting that Black identity is inextricably intertwined with the history of Black people in the United States. They theorized that Black identities are formed in the context of continuing racist views and racist institutions, and that the ability of Blacks to cope with and rise above these realities is what strengthens them.

Let us turn for a moment to the nomenclature used. Views differ about the term used to describe this group: *Black, African American,* or *African* (De Walt, 2011; Porter & Dean, 2015). Porter and Dean's (2015) recent phenomenological study of Black undergraduate women found that the women themselves chose the terminology they wished to use for self-description in context or juxtaposed against what they felt the social environment called for and the expectations of others. De Walt's (2011) study of first-generation Africans in the United States revealed their consternation about the terms and how the different terms themselves had meaning for the extent to which Blacks in the United States felt connected to their African roots.

Sanders Thompson (2001) emphasized the collective aspect of African American racial identity, suggesting that acceptance of self as a member of the group was paramount to their identity. Similarly, in Porter and Dean's (2015) study, the participants assigned great importance in the formation of their racial identities to their encouraging family relationships, especially their mothers, and their supportive interactions with other African American women.

Latinx

Although categories are useful in framing our understanding of ethnic identity, they cannot account for the full diversity of people, including monoracial and multiracial individuals. Latinx individuals, for example, face a dilemma in that they do not fit neatly into the traditional racial categories and often are said to be somewhere in the middle of Black and White (Gallegos &

Ferdman, 2007). Gallegos and Ferdman (2007) described six different orientations for Latinxs, which range from an undifferentiated sense of racial identity to identification with Whites or to a subgroup within the Latinx community (e.g., Puerto Rican or Colombian). The existence of subgroups within the Latinx community makes generalized assumptions difficult and yet reminds us that each of us has our own personal orientation to our race and ethnic backgrounds. The degree to which our racial and ethnic identities are visible or invisible, irrelevant or somewhat relevant, or core to who we are, also varies.

Multiracial

Models have also been created to better understand the ways in which individuals from multiracial backgrounds develop their identities. Multiracial individuals face the challenge of added complexity in their search for racial and ethnic identity. They may experience an existential struggle relative to which aspect of their background is visible; accepted by others; and more or less salient in their everyday lives, family, and relationships.

Renn's (2008) model posits that individuals begin with a monoracial identity and move through stages whereby they come to understand and accept different racial identities as part of their core. At that point they internalize both identities and feel comfortable in situations where either or both of these identities are lived outwardly. Wijeyesinghe (2001) described several internal and external factors that influence an individual's choice of multiracial identity: racial ancestry, physical appearance, early socialization, cultural attachment, spirituality, other social identities (e.g., gender, sexual orientation), and social and historical context.

LGBTQ Identity

Theoretical models of LGBTQ identity range from traditional stage theories to medical models, contextual models, and postmodern models (Bilodeau & Renn, 2005). Cass (1984) developed a frequently cited stage model that involves a process of changing self-perceptions. Her six-stage model begins with *identity confusion*, where individuals first become aware of their own homosexual thoughts and feelings, causing confusion about who they are. In this stage, individuals can choose to deny or repress those feelings, or they may decide to cope with this new self-awareness. The second stage, *identity comparison*, involves a focus on difference between who they thought they were and who they are becoming. They begin to distance themselves from their previous thinking about their own sexuality. The third stage is *identity tolerance*, a stage in which individuals accept who they are and begin to seek out social relationships. In the tolerance stage, individuals are neither fully engaged nor disclosed. The fourth stage is *identity acceptance*, where individuals develop the comfort and confidence to disclose to close family and friends, yet may still withhold this new identity in public. In the fifth stage, *identity pride*, individuals take public pride in themselves and in their new community, often feeling greater confidence in their ability and responsibility to speak out against bias. The sixth stage is *synthesis*, at which time individuals are able to integrate their private and public LGBTQ selves and see this aspect of who they are as just one aspect of their identities. As with Marcia's identity achievement status, identity achievement in this model also results from exploration, crisis resolution, and commitment.

Stage models like this have been critiqued for not acknowledging the complexity surrounding sexual identity development due to the intersections of multiple aspects of identity, such as race, gender, and ethnicity, as well as the cultural, social, and organizational environments in which this development occurs (Croteau, Anderson, & Vanderwal, 2008; Shapiro, Rios, & Stewart, 2010). LGBTQ individuals may face individual or organizational silencing forces, where culture, religion, family, and tradition may prevent them from expressing their sexual identity (Shapiro et al., 2010). Even pop culture may be a silencing force—consider, as examples, the portrayal of women in the media, or the reinforcement of traditional behaviors based on gender, race, and social class. Organizations such as colleges and universities, and departments within, can be oppressive, tolerant, or accepting. Supportive attitudes can be shared publicly through equity policies using affirming language. Social affirmations by colleagues can also contribute to a supportive campus climate for LGBTQ students (Croteau et al., 2008; Shapiro et al., 2010). Croteau and colleagues' (2008) synthesis of the literature on coming out at work suggested that "LGB workers are seen as more likely to reveal their sexual orientation when there is concrete evidence of support for diversity, including development and enforcement of nondiscrimination policies and positive treatment of others who have revealed their identity" (p. 541).

Individuals With Disabilities

Traditional higher education views on disability emerged from a medical model that viewed people with disabilities as having an illness that rendered them dependent upon healthcare professionals for support and survival. These views then morphed into a social pathology model in which people with disabilities were considered disadvantaged to the point of dependence on social programs (Peña, Stapleton, & Schaffer, 2016). Later, the supercrip model ascribed near superhuman power to people with disabilities who overcome great adversity to achieve success (Zhang & Haller, 2013).

In a recent review of literature on identity development for students with disabilities, Peña, Stapleton, and Schaffer (2016) noted a dearth of studies on the topic. They attribute this in part to the diversity of disabilities, such as learning, psychiatric conditions, mobility, hearing, seeing, and autism, to name a few. Such diversity, they suggest, makes for a vastly different experience for each student. They advocate for a critical framework, where the disability is not person-defining; the disability intersects with other aspects of identity, such as race, ethnicity, gender, and sexual orientation. Using a critical perspective can help us interrogate oppressive social and political contexts.

> Rooted in critical disability theory, it is the responsibility of all practitioners to engage students in conversations about their needs within and outside of their disability. In doing so, they facilitate intentional interactions and engagement with students as diverse beings with intersecting identities. (Peña et al., 2016, p. 90)

These differences notwithstanding, Dominiak-Kochanek (2016) posits that individuals with disabilities face three major influences on identity development: parental overprotection, peer networks, and lack of balance between family and peer socialization. Parental overprotection, while understandable, may delay the development of autonomy or interdependence in people with disabilities and may also restrict their socialization and creation of peer networks, leading to a limited exposure to diversity (Dominiak-Kochanek, 2016). She attributes these factors to her finding that higher percentages of students with disabilities were shown to be identity diffuse, where, using Marcia's framework, they experienced low levels of exploration and low levels of commitment. She suggests that exploration may prove difficult due to access barriers, and as such, educational institutions can be more purposeful in creating opportunities for students with disabilities to explore.

Zhang and Haller's (2013) study of media images of people with disabilities revealed a definitive impact on self-concept. Negative media imagery about people with disabilities contributed to misinformation, inaccurate stereotyping, and actual oppression, which negatively impacted self-esteem. Conversely, positive media images of people with disabilities who see past their limitations contributed to feelings of improved self-esteem and motivation to rise above disadvantage and negative stereotyping.

Although more research is needed on identity development of students with disabilities, it seems clear that student employment professionals might find a strengths-based approach useful in helping these students understand themselves in the fullest sense, inclusive of their disability and other aspects of their identities.

Higher education professionals readily acknowledge that while the afore-mentioned theories may fit a large number of people within these socially constructed groups, they should not be viewed as stereotypes. In fact, we must first understand our own gender, racial, ethnic, sexual orientation, and ability identities and how each part of our identity informs our worldviews and influences the way we react to people from other groups, such that we may be more open to understanding the differences in the identities of oth-ers. Note, too, that the degree of importance or salience you assign to each aspect of your identity may change over time.

Using These Theories With Student Employees

Taken together, gender, racial, ethnic, sexual orientation, and disability iden-tity theories have some commonalities. They involve a discovery and rec-ognition of being different and exploring that difference, as well as choices about accepting difference, along with reflection and action to integrate these aspects of self into their overall self-concepts. Recall Phinney and Ong's (2007) four components: self-categorization, commitment and attachment, exploration, and salience. Identity exploration occurs in sociopolitical con-texts, and as such is influenced by these contexts, the environment, and the communities in which the exploration occurs. Yet there are also some differ-ences, as noted previously. In particular, the authors acknowledge the fact that some identities are clearly visible and some are invisible.

Student employment practitioners and supervisors of student employ-ees can influence identity development by creating a welcoming environ-ment where students are accepted, respected, and celebrated for who they are and where personal narratives are shared (Allen et al., 2012; Tatum, 1992). Allen and colleagues (2012) suggest that we explore our identities in a supportive environment and discuss all aspects of our identity, those vis-ible and invisible, and the extent to which each has salience for us. Student employment practitioners can structure opportunities for students to express themselves—their true selves—at work in ways that positively contribute to mature interpersonal relationships, interdependence, and team building. Tatum (1992) suggests that we create opportunities for students to generate their own knowledge about racial identity, to situate their development in context, and to feel empowered to become change agents in the fight against discrimination and oppression. In a practical fashion, student employment practitioners would not need to go so far as to organize student involvement in political action, yet they may very well encourage their student employees to get involved in social justice efforts on and beyond the campus.

Students may be invited to explore their own views of these aspects of their identities while simultaneously exploring and understanding the views of others. Student employment practitioners might consider facilitating students' reflections on these aspects of identity as part of a commitment to understanding workplace diversity. We may challenge student employees to consider the ways in which gender and racial dynamics exist in the workplace, and observe how differences in these aspects of identity are folded into and represented by organizational culture. We may prompt our students to use a disability awareness lens to assess the accessibility of our facilities and programs. Invariably, our student employees will enter a world postcollege where they will be expected to work with and for persons who are different from them, and the opportunity for students to explore diversity in a safe and supportive campus environment can help them orient and acclimate to future professional environments.

Multiple Dimensions of Identity

At this point, it should be clear that the concept of identity development is far more complex than it may seem at first glance. Everyone has multiple dimensions of identity (Jones, 1997). These dimensions develop over time and take on more or less salience as we relate to others; experience negative stereotypes, racism, and oppression based on various aspects of our identities; and reflect upon our inner selves.

Jones and McEwen's Core Model

Jones and McEwen (2000) created the core model (see Figure 2.1), emphasizing the idea that aspects of identity most salient to us are ones that we think about and experience most often.

Jones and McEwen (2000) envisioned identity dimensions as intersecting rings around a core such that no one dimension may be understood singularly; each can be understood only in relation to other dimensions. How these multiple aspects of identity intersect is not only unique but also fluid, for each person changing over time based on changing contexts, social circumstances, and individual experiences. The value of understanding this model for ourselves and for our students is the capacity we build to identify, acknowledge, and understand external influences and how they shape us, and the extent to which we have accepted, rejected, or modified those aspects of self based on reflection and introspection.

Figure 2.1. Jones and McEwen's core model.

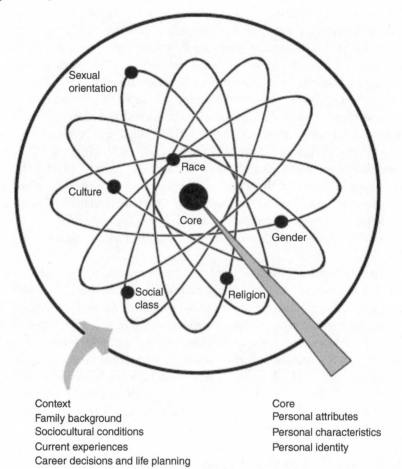

Context	Core
Family background	Personal attributes
Sociocultural conditions	Personal characteristics
Current experiences	Personal identity
Career decisions and life planning	

Source. Jones and McEwen (2000). Reprinted with permission.

Self-Authorship

Marcia Baxter Magolda (1999, 2008) took a constructionist perspective and built upon the work of other human development scholars, particularly Robert Kegan. Through a longitudinal study of college students that took place over 20 years, she developed a theory of personal meaning making and identity that built upon Kegan's ideas around self-authorship. *Self-authorship* is the "internal capacity to define one's beliefs, identity, and social relations" (Baxter Magolda, 2008, p. 269). She found that students first defined themselves based on external forces such as family, peers, and societal expectations. Over time and through experience, these students discovered that their identities could be based on their internal ideas about themselves. Through her research she noticed that her participants were moving from an external locus of control, where they made decisions based on an external view or pressure, to an internal locus of control, where their internal ideas or their own personal code formed the basis of their decisions and behaviors. Baxter Magolda (2003) called this "internal identity" (p. 233) and an "internal sense of self not threatened by difference" (p. 234). Over time these participants became less concerned with controlling what was happening around them and more concerned with their reactions and the personal meaning they derived from their circumstances. "They [the participants in her study] recognized that they could create their own emotions and happiness by choosing how to react to reality" (Baxter Magolda, 2003, p. 271).

Becoming self-authored is a process of experiencing tension, then resolving that tension by making a deeper commitment to your core self. Over time you become more confident in who you are at the core: You have integrated the multiple aspects of your identity; you readily accept responsibility for your feelings, decisions, and behaviors; and you are comfortable with standing up for your beliefs, even under pressure from others. You are also comfortable with the idea that identities continue to form and re-form, as people—including you—discover more about themselves, face new challenges and tensions, and reflect upon their individual ways of finding meaning in those various contexts.

Application With Student Employees

Student employment practitioners can help students become more self-authored by encouraging them to consider and reflect upon the multiple dimensions of their identity as they learn more about themselves through their work. Baxter Magolda (1999) believed that "campus supervisors could serve as those external authorities to help students work through dissonance, analyze their values in relation to the type of work settings, and learn to deal with political realities" (p. 642). One technique often cited in the experiential education literature is a review of a critical incident (Inkster & Ross, 1995), which begins with asking students to describe a significant or critical incident in terms of what happened and how they felt about it. Questions can then be raised that prompt students to think about any external pressure that challenged their sense of self and their decisions and actions as a result. Students may also be prompted to reflect upon which aspects of their identity they believe are core, those characteristics that make them proud, and those that remain intact in the face of challenges or adversity.

Student employment practitioners may also use a three-phrase conversation created by Baxter Magolda and King (2008) to create a trusting relationship that makes students feel more comfortable sharing aspects of their core identity. The first phase is getting acquainted. Ask student employees about their expectations for college overall and how things have been going for them. The goal in this first phase is to help students feel comfortable, knowing that they can share things and describe their feelings, building trust. The second phase is encouraged reflection. Ask students to describe experiences they deem significant and prompt them to recall the aspects of those experiences that made them so. You might ask student employees about their experiences with difference: genders, races, ethnicities, abilities, sexual orientations, value systems and beliefs, worldviews, politics, religious views, and so forth. Prompting student employees to reflect upon their experiences with difference can help them better understand themselves and find value in the other. The third phase of the conversation is interpretation. You might ask your student employees to interpret the meaning of these experiences in terms of their own growth and development—perhaps how these experiences are influencing their thinking about choice of major or career, or their larger purpose in life.

Identity development does not occur the same way or at the same speed for all students. Students are individuals who need to understand not only who they are but also how they have come to be and whom they wish to become. Jones (2009) encourages us to think of our own identities: Our ability to understand ourselves; the intersection among various aspects of our multiple dimensions of identity; and the social, racial, ethnic, and cultural contexts in which we were raised and educated that formed our identities and continue to influence our identity development. Moreover, we should be thinking about how we present ourselves to the various social groups we occupy (e.g., such as our family, friends, coworkers, peers, and partners) and in what contexts our presentation might change as a result of difference in gender, race, ethnicity, culture, sexuality, disability, spirituality, and social class. After careful thought and reflection upon our own identities, we are much better positioned to help student employees consider their own.

A Sociological View of Identity

Kaufman and Feldman (2004) sought to understand how student identity formation occurs using the lens of sociology, vis-à-vis how the social environment and social interactions influence identity. They interviewed 89 students about their college experiences, categorizing the identity domains into 3 major areas: intelligence, occupation, and cosmopolitanism.

With regard to *intelligence* students readily expressed that their college experiences inside and outside the classroom contributed to their ability to think differently, more expansively, and more critically about subjects and issues. Students also described their own realization that they were improving their intellectual capacity and recognizing that, in some social settings, such as with their high school friends and family, they purposefully changed their language patterns to fit in better, "talking smart" (Kaufman & Feldman, 2004, p. 473). Conversely, other participants reported feelings of inadequacy relative to the intelligence they perceived their peers to have versus their own as a result of their college experience.

Occupation as identity relates to career goals and to the social class identity one develops as a result. Kaufman and Feldman (2004) learned that students whose peers were career focused and goal oriented provided a measure of positive motivation. A participant in this study emphasized the "importance of her social group in reinforcing both her identity as a future professional and the self-presentations that will allow her to successfully enact and achieve such an identity" (Kaufman & Feldman, 2004, p. 478). Undecided students can benefit from having peers on the job who are goal oriented and career focused; the peers serve as role models and as sounding boards for feedback on others' career thinking. Students may expect their future status as college graduates and corresponding occupational choices to move them into a higher social class.

Cosmopolitanism refers to the idea that students are developing sophisticated thinking about their place in world. Sometimes this idea is referred to as becoming a citizen of the world. Experiences with a full range of diversity, exposure to the traditions and values and ideas of others, and how those exposures influence who they are invariably expands people's thinking of who they wish to become.

Applying a Sociological Lens to Student Employees

Student employment practitioners might consider ways to bring in conversations about social phenomena that may impact the student employees as individuals and as employees. A civic engagement office, for example, would be particularly attuned to community issues and likely could engage student employees in discussions about local problems the department may be interested in addressing, such as homelessness, food insecurity, or racial unrest. As part of their work these students might also be invited to build greater awareness of social issues by engaging peers on campus in conversations and motivating them to get involved. Student employees in any campus department could be invited to participate in holiday season community projects, where they raise money, collect canned foods, run toy and book drives, or cook meals for people in need. Just as many companies have corporate social responsibility initiatives, higher education institutions promote community and civic engagement among faculty, staff, and students. Student employees could be invited to stay abreast of current events focusing on social issues in their communities and periodically brainstorm ideas for how the campus might serve them more effectively. Supervisors may also prompt employees to reflect upon and discuss societal issues and how individual identity informs perspectives, influences thinking, and guides behavior.

Let's pause for a moment and reflect upon the identity theories presented in this chapter. Student employment practitioners need not feel pressure to become experts in these theories or in all aspects of identity development. However, it is important for us to understand that student employees are not simply employees; often they are emerging adults, or perhaps adults reconsidered. While acquiring academic knowledge and work-relevant skills, they are also learning about themselves—exploring various aspects of their identities, exposing themselves to difference, and reconciling all they are learning about themselves and others in a period ripe for self-examination, which occurs before, during, and after work, on campus and in their communities. Events, situations, and relationships that student employees experience at work may prompt them to reflect upon these multiple dimensions of their identity. As such, we must be ready to provide the support they need to safely question, evolve, and discover all aspects of themselves.

Moral and Ethical Development

We turn now to theories of moral and ethical development, a topic of serious concern for educators who seek to cultivate citizenship, as well as for employers who wish to recruit talented graduates possessing the highest levels of integrity. As we did with identity development, we provide examples of ways to apply the theories with student employees.

Zhu, Treviño, and Zheng (2016) posited that morality is a way of being; it becomes part of who you are. One could say that morality is part of identity: "The extent to which people believe themselves to be ethical and the degree to which moral traits, such as being caring, compassionate, fair, friendly, generous, helpful, honest, and kind are important and central to their self-definition" (Zhu et al., 2016, p. 97). Student employment practitioners are well situated to provide opportunities for ethical and moral development among students. As program managers, supervisors, coaches, and mentors, we can help students learn about ethical behavior in the workplace and develop a professional character that can guide them through their work lives. Astin and Antonio (2000) define *character* as "the values and behavior as reflected in the ways we interact with each other and in the moral choices we make on a daily basis" (p. 4). Note how similar character development is to integrity development reviewed earlier in this chapter, whereby students reflect upon the values and beliefs they bring to college and, through experience, clarify, expand, and adjust these beliefs (Chickering & Reisser, 1993).

Morality, character, and ethics inform a person's values and actions. Student employment practitioners can help their student employees develop their own sense of principled and ethical reasoning, and articulate the values and ethics upon which their behavior is based. In the following section, we describe the seminal theories of moral development and present a more recent theoretical framework that can help structure thinking when confronted with moral dilemmas.

Kohlberg's Theory of Moral Development

Perhaps the most well-known among theories of moral development was developed in the late 1960s by Lawrence Kohlberg (1973), who conceptualized the way individuals view and respond to moral dilemmas as a series of six stages grouped into three levels of reasoning. He posited that these stages and levels are linear, in that an individual progresses from a lower level to higher levels of development. Level 1 is called *preconventional morality* and includes a "punishment-and-obedience orientation" (Kohlberg, 1973, p. 631). At this basic level, moral dilemmas are viewed in the context of an authority or external standard. A student solely concerned about whether he or she would be punished for immoral behavior would be categorized as preconventional. Level 2 is *conventional morality*. At this level, moral dilemmas are viewed in the context of societal expectations and a personal interest in complying with rules as a societal standard. Beyond simple acquiescence to an authority or external standard, students concerned with how their actions would violate societal rules and be viewed by others would be categorized as conventional. Conforming to peer group expectations is an important consideration in the conventional stage. Level 3, *postconventional morality*, is the most advanced. Students who have developed to this point understand that moral dilemmas are about more than simple risk of punishment, the existence of rules, or peer expectations; the highest level of morality includes universal concerns for individuals, the public good, and humanity. Most higher education professionals strive to bring students to this sense of universal moral judgment. Kohlberg (1975) described moral judgment in terms of principles being "distinguished from rules," and described morality as justice, involving "liberty, equality, and reciprocity" (p. 50). Although aptly critiqued for its sole basis in men's moral judgment, Kohlberg's theory is still useful in conceptualizing student moral behavior.

Gilligan's Theory of Women's Moral Development

Carol Gilligan (1982) believed that women develop a sense of morality differently than men do. Rather than a concern for justice, women's sense of morality, according to Gilligan, is based on an ethic of care and concern, rooted in relationships. Through her research on adolescent boys and girls, she demonstrated that an ethic of care is an equally valid framework through which individuals view, relate to, and work through moral dilemmas. Her three-stage model begins with decision-making based on concern for self and survival. In Stage 1, a student's behavior would be based on care of self and the predicted impact that a decision would have on her personally. In Stage 2, moral decision-making is based on self-sacrifice and care for others. Before making a moral decision, a student in this stage would consider the impact of her decision on others. In Stage 3, individuals consider the principle of caring as universal, including both care for others as well as care for self. At this highest level of moral development, women can see interconnectedness and take responsibility for others without subjugating their own voice. Held (2014) described Gilligan's ethic of care as viewing responsibility to others as well as responsibility to self.

Gilligan (1995) described her theory as a feminist ethic of care. She suggested that such an ethic is universal, in that moral decisions at the highest level should be based on what is right for the community, for society, even for humanity. A universal feminist ethic of care requires empathy so that we can take the perspective of the other, enabling women to confidently use their voices to call out discrimination and oppression, as well as shed light on unethical behavior.

Using These Theories With Student Employees

When considered together, Kohlberg and Gilligan present models that frame the cognitive process of moral and ethical reasoning as a series of progressive steps, where an individual moves from a focus on self, to a focus on society and others, to the incorporation of a set of universal principles. Kohlberg's theory was based on a seemingly context-free notion of justice and duty, while Gilligan believed that morality is based on relationships and can only be subjective (Linn, 2001). The authors of this book believe it can be both.

Student employment practitioners can use both Kohlberg's and Gilligan's models, not exclusively as male-female, but as a way to contextualize ethical decisions at work. Are student employees using the justice lens or the care perspective when making moral decisions? To what extent can we help students see their own perspectives and develop the capacity to view moral dilemmas using both lenses at the highest levels? For example, let us consider Sophia's situation. Sophia works for the telefund of her college, where she calls alumnae three nights per week for donations. She is well compensated for this work, as this position requires strong communication and persuasive skills. Sophia earns bonuses based on the number of pledges she secures each week, all of which are documented in the college's telefund database. Lately Sophia has not been doing so well; the last two weeks she did not meet her quota, let alone earn a bonus, and she is concerned about her cash flow. One week she felt pressure to earn a bonus and proceeded to falsify pledges in the system, showing that she exceeded her goal for that week when, in fact, she had not. She knew that her supervisor would be unable to verify these pledges, and she figured that it wasn't that big of a deal because the college telefund was doing well overall. If you were Sophia's supervisor and discovered that the pledges had been falsified, what would you do? How might you use Kohlberg's and Gilligan's frameworks to support your conversation with Sophia?

In this situation, what Sophia did, while unethical, did not cause immediate harm to another individual. In many instances, unethical or immoral behavior may not harm others. Consider the following examples:

- A student working for the advising center has access to individual student transcripts and tells a friend about the superior academic performance of another student.
- A dining employee is asked by his roommate to provide extra large portions without extra charge because the roommate does not have enough money on his meal card.
- After taking a two-hour break from work to visit a professor during her office hours, a student employee only documents a one-hour break on her timesheet.
- A student working at the career center is reviewing a peer's résumé and notices that he lied about his grade point average (GPA).
- A student working in the athletics department finds himself among a group of male players making lewd and inappropriate comments about female athletes.
- A student working in the activities office observes her supervisor leaving for the day. She then spends the rest of the afternoon on Facebook and Instagram.

Student employment practitioners play an important role in guiding students in thinking through everyday moral and ethical dilemmas; they do not need to be life-or-death scenarios. Although Kohlberg's and Gilligan's frameworks are well known and often used, several lesser-known theories can also be used to frame these situations for students.

Rest's Four-Part Framework

Rest (1984) described moral decision-making as a complex process involving the following four components:

1. *Moral sensitivity*—The ability to recognize that a situation does indeed have a moral or ethical component. Individuals who have developed moral sensitivity recognize and can articulate their personal feelings about the matter, as well as understand the people involved in the situation, along with their perspective and feelings. Being morally sensitive enables a person to generate potential solutions while considering how each option might impact each participant.

2. *Moral judgment*—The capacity to use reasoning to make a moral decision using a deeper investigation of the facts and circumstances involved. Exercising moral judgment relies on the individual's internal sense of fairness, justice, and care.

3. *Moral motivation*—Internal conscience and commitment to taking action.

4. *Moral behavior*—Action steps taken, even if the action is viewed as unpopular.

Anderson, Wagoner, and Moore's Model of Ethical Choice

Anderson, Wagoner, and Moore (2005) introduced a model that complements Rest's (1984), suggesting that personal character, moral reasoning capability, ethics training, and a personal ethical identity all contribute to an individual's ability to make ethical decisions. They describe personal character as the moral compass an individual possesses, which is likely formed over time and influenced by family, school, religion, mentors, peers, and personal experience. Personal character—an individual's innate sense of right and wrong—and moral reasoning capability are where ethics training and the examination of a person's ethical identity begin.

This model of ethical choice, which the authors describe as "an outcome of being, becoming, and doing" (Anderson et al., 2005, p. 51), includes four components, which closely mirror Rest's (1984) model:

1. *Ethical sensitivity*—An acute awareness of the situation; that is, who is involved and the extent to which issues of oppression or discrimination exist. Gut feeling is acknowledged as an important part of this stage, vis-à-vis whether something instinctively feels right or wrong.

2. *Ethical thought process*—A logical process of carefully reviewing the specifics of the situation, determining missing facts, and taking the perspective

of each party involved. This process also involves looking for established ethical guidelines and people who direct behavior in that situation.

3. *Ethical motivation and competing values*—At the core, self-awareness and the recognition of internal conflicts felt about the situation—an individual's capacity to reflect upon personal values and the extent to which those values are being challenged or threatened by the situation, along with the motivation to make the dilemma and reasoning transparent.

4. *Ethical follow-through*—Taking action, making the decision, and communicating the decision and rationale to those involved.

Anderson and colleagues (2005) applied this model to coaches, suggesting that coaches can use these steps when confronted with ethical dilemmas. They defined an *ethical coach* as one who possesses the following five personal characteristics: good judgment, integrity, trustworthiness, respectfulness, and compassion. Coaching is a natural part of supervision, and while the authors have been describing here ways supervisors can impact student development, we discuss the supervisor's role in much greater detail in chapter 6.

Johnson's 5I Format

Johnson (2006) created an easy mnemonic to use when confronted with a moral or ethical dilemma. This approach nicely connects with the frameworks of both Rest (1984) and Anderson and colleagues (2005): identify, investigate, innovate, isolate, and implement.

1. *Identify the problem*, using moral and ethical sensitivity as well as gut feeling. Johnson (2006) compared the gut feeling to the "mom test" (p. 76), suggesting that an individual might consider how one's mother would view the situation.

2. *Investigate the problem*, using moral judgment and an ethical thought process to gather facts and perspective to understand the problem, its components, those involved, and the impacts.

3. *Innovate*, using moral and ethical motivation to generate multiple creative solutions that could meet ethical standards of behavior and work for the parties involved.

4. *Isolate*, using moral and ethical motivation and an awareness of the competing values that are involved in the situation, as well as an understanding of the internal and external presses. Surfacing negative emotions and feelings of anger or resentment—and then clarifying these emotions aloud with someone else—can help differentiate among the innovation solutions proposed to select the best fit.

5. *Implement*, the action step, the moral and ethical follow-through, taken with the confidence to confront others whose behavior is antithetical to universal ethical standards and the self-assuredness to persist in spite of obstacles. Implementation also involves a review of the outcomes and an opportunity to reevaluate the solution.

Evans's Framework for Fostering Moral Development

Johnson's (2006) format is useful for individuals in their decision processes; Evans (1987) created a planning framework for organizations, specifically higher education professionals, to use in fostering the moral development of others. It includes four approaches, including explicit, planned interventions; explicit, responsive interventions; implicit, planned interventions; and implicit, responsive interventions. As the names suggest, planned interventions are those we purposefully create to encourage student discussion about moral issues, helping them explore their own views and become aware of their own moral reasoning, as well as listen to the views and reasoning of others, which may prompt students to refine their own reasoning. Responsive interventions arise in direct response to an incident or occurrence, as in Sophia's case. Responsive interventions help students process and confront behavior in the immediate aftermath so that they may have a fresh recollection of the incident and reflect upon their own reactions to that event as well as the values upon which their reactions are based.

Using These Theories With Student Employees

So far, we have reviewed two complementary theories of moral and ethical development and two frameworks that can be used to evaluate moral dilemmas and take action. Now we present several ways that student employment practitioners can apply these theories: coaching and supervision, structured training and ongoing professional development, leveraging institutional policies and values, and individual role modeling.

Coaching and Supervision

To use Anderson and colleagues' (2005) terminology, student employment practitioners may be viewed as workplace coaches. In a practical fashion we nurture the development of skills, attitudes, and behaviors that constitute professionalism in the workplace. Ethics in decision-making is an essential piece of workplace professionalism. Modeling these characteristics—sharing examples of how we ourselves have worked through ethical dilemmas using sensitivity, judgment, motivation, and the courage to follow through transparently—can help our student employees internalize these principles and incorporate these steps into their own ethical decision-making processes.

Returning to the case of Sophia, a supervisor as coach could review each of the four elements in Rest's (1984) and Anderson and colleagues' (2005) models using Johnson's (2006) five *I*s to frame the conversation. Sophia likely possessed the sensitivity to know that her choice to falsify pledges was unethical, but that in itself can also be discussed vis-à-vis identifying the problem. Sophia's supervisor would probably want to spend the most time on her judgment and motivation, helping Sophia think through the innovation and isolation steps to better understand her behavior, the consequences, and the risks if she continues to make similar choices.

Training
Using Evans's framework, supervisors can create work environments that explicitly clarify expectations for what constitutes acceptable, ethical behavior and unacceptable, unethical behavior. Planned interventions can be part of training. Case studies involving ethical dilemmas could be presented in which student employees consider the available and missing facts, use Johnson's five *I*s, and process the dilemma using an ethic of justice, an ethic of care, or both. Group work can provide a venue for student employees to learn from their peers and gain the ability to take another's perspective, as well as discuss personal characteristics that may negatively influence moral behavior. Characteristics such as insecurity, greed, ego, and pressure to make immediate decisions without full consideration may lead to unethical behavior (Johnson, 2006). Self-interest and opportunity for personal gain can tempt individuals to engage in unethical behavior and then excuse such behavior by displacing responsibility away from self, blaming another, or distorting potential consequences (Kish-Gephart, Detert, Treviño, Baker, & Martin, 2014).

Following are several ideas for case studies that can be used in student employee training. These examples cover ethical dilemmas confronting the student and the supervisor:

- A student tutor is asked to do her client's homework.
- A student is told to begin work before being formally cleared through payroll.
- An international student accepts a job on campus to acquire a Social Security card, then promptly resigns to take another position.
- A student misrepresents work history on a résumé or job application.
- A student divulges information about another student that may not be officially labeled as confidential (e.g., academic records) but is nonetheless personal (e.g., life goal or sexual orientation).

- A student places blame on a colleague for his own mistake.
- A supervisor blames a student for something she did not do.
- A supervisor fails to address safety issues.
- A supervisor does not approve work hours in time for a student to get paid.
- Inappropriate romantic relations are taking place between a staff member and a student.
- A staff member reveals information about one student to another student.

Personal reflection time should be incorporated into training to allow students to reflect upon their own values and moral identity. Students should be given opportunities to explore their conscious and unconscious belief systems, surfacing the sources of those beliefs and the role models who influenced them. Then students can examine how those beliefs support or conflict with their emerging sense of morality.

Ongoing Professional Development

Ethical and moral development training does not solely exist in a presemester series of workshops; student employees can always benefit from ongoing conversations about ethics in the workplace and universal ethics. Student employees may bring ethical dilemmas they face outside of work for discussion. In fact, making ethics a regular part of communication and feedback sessions, as well as the focus of periodic professional development activities, would reinforce the institution's commitment to living by its stated values as well as the supervisor's commitment to workplace ethics. Role-play can be used as a strategy to encourage students to take the other's perspective and see a situation through a different lens, leading to increased moral and ethical sensitivity. Supervisors could invite student employees to reflect upon difficult situations that arise during work shifts and process those situations together, enabling students to express their views of a situation and prompting questions about the extent to which there may have been potential oppression or discrimination involved. By providing a safe and trusting environment for students to raise these issues, describe their feelings, and process their reasoning using multiple lenses, student employment practitioners can help students further develop their moral compass and their capacity to behave ethically, even in challenging situations.

Leveraging Institutional Support

Supervisors, however, should not be doing this work alone. Developing moral and ethical student employees is just one piece of the institution's values in action. Support from institutional leadership is also important: Values statements espoused by leadership, policies that reward ethical behavior and discipline the opposite, and public statements of values work throughout the organization all attest to moral behavior as an institutional imperative. Leaders could examine the extent to which policies and practices speak to moral and ethical sensitivity and explicitly clarify institutional responses to immoral and unethical behavior. Leaders might also share examples of the complex decisions they face regularly and how they have applied principled, ethical decision-making practices to solving them. A short video from the president, provost, divisional vice president, or other executives sharing their perspectives on character, integrity, and ethics would reinforce the institutional message. Open and honest discussion about institutional values, ethics, and the personal characteristics that support ethical decision making—including respectfulness, compassion, and trustworthiness—bolster awareness of these important concerns. Gehman, Treviño, and Garud (2013) use the term *values practice* to describe how individuals within an organization live their values and the extent to which the behaviors reflect and align with the espoused organizational values. Gehman and colleagues' study of a university's process of creating an honor code found that the connection of living values was practiced in two ways—first, a top-down approach through policy and behavioral modeling from the leadership, and second, individuals at all levels of the organization choosing to champion values practices. The researchers described their findings in terms of values work as "a distributed, relational, interactive and ongoing process" (Gehman et al., 2013, p. 97).

Individual Role Modeling

As we consider how the espoused organizational values are lived throughout all levels of our institutions and the ways in which we engage students in reflecting upon their moral sensitivity, judgment, motivation, and actions, we may also look inward and contemplate the extent to which we as individuals are modeling ethical thinking ourselves. "Role modeling must consistently be confirmed by those around them if we expect individuals to change" (Feller & Whichard, 2005, p. 98). To what extent are we demonstrating moral and ethical sensitivity? To what extent do we articulate our own ethical thought processes, motivation, and follow-through? Do our student employees see us living our values consistently, or do they see us telling them one thing and doing another—as sometimes we hear parents say, "Do as I say, not as I do"?

In fact, parents and family members are often our very first role models. Our ethical thinking and moral compass start with them and extend to other role models we have in childhood, like teachers, religious leaders, coaches, peers, and siblings. Brown and Treviño (2014) studied corporate managers and their employees and sought to understand the extent to which having an ethical role model matters to perceptions of ethical leadership. They found that managers who reported having positive ethical role models were rated more positively as ethical leaders than managers who had fewer ethical role models. "Followers of ethical leaders . . . are themselves higher on moral identity and moral attentiveness, suggesting a kind of moral uplifting role for ethical leaders who act as attractive, legitimate, and credible role models for their followers" (Zhu et al., 2016, p. 108).

As student employment practitioners, we play two roles: facilitators of moral and ethical development and role models of the highest ethical standards. Inasmuch as we hope our student employees will internalize ethics, basing their decisions and actions consistently over time upon the universal ethics of care and justice, we must also be realistic. A moral compass develops over time through experiences, as does a deeper sense of moral and ethical identity. Ethical people sometimes make the wrong call for a variety of reasons. Students may falter on occasion, lapsing in judgment and attempting to justify selfish interests over ethical behavior. Student employment professionals should proactively and openly engage students in conversations about those very experiences, helping them process their thinking and feelings, and the values that drove their decisions and behaviors, thereby helping them learn from mistakes and move forward.

Higher education professionals across campus and throughout the organizational chart are confronted regularly with student moral and ethical dilemmas. Cheating is probably the most commonly mentioned ethical concern, but there are others: excessive alcohol consumption; romantic relationships between students and faculty; confidentiality breaches; unfairness; and disciplinary actions that may involve privilege, favoritism, racism, sexism, or other overt or discreet discrimination (Dalton, Crosby, Valente, & Eberhardt, 2009). Higher education professionals have a great deal of influence in organizing out-of-class activities that have been shown in the literature to contribute to character development: cultural, ethnic, and religious activities; social activities including students from a variety of backgrounds; volunteer work; and leadership training (Astin & Antonio, 2000). Options to create experiences for students to confront these issues abound. Thompson and Epstein (2013) astutely concluded, "There is no one setting that will produce the results that one might expect with regard to the enhancement of student character development" (p. 95). It is a matter of providing multiple opportunities for students to face and work through different moral dilemmas and ethical challenges in a supportive environment.

Career Implications of Moral and Ethical Development

The majority of our student employees will graduate and enter the workforce directly or following graduate school, and they must be ready to face the working world. We have seen all too well what corporate greed, unethical business practices, and immoral abuses of workers have done to society. Because the twenty-first-century world of work is predicated on change as constant, our graduates are entering a world in which reliance on self for career success is expected, rather than reliance on an employer for life's work and wages. In their book, *Knowledge Nomads and the Nervously Employed*, Feller and Whichard (2005) describe future work as requiring an advanced set of applicable and constantly tuned technical and interpersonal skills, an understanding of globalization, and careful attention to an individual's ability to adapt to changing circumstances and take advantage of serendipitous opportunities. These authors are concerned about the workforce of the future and the ability of individuals to sustain themselves and live meaningful lives in the face of ever-changing economic conditions, political corruption, and corporate greed. "Character development," Feller and Whichard (2005) write, "moral, ethical, affective growth—is equally important to technical skills and academic achievements" (p. 79).

Chickering (2010) also cautioned the higher education community about the increasing focus of students and parents on college as a vehicle for personal gain and career success, rather than as a place to develop a sense of social responsibility: "The larger issues of interdependence, identity, purpose, meaning, and integrity have been eclipsed by short-term goals oriented toward securing a well-paying job upon graduation" (p. 58). He called for higher education to return to its roots as fundamentally preparing students for responsible civic engagement. Interpersonal competence, emotional intelligence, integrity, and motivation are necessary for individuals to become responsible contributors to democratic society (Chickering & Stamm, 2002).

Indeed, as educators and student developers, we strive to give students the ethical foundation upon which their future actions will be based. Student employees undoubtedly encounter situations throughout their college careers that require ethical choices. Student employment practitioners can structure purposeful, explicit interventions during training and throughout the semester to help students confront ethical dilemmas, examine their views and values, and process decisions using the ethic of justice and the ethic of care. We can also reinforce institutional values while creating a nonjudgmental environment where students can share their moral dilemmas and process their thinking and feelings with us. Supervisors have a special obligation to serve as role models for the moral decision-making process and ethical behaviors we wish to instill into our students, not only for microlevel decisions on the job but also their future as citizens in a socially just democracy.

Conclusion

Students develop in a number of ways during their college experience. They develop a core identity, learning more about who they are as individuals in multiple aspects of their identities, which aspects are most salient, what they stand for, and what values they hold dearest. They develop competence and the ability to manage emotions and acknowledge their feelings of insecurity, of being in-between. They learn to develop mature relationships and become interdependent. They build their personal character based on integrity. They develop their capacity to identify and understand ethical issues, make judgments, and take actions using ethics of care and justice. Through it all they begin to establish a sense of self, integrate these multiple dimensions of their identities, and begin to feel comfortable as themselves in a variety of social and environmental contexts.

As student employment practitioners we can set the tone for trust and openness so that students feel comfortable in bringing their full selves to work. We can design interventions that prompt students to develop competence and build character, and that challenge thinking about ethical behavior while responding to situations that arise. We can live our values and serve as role models, enacting the attitudes and behaviors we wish to instill in our student employees. We can ensure that institutional values and expectations are visible and honored every day through our example.

3

CAREER DEVELOPMENT AND CAMPUS EMPLOYMENT

This chapter focuses on career development and student employment on campus. Seven theories of career development are discussed. Two are more traditional and still very popular; five are contemporary theories that consider career development in context of the present-day economy and new ways of thinking about work. As with the previous chapter on identity and moral development, we present several approaches that student employment practitioners can use when applying these theories with their students.

Careers

According to journalist John Morrish (2015), the term *career* was first used in the sixteenth century to describe a short horse race. The *Oxford English Dictionary* defines *career* as a "an occupation undertaken for a significant period of a person's life and with opportunities for progress" (Career, n.d.a) and *Merriam-Webster's Dictionary* offers the following definitions: "A field for or pursuit of consecutive progress achievement especially in public, professional, or business life" and "a profession for which one trains and which is undertaken as a permanent calling" (Career, n.d.b).

The term *career* has a history. How did the term *job* evolve? Gewirtz (2009) writes that a job is "a trade of time, skill and spirit for something of value, usually money." Put in historical context, as societies began moving from agrarian to more industrialized economies, a person's time, skill, and spirit were most often exchanged for food, shelter, and perhaps money. In early colonial times, an individual's effort was sometimes exchanged for training, often with respect to trades, such as carpentry, ironwork, and shoemaking. These exchanges were known as *apprenticeships*. Apprenticeships in the United States trace back to 1716 (Jacoby, 1998). Before technical and vocational schools were established, work in the trades was limited to those who could apprentice. As vocational training via schooling became more popular and industry expanded, there was a greater need to help match individuals with the jobs available. Flexibility was limited and choices were few. In those early times, jobs and work were keys to survival, not at all considered vehicles for personal self-fulfillment.

In today's times, a career implies a type of job or series of jobs, perhaps related but not necessarily so, in which individuals engage over the course of their lifetime. Views of work are more expansive, and choices for job and career options abound. In the early 1900s, colleges began providing placement services to their students (American College Personnel Association [ACPA], n.d.). You might have been surprised to learn in chapter 1 that one of our national associations, the ACPA, has its roots in career development. The "ACPA" label was coined in 1931, but it was first founded in 1924 as the National Association of Appointment Secretaries by May L. Cheney from the University of California at Berkeley to place new teacher graduates in jobs (American College Personnel Association, n.d.). Career development is gaining more attention as parents and families are looking for tangible career outcomes from their students' college educations (Cruzvergara & Dey, 2014).

Although concerns raised in the previous chapter about the risks of contemporary views of college as primarily a vehicle for career success (Chickering, 2010; Feller & Whichard, 2005) versus character development are justifiable, higher education administrators and student employment practitioners can still help students connect their college experiences to career possibilities. In fact, student employment practitioners can benefit from a deeper understanding of contemporary career development theory and ways in which working on campus can influence the development of career thinking, exploration, and planning.

Traditional Theories of Career Development

Two well-known career development theories, Holland's (1959, 1985) theory of vocational personalities and Super's (1953, 1975) life-span/life-roles theory of career development have stood the test of time. They are deemed traditional as they represent the first theoretical models of career decision-making and development, and both are still quite useful and relevant today.

Holland's Theory of Vocational Personalities

When considering seminal career development theories, John L. Holland is often the first name that comes to mind. Holland's work experience as a personnel assistant in the U.S. Army, where he matched enlisted men with a variety of jobs, greatly influenced his thinking about jobs and careers. His original theory of career development was published in 1959, and he spent the rest of his career studying, testing, and further refining it. The theory states that vocational choice and job satisfaction are outcomes of interactions between people's personalities and their work environments (Holland, 1959). Career choices are an expression of personality and are best made by people with adequate information about themselves and occupations (Holland, 1985). This idea is at the heart of the idea of making a good match or fit between person and position. In choosing, Holland (1997) thought, people are ultimately making "an expression of personality" (p. 7). This matching idea was not entirely new at that time; the idea that a good career choice is made by comparing aspects of self to aspects of work was first described in 1909 by Frank Parsons, known as the father of vocational guidance (Pope & Sveinsdotir, 2005).

Holland took Parsons's matching idea and expanded it. He believed that a positive interaction between people's personalities and their work environments would lead to job satisfaction. People gravitate to work environments that are congruent with their personalities specifically because these environments support their style and attitudes, provide opportunities to use preferences and strengths, build confidence, endorse expressed values, and result in achievement and job satisfaction (Holland, 1997). A work environment consistent with one's personality would also encourage similar thinking and reward consistent behaviors (Holland, 1968).

To help people make good career choices, Holland sought to develop a categorization of people and work environments. He was especially interested in making sure that his theory was accessible to people who did not have access to professional psychologists, which is why he used lay terms when describing his typology. He defined the following six types of personalities and environments:

1. *Realistic* (R) personalities tend to prefer activities that involve things physical, such as machines, tools, or athletics. They value stability and practicality and enjoy solving concrete, tangible problems. Realistic environments are dominated by individuals with similar preferences. These environments reward values and behaviors that are consistent with a concrete problem-solving approach and manual work.

2. *Investigative* (I) personalities tend to prefer activities involving ideas, theories, scientific research, and mathematical analysis. They value independence and abstract concepts and tend to be curious, intellectual problem-solvers. Investigative environments comprise similar personality

types and reward activities that produce systematic, objective, and analytical approaches to intellectual and abstract problems.

3. *Artistic* (A) personalities tend to prefer aesthetic, creative, and unstructured activities, and they value imagination, self-expression, and originality. Environments categorized as artistic would provide opportunities for such self-expression; allow freedom for exploration and creativity; and be flexible to accommodate inspired, unconventional pursuits.

4. *Social* (S) personalities prefer activities involving the care, support, education, and influence of others and value cooperation, relationships, and community. Likewise, social environments provide opportunities to support, care for, teach, train, or cure others and reward those with helpful, person-centered dispositions, who consider the human element when making decisions and enjoy team-based activities.

5. *Enterprising* (E) personalities prefer entrepreneurial activities, such as risk-taking and leadership, and value status, influence, and financial success. Accordingly, enterprising environments provide opportunities for influence, encourage persuasion of others toward the achievement of organizational and personal goals, and reward those with ambition.

6. *Conventional* (C) personalities prefer organized and explicit activities involving record keeping, organizing data, and performing computations, and they value structure, order, and precision. Conventional environments reward organizational abilities, conformist attitudes, and practical solutions.

These six vocational personalities are often described by their letters—RIASEC—and can be categorized with a one-, two-, or three-letter code, with the first letter considered a dominant feature (Holland, 1996). RIASEC work environments are also categorized (Gottfredson, 1999; Holland, 1985) and demand like-minded activities, expect like-minded approaches to problem-solving, offer opportunities for expression of similar thinking and shared values, and encourage people to use their innate preferences and apply their strengths. The key for Holland was in the match, or as he later described, approximations of a match (Freeman, 1993).

Holland's theory is one of the most well known and widely researched among career development theories (Gottfredson & Johnstun, 2009; Nauta, 2010). Although several scholars have questioned the power of the theory to actually predict vocational outcomes (Brown & Gore, 1994; Spokane & Cruza-Guet, 2005; Tinsley, 2000), it is widely agreed that Holland's theory is well grounded, accessible, practical, and useful to people without extensive education in vocational psychology (Gottfredson, 1999; Nauta, 2010; Tinsley, 2000). Accessibility and affordability, as well as the variety of instruments available to measure both personality and work environments, make it a popular theory that career counselors have long used with clients (McDaniel & Snell, 1999). This theory is especially good to use with students who have made no attempt at self-exploration and have made no decisions. If we recall Marcia's identity statuses, such students might be considered diffuse—low on exploration and low on commitment. Holland's theory is a great starting point to motivate these students to begin the process of self-discovery.

Super's Life-Span/Life-Roles Theory

Donald E. Super was a contemporary of Holland who viewed vocational choice differently. Rather than see choice as a match at one point in time, Super envisioned a series of choices that occur throughout a lifetime as roles evolve. He described this series of choices as a process of adjustment (Super, Savickas, & Super, 1996). In fact he preferred the word *development* instead of *choice* (Super, 1953, 1975). Super acknowledged the value of Holland's fit between person and environment and added that people may have multiple outlets through which they apply their interests and skills, such as in their leisure time or community work. He called his theory a life-span/life-roles theory and created the life career rainbow (see Figure 3.1), which describes five stages of career development that occur over a lifetime and align loosely, but not exclusively, with age.

1. *Growth* (ages 0–14)—This stage is characterized by the development of a self-concept.
2. *Exploration* (ages 15–24)—This is a period for further development of self-concept, through trying things out, along with initial choices about career.
3. *Establishment* (ages 25–44)—This is a period of stability in work and life, professional reputation.
4. *Maintenance* (ages 45–64)—This is a time of refined improvements and adjustments of life roles.
5. *Decline* (ages 65 and above)—Initially designated by Super to refer to the retirement stage, individuals in this stage would be withdrawing, or disengaging, from the work environment. However, Super himself wrote about his own rebirth of sorts after age 65, where he found new opportunities that reinvigorated his career.

These stages occur in sequence as one grows older and cycles through the various life roles and spaces, such as school, home, work, and community. Depending on a person's individual circumstances, one can re-cycle (Super et al., 1996) into an earlier stage, making a reverse loop in light of a changed

Figure 3.1. Super's life career rainbow.

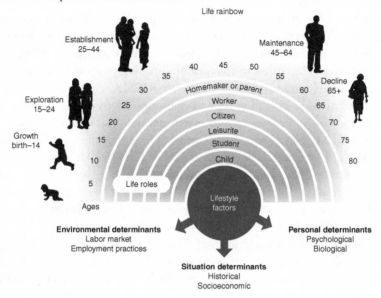

Source: Careersnz (2017).

situation. One particularly relevant application of Super's theory is with adult learners who may, as they enroll in college after a period of full-time work, be recycling or looping back from the establishment to the exploration stage. As these adults also take on various roles in life (student, worker, spouse, or parent), their self-concept and career satisfaction are affected (Freeman, 1993). This idea is still very much relevant in today's world, where students often balance many roles simultaneously.

Super believed that career development involved a process of exploration through experience, where individuals have an experience (in today's career development circles we would use the term *internship*) and learn more about themselves from that experience. Development occurs as people continue to refine their self-concepts based on the experiences they have (Super, 1953). Here is Super (1953) in his own words, which align perfectly with present-day career development:

> The process of vocational development is essentially that of developing and implementing a self concept: it is a compromise process in which the self concept is a product of the interaction of inherited aptitudes, neural and endocrine make-up, opportunity to play various roles, and evaluations of the extent to which the results of role playing meet with the approval of superiors and fellows. (p. 190)

Using These Theories With Student Employees

Holland's theory of vocational personalities and Super's life-span theory are traditional theories that still hold relevance today. Student employment practitioners can use Holland's RIASEC model to give students a starting point. The authors call attention to the idea of a starting point as we do not want students to feel boxed in by one of the six RIASEC categories. Rather, the categories might be viewed as broad beginnings. Many free tools and games explain the Holland codes, and an Internet search quickly reveals them. We recommend My Next Move, a free web resource that the U.S. Department of Labor (n.d.) created for the general public. The "Tell Us What You'd Like to Do" section offers a quiz of 60 questions that takes about 3 minutes to complete; results generate a 3-letter Holland code. The companion website, O'NET Online, can then be used to browse occupations based on the Holland codes (National Center for O'NET Development, n.d.).

It might be particularly impactful in a student employment setting to invite the student employee to assess the work environment using Holland's terms, and then consider the extent to which there is reasonable alignment or misalignment with his or her own Holland personality type. If the work environment provides opportunities for student employees to live out their personality preferences and apply their strengths on the job, according to Holland (1985), they will experience greater job satisfaction. Supervisors may discuss the opportunities student employees have at work to stretch their thinking and develop new skills in areas that feel less comfortable for them.

Note that Holland's theory and the instruments and quizzes used to determine a person's Holland code are based purely on expressed interest, not vetted skill or education or degree level. Therefore, the authors reiterate that RIASEC is a terrific starting point for students; it is not a predictive model of career choice. Holland's RIASEC can be used to gain self-awareness, explore possible careers, and acquire language students can use to describe themselves and their interests. It is not meant to prescribe careers or assign work environments.

Super's theory is applicable to students of all ages and stages in their career development because it focuses on individuals, their stage in life, their roles, and the spaces in which they exist and function. Recall from chapter 1 the idea that college student employees can be understood, depending on their life circumstances, as either students who work or as workers who study. Nontraditional students may be more likely to consider themselves workers who study, and Super's theory can help them examine how the role of student is incorporated into the bigger picture of their life roles. Super was one of the earliest to introduce the idea that one could learn more about oneself and further self-concept from experience; a campus job is certainly an experience through which students can learn about themselves. Chapter 4 of this book is devoted to learning and campus employment.

Supervisors may share Super's life career rainbow with students and ask them to consider their life stage and roles and the ways their campus jobs, academic experiences, and cocurricular experiences fit together. Adult students in particular might be invited to share more about their life experiences— how those life experiences have shaped their identity and are now contributing to their academic experience. Students may also be prompted to use Holland and Super together, by considering how their Holland personalities have matched their life experiences and roles to date and relate their unique experiences and personalities to their future career plans. Some students may see a good fit between their primary RIASEC code and their community or leisure pursuits. Others may purposefully enter a work environment opposite of their primary RIASEC code as a challenge to develop new interests and skills. A campus job can endorse or challenge students' preferences, thereby enhancing their development.

Contemporary Theories of Career Development

Now we shift to more contemporary views of career choice and development: Gelatt's (1989) theory of positive uncertainty, Krumboltz's (2009) theory of planned happenstance, Bright and Pryor's (2005) chaos theory of career development, Savickas's (2013) theory of career construction, and Bluestein's (2006) relational theory of working. This set of theories is grounded on the paradoxical notion that change is constant, and as a result, our students need to be prepared to adjust quickly to changing conditions.

Gelatt's Theory of Positive Uncertainty

H. B. Gelatt is a contemporary career development theorist concerned about what he views as an outdated way of making career decisions. Gelatt (1989) argues that career decisions are far more complex than is reflected in Holland's person-environment matching process, and also more than Super's view of work in balance with multiple life roles. In the late 1980s Gelatt introduced his theory of positive uncertainty, which accounts for the reality that career decisions are often made in unstable and unpredictable economic conditions. Positive uncertainty, he wrote, is "a decision and counseling framework that helps clients deal with change and ambiguity, accept uncertainty and inconsistency, and utilize the non-rational and intuitive side of thinking and choosing" (Gelatt, 1989, p. 252).

Positive uncertainty involves two simple principles, or as Gelatt termed them, *attitudes*: first, that uncertainty is certain and should be accepted as such, and second, that in spite of uncertainty and constant change, people should remain positive and self-confident in their ability to navigate the changes that arise. In fact, positive uncertainty carries several clever paradoxes. Gelatt (1989) described the first as "Treat your facts with imagination but do not imagine your facts" (p. 253). This paradox encourages people to be skeptical of what they hear and what they believe they know. Facts presented may not necessarily represent a full picture of any situation. Healthy skepticism is important. In the present day, these ideas are often discussed in the media, as we are bombarded with opinions and slanted reporting presented as objective journalism. Gelatt's (1989) second paradox is, "Know what you want and believe, but do not be sure" (p. 253). This paradox invites us to be goal oriented but to leave some room to adjust course or to reconsider goals once new information or new circumstances arise, as they often do in today's society where new information flows continually. Note that this concept applies to career and any type of goal, such as an academic or personal goal or a work-related goal. Gelatt's (1989) third paradox is, "Be rational, unless there is a good reason not to be" (p. 254). Clearly Gelatt is not advocating for haphazard decision-making or irrational behavior; he suggests here that one's gut is not to be summarily ignored. Feelings about decisions and actions matter and should be valued, explored, and also vetted. Gelatt (1989) encouraged people to view career decision-making as "as much a process for discovering goals as for achieving them" (p. 254). This idea of career discovery aligns well with Super's life-span theory and adds the recommendation of remaining positive in the face of ambiguity and confusion.

Krumboltz's Theory of Planned Happenstance

At age 81, John D. Krumboltz (2009) described his own career in the following:

> Over the course of my lifetime so far, I personally have been employed as a gardener, magazine sales person, chauffeur, farmer, drill press operator, aluminum foundry worker, cereal packager, railroad loader, elevator operator, chemist's assistant, pancake taster, book publisher's assistant, radio announcer, teaching assistant, tennis coach, camp counselor, career counselor, high school counselor, algebra teacher, military officer, test construction specialist, research psychologist, professor, and author. I did not, and never could have, predicted this pattern of employment. And who knows what I will do next? (p. 136)

You may be wondering if Krumboltz was actually able to keep a job, but poor performance was not an issue in his case. He used his own story to exemplify the myriad of opportunities he took advantage of as a young man before beginning his career as a psychologist and professor. If you are thinking that planned happenstance sounds like a paradox, you are correct! Krumboltz, like Gelatt, viewed the world, economy, and jobs as constantly changing. He believed that career development is not about a choice in time or about choosing one career; rather, it is an ongoing process of learning and development, of self-discovery, and of making the most of opportunities that present themselves, vis-à-vis happenstance (Mitchell, Levin, & Krumboltz, 1999). Also, like positive uncertainty, the theory of planned happenstance encourages openness to opportunities one can neither plan for nor predict. Take note that happenstance, according to Krumboltz, is not simply about luck or chance; it is about being ready and able to take full advantage of unplanned events. Mitchell, Levin, and Krumboltz (1999) suggest that to best position oneself and be ready to take advantage of happenstance, one should develop five skills: curiosity, flexibility, optimism, risk-taking, and persistence.

Student employment opportunities on campus can be shaped in ways that encourage students to develop these skills. For example, the college library hires a student employee, Liam, to work on social media campaigns that will bring more visibility to library resources and services. He brings to the job the social media skills he developed as part of his social world, not work. Liam's supervisor asks if he would be willing to learn WordPress as part of the library's new initiative with faculty blogging. Liam is curious, and while a little anxious about a responsibility he has never had, he willingly takes a risk and accepts the challenge with great optimism. Liam finds that WordPress is not very difficult to learn. In a few weeks he has designed the blog site and manages the content. Liam might have predicted that he could learn a new program, but he could not have predicted the number of requests that came in from new faculty bloggers who needed his assistance. Liam's willingness to take on a new responsibility on the job resulted not only in learning a new skill but in expanding his relationships with faculty on campus, and refining his tutoring abilities as well. Whether Liam's next position involves WordPress is not as important as the attitude he had about taking a risk, learning a new task, and being open to opportunities that arose as a result.

The idea of being open to opportunity is the happenstance part. As we consider the uncertainty of today's economy, the churning of business, and the speed with which entrepreneurial ventures and start-ups are taking hold, we want our students to be aware of what is happening around them. We want our students to be listening for and looking for ways to optimize their options through willingness to make adjustments from their plans and take a risk by taking action.

Bright and Pryor's Chaos Theory of Career Development

A similar way of thinking about careers was termed the *chaos theory of careers* (Bright & Pryor, 2005). Bright and Pryor (2005) compared modern careers to the chaos theory used in mathematics and science, which states that very small changes in complex systems can have large effects. They suggest that because careers no longer follow a predictable linear path, individuals need to learn how to react to unplanned events and overcome adversity. "We want to move away from this predict and control attitude. . . . We need to equip people to continually reinvent themselves and to deal with the changes they are going to face . . . to take advantage of opportunities that present themselves . . . and to get back from the setbacks" (Bright, 2013, 2:01).

Chaos theory is simply another way of describing the uncertainty of our future and fortifying the need for our graduates to manage through chaos and uncertainty, find positive opportunities, and successfully cope with and rebound from the setbacks. Pink (2001) posited that twenty-first-century work would involve fewer long-term employers offering lifetime employment and far more individuals who act like free agents, moving swiftly from work project to work project, where different professionals come together, form a team to complete a project, and then re-form with others for other projects. Krumboltz (2009) decried the traditional question often asked of college students about what career they have chosen to pursue: "Naming a future occupation is amazingly simple and can easily be faked," he wrote (p. 142). All students can benefit from reframing undecidedness and open-mindedness; this way of thinking allows them the freedom to discover more about themselves and their purpose in life without the restriction of a career box based on what is known about careers at the moment.

Applying These Theories to Student Employees

These theorists not only acknowledge but also celebrate the accelerated pace of change in today's society. Without a doubt, our students will face many changes long after they graduate. If they become more comfortable with uncertainty and remain positive about the exciting opportunities that await them, rather than becoming paralyzed with anxiety about things they cannot and will not ever be able to control, they will be ready to manage during the uncertain times that occur throughout their life span.

Student employment practitioners can use these theories to help students think about their campus job as an opportunity to develop the skills they need to face uncertainty and happenstance: curiosity, flexibility, optimism, risk-taking, and persistence. Not surprisingly, these five skills are also needed in the workplace off campus. Helping students develop these skills also assists them in becoming better employees now and in the future. Supervisors can share examples from their own careers as well as in present workplaces of when unplanned events occurred and how they reacted, adjusted, and moved forward in spite of surprise. We can focus our mentoring conversations on skill development and attitude, rather than on a point-in-time choice relative to career, helping our students to perform at higher levels on the job and to position themselves to take advantage of opportunities that materialize in the future.

Having reviewed the aforementioned career development theories, we now know that our students will not make a single career choice; they will engage in career development throughout their lives. Some of this development will result from goals set and actions taken toward those goals; other developments will arise from uncertain circumstances and unplanned events.

Savickas's Theory of Career Construction

Mark Savickas is known as a postmodern theorist. Like Gelatt and Krumboltz, he embraces the complexity of work in the modern era and acknowledges the constant change expected in one's work and life. Savickas (2013) defines *career* as "the construction of meaning through work-role self-consciousness" (p. 654) that emerges from individuals as they review their life situations and stories; reflect upon the what, how, and why behind choices they have made; and recall how they reacted and adapted to unplanned negative events. Such negative events could include failure—large or small—loss of employment, and even personal or health issues.

This process of storying, reflection, and pattern identification can help individuals more deeply understand their own motivations and behaviors and the meaning they personally derive from work. You may recall that the reflection process was highlighted in chapter 2 as a key method for helping students with identity development and moral and ethical decision-making. Especially important to the process of career construction is reflection on and understanding of how individuals exhibit resiliency in the face of challenging circumstances. Because the modern-day era is one of constant change, Savickas (1997) claims that adaptability is key to career satisfaction: "Career adaptability is the readiness to cope with the predictable tasks of preparing for and participating in the work role and with the unpredictable adjustments prompted by changes in work and working conditions" (p. 254). Key to adaptability is an individual's perspective on change and willingness to accept that change is the norm. Individuals may look forward in anticipation of what could be while remaining alert for changing conditions that will require them to adapt and continuing to prepare and position themselves for that next responsibility or role.

Consider the term *career construction*. The word *construction* makes us think of intentional and planned creation, as if one is constructing an edifice or bridge. When related to career, the connotation is the same: constructing one's career over a lifetime, or as Savickas has described it, designing one's life

(Savickas et al., 2009). The term *construction* "emphasizes narratability to tell one's story coherently, adaptability to cope with changes in self and situation, and intentionality to design a meaningful life" (Hartung, 2013, p. 11). About now you may be thinking about Baxter Magolda's theory of self-authorship relative to identity; conceptually the creation of identity and the creation of career share commonalities. The ability for individuals to construct their careers and design meaningful lives emerges from two viewpoints, looking back and looking ahead (Savickas et al., 2009). Looking back enables us to remember and retell our stories, recalling critical incidents in our lives that have shaped our identities—decisions and circumstances; experiences that helped us understand ourselves better; our motivations, interests, values, priorities, skills, and talents—as well as individuals and their roles in our lives. Looking ahead gives us the opportunity to envision our ideal futures with an eye toward real restrictions and practical limitations, such as with a specific geographical area or the job market and employment opportunities available. The idea of *career construction* or *life design*—whichever term you choose—is meant to be a liberating examination of who we are and whom we wish to become.

At this point you may recall that Cote (2014) critiqued Arnett's theory of emerging adults as excluding people from lower socioeconomic strata who do not have the time nor the freedom to explore new possibilities. You may be wondering who in our society has the freedom to construct their careers and design their lives. Blustein's relational theory of working takes a social justice perspective on work that can prompt your own thinking about work and its role in your life and the lives of your student employees.

Blustein's Relational Theory of Working

David L. Blustein is a scholar, a counseling psychologist with a private practice, and a contemporary of Savickas. As such, he is positioned to understand the theoretical and practical aspects of career development. He suggests that, to a large extent, traditional career development theories and, to a smaller extent, even the contemporary and postmodern-era theories are limited, as they tend to apply to highly educated populations who live in advanced economies (Blustein, 2006). Despite the increasing lack of stability in first-world countries relative to economies and job prospects, highly educated people in industrialized nations still, by and large, have many more options for jobs, careers, and callings. In the United States we have the luxury of living in a country where opportunities exist. Blustein has argued that work is not necessarily about fulfilling one's dreams, designing one's life, or becoming self-actualized; work for many around the globe is simply about survival. Work, according to Blustein (2006), fulfills three basic human needs: survival, social connectedness, and self-determination.

How, then, is *work* defined and viewed? A quick scan of *Thesaurus.com* reveals more than 30 synonyms for the word *work*, almost half of which—including *toil, grind, drudge, slogging,* and *struggle*—have negative connotations and relate far better to work for survival than for the other needs. For most of us, working is likely necessary for survival, yet the extent to which we work solely for survival is another consideration. Higher education professionals often describe our work as a calling, or in Blustein's language, self-determination.

What needs does work fulfill for our students? Knowing how they view work can enable students to better understand the opportunities work presents. If, for example, your student Odelia is working solely for survival, she may not give much thought to any other benefits she may derive from her campus job in food service. She may view her campus job as just a job that pays the bills, so to speak, and disregard opportunities for professional development if her basic survival needs are met. In other words, if Odelia's job satisfies these survival needs for her, she may not consider investing more of herself in the role because she does not see an additional need for that. Let us consider how Odelia's experience with her food service job could be different if she views work as an opportunity for social connection. In this case, Odelia may be highly motivated to learn more about customer service, to go above and beyond for her customers who are also her peers, and she may be an enthusiastic participant in group training sessions and department get-togethers. Odelia may volunteer to serve with other students on committees that review student dining concerns and create policy recommendations. Finally, in Blustein's language, Odelia might also view her job as fulfilling her need for self-determination. As such, she may be acutely aware of the career-building opportunities within campus dining and afterward with the sponsoring corporate partner. This attitude may motivate Odelia to put forth maximum effort into her job to be recognized, to be offered higher levels of responsibility, and to gain the business skills she knows are needed to progress in her postcollege future. Odelia's example demonstrates how a person's view of work will likely influence the type of experience he or she has.

Blustein (2011) also points out that work is more than service to individual needs for survival, connectedness, and self-determination. Work is rooted in society and in culture. It is relational, in that family traditions influence our views of work, as do social class, gender, and race. Our choices about work and career are influenced by these relational factors as well as the needs that work fulfills. Consider Tomás, a first-generation college student who came to the university as part of a bridge program for students from underserved high schools. Tomás got his first job on campus in an office where he was left alone to do filing for most of his shift each day. The filing itself was not so bad and his supervisor was nice, but Tomás realized that he needed more people contact and was tempted to quit. His mother was very upset and tried to dissuade him from leaving that position. She feared that he would be unable to find another job and lose an important source of income. His father agreed. Tomás tentatively approached his college success counselor about his concerns and shared his parents' opinions. The counselor understood the source of the parents' concern and was able to help Tomás find a new position at the same rate of pay in another department where he would have peers working alongside him on a daily basis. Tomás needed his job for survival, but he also clearly recognized that he needed social connection more.

Applying These Theories to Student Employees

This last set of postmodern career development theories can be thick and complex, yet they are presented here for the generalist student employment practitioner. You may be concerned that these theories are meant only for professional career counselors. Not so. Supervisors and mentors of student employees can invite students to reflect on their own stories with all aspects of their identity; the richness of their background and traditions; and the unique experiences they have had, in school and at work. We may prompt students to consider the ways in which their campus job also influences their career thinking and life purpose. Giving our students opportunities to reflect on and tell their stories not only validates their narratives but brings us closer to them; we learn more about who they are and what is really important to them. This exercise has a career benefit as well: Sharing their past stories will also help them prepare for future interviews for internships, fellowships, full-time positions, or additional schooling and ultimately empower them to design their futures.

Student employment practitioners can use Blustein's relational theory of working to engage student employees in reflective conversations about their personal views of work and the views of family members. One simple exercise is to have students create a work genogram—a diagram of members of their family tree, labeling each with a primary or significant career or job, as well as their views of work. Invite students to share their genograms with each other and discuss their own personal views of work and the ways in which family views have influenced their thinking.

We offer one final recommendation for student employment practitioners who wish to focus on student career development: Engage the experts in your career center. Career counselors can work with you to design customized programming that honors the unique aspects of your work environment and meets the needs of your student employees. Career services professionals often have a wealth of industry contacts—employers and alumni—who could be invited to share their career stories with your student employees, offer career advice, assist in an internship or job search, and provide access to industry opportunities for internships, co-ops, or full-time jobs. Leverage the resources and the experts on your campus to help your student employees explore career options, consider the fit between their personalities and potential work environments, and actively design and pursue career goals while remaining open to happenstance and unexpected opportunity.

Conclusion

As student employment practitioners, we can draw on theories of career development to prompt student thinking about their views of work, their life's purpose, and their practical development of transferable skills. We can partner with institutional experts to help students access and utilize career resources, and we can support their dreams for career and for life. Review these theories a few more times to familiarize yourself with them. Think about the extent to which these theories align with your personal and professional experiences. Consider the examples we have shared throughout the chapter, and reflect upon how these theories might come alive in the lives of your students.

Not all individuals develop in the same way at the same time. Not all theories fit your student employees exactly, and not all student employees fit the theories exactly. The usefulness of any theory in working with a student depends on our ability to apply, adapt, or reject it based on our knowledge of and interaction with that student.

4

CAMPUS EMPLOYMENT AND STUDENT LEARNING

S everal prominent foundations—including Lumina, Ford, Teagle, and Carnegie—funded a large-scale research project in 2011 examining what students learned in college. Investigators looked at survey responses, transcript data, and scores on the Collegiate Learning Assessment. The results as reported were alarming: "Students are likely to learn no more in the last two years [of college] than they did in the first two, leaving higher education just slightly more proficient in critical thinking, complex reasoning, and writing than when they entered" (Arum & Roksa, 2011, p. 37). This study created quite a controversy among scholars and practitioners in higher education. Critics questioned the researchers' methodology, statistical analyses, and conclusions (Astin, 2011; Igo, 2011; Lederman, 2013). Despite convincing critiques, the study served a practical purpose—prompting colleges and universities to revisit their curricula inside and outside the classroom to discover, document, enhance, and expand the teaching and learning strategies that positively impact student learning and success. Two findings from this study speak directly to campus student employment. First, students who worked about 10 hours per week on campus improved their critical thinking scores. Second, academic and social climates with high expectations of student performance and greater amounts of reading and writing contributed positively to student engagement (Arum & Roksa, 2011).

This chapter explores the nexus between student learning and student employment on campus. Having just digested chapters devoted to student development and career development and given that development and learning are sometimes conjoined or considered as one process in the literature of higher education, readers may be wondering why we have chosen to separate the topics into distinct chapters. What are the differences between learning and development as we see them? Learning and development are both continuous processes occurring throughout our lives. We believe the two concepts are inextricably linked. In fact, we even define *learning* in this chapter as cognitive and intellectual development. However, we also believe that development and learning are distinct from one another in an important and meaningful way. One can undevelop, so to speak, in that we can regress in our development—or re-cycle, as with Super's life-span/life-roles theory of career development. The authors submit that while one can certainly forget facts, once something is learned, is it actually possible to unlearn it? This perspective prompted us to separate development and learning in this text.

An important point of commonality between development and learning is that both processes can take place without the benefit of purpose or guidance, but both can be far better with purpose and guidance. We know that student development can be fostered if someone—a mentor, coach, or supervisor—helps a student through. The same is true of learning. With this idea in mind, we present this chapter on student learning and campus student employment.

In this chapter, we define *learning* as "a comprehensive, holistic, transformative activity that integrates academic learning and student development," occurring "throughout and across the college experience" (Keeling, 2004, p. 4). Learning is not location specific, vis-à-vis classroom only; learning can take place anywhere. Moreover, if we consider learning to be a holistic activity in which learning and development are both intertwined and interdependent, the authors are less concerned with demarking lines of difference between these concepts and more concerned with giving student employment practitioners an understanding of how students learn and develop. Therefore, this chapter is presented with the hope that student employment practitioners can construct programs, goals, responsibilities, and interventions to move students forward in learning, personal growth, and professional development.

Lastly, if we consider Keeling's use of the word *transformative*, we are accepting a big responsibility: transformation. Transformational learning is a complex process involving awareness, recognition, transformation, application, and integration (Eraut, 2004). In other words, an individual would become aware of a new situation, recognize the knowledge and skills required to function in that situation, transform the skills and knowledge, apply them to the new situation, and integrate the adapted knowledge and skills with what they now know and know how to do. Clearly, this is not as easy to do as it is to say.

In this chapter we introduce theories of learning and cognitive development that can be applied to student employment. Several seminal learning theories are presented first, including those of Bloom, Perry, and King and Kitchener. A review of the essential learning outcomes of a college education and a primer on writing effective learning outcomes for student employees follow. The next section is devoted to theories of experiential learning and work-integrated learning, with a focus on reflection. Transitioning from experiential and work-integrated learning, the skills and qualities employers are expecting from college graduates overall, regardless of academic major, are identified. Next, we introduce the T-shaped professional, a model that has been used primarily in industry and recently has gained traction among higher education professionals. We conclude the chapter with a series of institutional and individual strategies to pursue to improve student employee learning outcomes.

Seminal Theories of Learning

We begin with an overview of two of the most popular learning theories, Bloom's taxonomy (Krathwohl, 2007) of educational objectives and Perry's (1970) theory of intellectual development. We then transition to reflection models, including King and Kitchener's (2004) reflective judgment model and Chickering's (2006) 3R model of reflection. Lastly, the needs of adult learners and the funds of knowledge model are explored. We acknowledge that other models of cognitive development exist, but we have selected these theories because we believe they are particularly salient to working with student employees.

Bloom's Taxonomy of Educational Objectives

Benjamin Bloom developed his taxonomy in the early 1950s. What has come to be known as Bloom's taxonomy has been used ever since in education, elementary through postsecondary, to create and structure learning goals (Krathwohl, 2007; Wilson, 2016). This framework comprises two domains: knowledge and cognitive process. It is meant to be cumulative. Learning goals at the lower level are basic, and as one moves up the levels, the complexity of learning goals increases (Krathwohl, 2007). Anderson and Krathwohl (2001) modified Bloom's taxonomy and built upon it, expanding and clarifying the original levels of knowledge and creating a user-friendly tool to help educators structure their learning goals within the framework. Figure 4.1 depicts the pyramid, showing the levels of cognitive processing from "remember," the beginning level at the bottom, to "create," the highest level at the top.

Many online resources are available that provide examples of Bloom's taxonomy to support the work of student employment practitioners in translating student employee learning goals into a series of increasingly complex learning outcomes. One such example comparing the original cognitive taxonomy and the revised taxonomy is available through a website hosted by

Figure 4.1. Bloom's taxonomy.

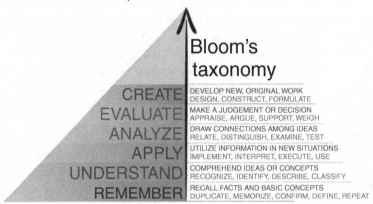

Source. Adapted from Vanderbilt University Center for Teaching (2007), https://cft.vanderbilt.edu/guides-sub-pages/blooms-taxonomy/

Leslie Owen Wilson at the University of Wisconsin–Stevens Point (Wilson, 2016). Another example comes from the Iowa State University Center for Excellence in Learning and Teaching (n.d.), which offers an interactive online tool depicting examples of the dimensions of learning with a chart of learning skills sequenced from lower levels of thinking to higher levels. We also recommend the Center for Teaching and Learning at the University of North Carolina Charlotte's (n.d.) comprehensive webpage dedicated to developing learning outcomes using Bloom.

To assist you in structuring learning goals based on levels of knowledge and the cognitive process, review Table 4.1, which shows the two dimensions of learning in tabular format.

TABLE 4.1
Structuring Learning Goals

Bloom's Dimensions of Learning						
Knowledge	**Cognitive Process**					
	Remember	**Understand**	**Apply**	**Analyze**	**Evaluate**	**Create**
Facts						
Concepts						
Procedures						
Metacognition						

Perry's Theory of Intellectual Development

One of the most influential and well-known theories of intellectual development is that of William G. Perry, a Harvard-educated psychologist who studied college student development in the 1950s and 1960s. A theory developed in the 1970s may seem dated to today's readers, but it still provides a useful lens through which to view cognitive development. Perry's (1970) framework includes four positions, or stages, as follows.

Dualism

During this beginning stage, knowledge is viewed in absolutes (right or wrong, good or bad) and also viewed as being known by an authority. Students in this stage believe that all questions have a correct answer, all problems have a best solution, and that the authority (their faculty, or in the case of student employees, their supervisors) have the correct one. Dualistic thinkers are not yet able to see gray; they think in terms of black or white. Student employees in the dualistic stage of thinking look to the supervisor or other authority (e.g., a department head) for rules, instruction, and specific direction. They believe that there are right and wrong answers at work, and that the supervisor is the person who has all the answers. If you consider dualism in the context of Bloom's stages, a dualistic thinker may be ready to remember and understand facts and concepts and perhaps apply concepts and follow procedures. They may be challenged by activities in the analysis stage. Dualistic-thinking student employees may not be ready to give their opinions or provide input into work projects, as they would not be confident in their own knowledge. They may also hesitate to take guidance from peers, unless the supervisor specifically ascribes expertise to those peers.

Multiplicity

During their college experiences inside and outside of class, students are exposed to new ideas, new ways of thinking, and different perspectives and backgrounds. Through these experiences, they become aware that not all knowledge is known or knowable. Students using multiplistic thinking are intellectually ready to experience diversity and accept multiple viewpoints, beliefs, and opinions, because in this stage everyone can have an opinion. Multiplistic thinkers may consider a variety of alternatives to problem solving, yet they may still look toward authority to help them sort out the exceptions from the rules. Students at this stage of cognitive development are ready to be challenged, so supervisors may consider assigning higher-level tasks to them. Drawing on Bloom's taxonomy, students using multiplistic thinking may be at the analysis stage and perhaps able to engage in some level of evaluation.

Relativism

In this stage, knowledge is accepted as uncertain and viewed as contextual. All opinions are no longer considered equally valid. As a result, right or wrong is dependent upon circumstance. Students using relativistic thinking are more open to contextual factors that lead to circumstances, problems, and potential solutions. Student employees in this stage could be invited to discover with a supervisor the differences between work performance that is acceptable and work performance that is outstanding. They may be open to engaging in a peer review process, as both feedback giver and receiver. However, relativistic thinking may also prompt students to question authority or authoritarian work styles, and supervisors must be ready to field these questions and create opportunities for students to think more deeply as they struggle with choices about whose opinions and facts they will value and follow. If we situate a relativistic thinker in Bloom's dimensions, we would expect this student to be able to analyze, evaluate, and create at the higher level of metacognition.

Commitment

A person in this stage has internalized the belief that knowledge is contextual and that multiple truths legitimately exist. During this stage, students make a personal commitment to their own internal set of values and beliefs that will guide their future thinking, judgment, and acceptance of knowledge in all of its contexts. You may recall from chapter 2 the concepts of self-authorship and moral motivation, where individuals form a sense of their own personal code, which then supports their decisions and actions. Student employees at the commitment stage are likely ready to reflect upon what they are learning on the job and how it applies to their lives outside of work. Supervisors may invite student employees in this stage to consider the connections between their campus jobs and their classroom experiences. As with relativism, students functioning in the commitment stage would be expected to learn at the most complex levels of Bloom's taxonomy.

As mentioned earlier, Perry's theory is well known and widely used. Although practitioners who have studied these theories may be familiar with Perry's work, many student employment practitioners are not. Landrum's (2012) 20-minute video provides a useful summary of Perry's theory.

Applying These Theories to Student Employment

Let's consider these two seminal theories of learning and intellectual development with application to student employees. Bloom's taxonomy invites us to envision what we want our students to know and do in an orderly way, from the basic levels of remembering and understanding to the higher levels of applying, analyzing, evaluating, and creating. In a real-life example, Hakeem is an undergraduate student who secured a job with his college's information technology (IT) help desk. We can describe what Hakeem has learned during his work experience using Bloom's language (Voss, 2016):

- *remembering* facts about help desk hours of operations and departmental policies (e.g., no food or drink in the lab, no personal calls while on shift)
- *understanding* concepts about and being able to describe and explain confidentiality, information security, and the customer service focus of the department
- *applying* concepts and procedures to fix a paper jam in the printer and create a technical document
- *analyzing* complex concepts and mentally reorganizing them to diagnose and fix challenging computer problems
- *evaluating* new software packages to determine which would be the best purchase
- *creating* a new webinar to instruct students in using the new software

This is just one example of how a supervisor might structure learning goals for student employees in the IT department. Student employment practitioners in other departments can use Bloom's theory and the online resources and examples referenced in this chapter to describe and structure departmental and job-specific learning goals that begin at the base level and, as time goes on, require higher-level thinking.

Whereas Bloom is best used for the planning stages in structuring learning objectives, Perry is useful as a framework for structuring successively more complex tasks and as a lens through which to understand student employees' thinking. Earlier we shared a few ideas for how student employees in each stage might react to work assignments, but let us summarize. Perry's stages are cumulative; students may begin at the lowest stage of development, dualism, and progress upward through the stages as they increase their cognitive capacity. Student employment practitioners can use Perry's framework when planning orientation and training or when developing a series of work assignments that challenge students' thinking and move them up to high levels of complex thinking.

Consider the example of Angelo, a student who works in the alumni relations office. If Angelo is functioning as a dualistic thinker, he could likely absorb rules and procedures and be able to follow directions about concrete tasks, such as putting together gift packages for the alumni volunteers at the college admissions fair. When the task is straightforward and the instructions are clear, Angelo need only follow the procedure. If Angelo is functioning as a multiplistic thinker, he may be invited to participate in the planning meetings for the admissions volunteer program. During these meetings Angelo could help determine which alumni might be the best representatives for the admissions program and how they might structure the invitation and coordinate alumni representation across a number of locations. Relativistic thinking would enable Angelo to offer opinions about whether the admissions volunteer program should be the same everywhere, in all cities, at all high schools, or whether there would be a need to customize and differentiate the programs. In this case, Angelo might be invited to provide input into the parameters and differentiators. At the commitment stage, Angelo might find himself in the middle of team disagreement about the program plans, but because he is functioning at a high level of intellectual development, Angelo is not put off by the disagreement; he is willing to talk through all the angles and perspectives that each party represents. The extent to which Angelo is able to mediate this situation, however, is not part of Perry's scheme. Mediation might come more easily to a person functioning at the commitment level, but we cannot make assumptions about a range of workplace skills based solely on level of intellectual development.

Angelo's story is one example of how Perry's theory can be used to assess student employees' level of cognition and leverage their abilities by assigning higher-level tasks. Supervisors can look for signs of these various stages of thinking in their conversations with student employees and through observation of their work. Supervisors may also use reflection models to prompt higher level thinking. The following reflection models are particularly applicable to student employees.

King and Kitchener's Reflective Judgment Model

King and Kitchener (2004) connect the ways in which an individual constructs knowledge through reflective thinking. Their model consists of seven stages, which can be combined into three phases. The first phase is *prereflective thinking*, where knowledge exists concretely and can be obtained from an authority, even if initially it is accepted that the knowledge is not available at that moment. As student employees progress through this phase, they come to accept that some knowledge may not be absolute, but they still believe this situation is temporary. Consider this phase as complementary to Perry's dualism. The second phase is *quasireflective thinking*, where knowledge becomes less absolute. Students progressing through this phase come to see that knowledge is far more contextual and subjective than absolute. Compare this phase to Perry's multiplicity. The third phase is *reflective thinking*, where knowledge is constructed through an individual's interpretation of the information available. Reflective thinking develops over time. "Each stage is a dramatic shift in worldview in one's role as a knower" (King & Kitchener, 2004, p. 16). This phase aligns with Perry's highest level of commitment.

The essence of the reflective judgment model is helping students confront complex problems that are not well defined. Student employees need to understand how to identify the core of the problem (not just what might be presented), delineate who is involved in the situation and what their perspectives are, collect as much information as reasonable, evaluate that information in light of the specific situation and people involved, then make judgments and take action. Recall Johnson's *5I* model of ethical judgment from chapter 2: identify, investigate, innovate, isolate, and implement. Johnson was writing for ethical judgment, yet the activities in the *5I* model can easily be applied to other types of problems, prompting higher-level thinking by compelling the problem solver to generate multiple potential solutions, not just rely on the obvious or on the first solution generated.

Adult Learners

The aforementioned theories of how knowledge is viewed, acquired, and constructed are not limited to the traditional-age college student. Adults over age 25 are returning to college in greater numbers than ever, and their life experiences undoubtedly contribute to their own knowledge and motivation to learn. Life experience can benefit adult learners in that they may have already moved from dualistic thinking to multiplistic and relativistic thinking in Perry's (1970) language, or from prereflective to quasireflective and reflective thinking in King and Kitchener's (2004) language. Throughout life and work, adults may have already confronted and solved complex and ill-defined problems, met the challenges posed by having to balance multiple roles and responsibilities, experienced failure, and developed coping skills and resilience (Merriam, Caffarella, & Baumgartner, 2007). They may also have experience with training and professional development programs with previous employers that have taken place in person and perhaps online. Personal backgrounds of adult learners, including their ethnicity, race, social class, sexual orientation, ability, and experiences with power and privilege, may have already contributed to their understanding of knowledge as constructed in context. However, as Merriam and colleagues (2007) note, life experience alone does not enable an open mind; a life experience in which closed-mindedness and negative attitudes have been learned and cast in someone's views can actually detract from the learning process in college. They caution, "A single set of principles is not likely to hold true for the wide ranging diversity of learners and learning situations" (Merriam et al., 2007, p. 422).

Chickering's 3R Framework

Given the differences between traditional-age students and adult students, how might student employment practitioners honor differences without making assumptions that all adults have achieved similar levels of intellectual growth and reflective judgment? We can start by acknowledging that the life experience of adult learners contributes to their intellectual development. At the same time, we can also challenge them to continue to expand their knowledge and their views of knowledge. Chickering (2006) offers a simple 3R framework when working with adult learners: recognize, respect, and respond. Using this framework, we can *recognize* that adult learners have life experience that could inform their peer students as well as their own new learning. We can show *respect* for what they have learned thus far through life experience, and we can *respond* to the diversity of experiences these students bring with them by asking about them. The authors suggest adding a fourth R: *request*, in that we may request that our adult learners share what they know relative to the project, task, or learning activity so that they might contribute and add value to the learning experiences of their peer students.

The Funds of Knowledge Approach

Chickering's 3R framework for adult learners is similar to an approach that K–12 teachers have traditionally used but that has recently become more visible in higher education literature, called *funds of knowledge* (Moll, 2005; Ribeiro & Lubbers, 2015). Teachers using this approach flip their roles from teacher to learner by connecting with the students' families, respecting the knowledge students gain from their families, and creating trusting relationships through which they can help students incorporate that knowledge into their new learning at school. The funds of knowledge concept is described by one of its primary scholars as "the knowledge base generated by families on the basis of their experience, especially their work experiences, their social practices, and their social history" (Moll, 2005). Moll, Amanti, Neff, and Gonzalez (1992) advocated for this approach as a way to refute the perceived knowledge deficiencies in households of working-class families. Through their research they discovered that much was learned in these households, and that families demonstrated skills in dealing with change and developing resiliency in the face of hardship (Moll et al., 1992). The ability to manage through change and demonstrate resilience in the face of challenges are skills our students will need when they graduate and continue to the working world. At this point you might be thinking of chapter 2, considering that the funds of knowledge framework may also provide an opportunity to validate student identity.

Applying These Theories to Student Employees

Let us clarify straightaway that assessing and evaluating both judgment and learning have been vexing problems faced by educators at all levels for a very long time. Experts agree that no singular instrument, action plan, or rubric is the solution. Clearly, if pedagogical scholars have not quite figured this out, by no means are we suggesting that student employment practitioners generate such a solution. However, we can still incorporate aspects of these models into our work or attempt to assess learning outcomes. King and Kitchener (2004) developed a "reflective judgment interview" (p. 102) as a conversation guide. Some of the questions easily apply to student employees. For example, we could ask student employees about how they came to hold a particular point of view on a work-relevant topic and what supports their stance, prompting them to consider the possibility of others having a completely different and equally valid view. "As educators, we have the responsibility to teach students the 'habits of mind' associated with making interpretative analyses and thoughtful, reasoned arguments" (King & Kitchener, 2004, p. 222). If we consider the funds of knowledge approach, we may ask our students to share knowledge and skills they developed through family and personal experience before college. The goal of the reflective judgment interview is to get students to surface their experiences and the assumptions they bring to their thinking so that they can then scrutinize those assumptions and determine if they still hold up against new understanding.

Another way of fostering reflective judgment is to encourage supervisors to share examples of complex and ill-structured problems we face in our own work. For example, the career center director might share her frustrations about low participation rates by business majors in career preparation activities and employer networking events. Or she may present the dilemma of how the career center can best serve liberal arts students when the popular media consistently (albeit erroneously) reports that these students are working at the local coffeehouses after graduation because they are not employable. The director could invite her student employees to consider the different actors in these scenarios, including students, staff, faculty, employers, perhaps even parents, family members, and advisers. A task force of student employees working in different areas of the center could be formed to investigate these problems and generate potential solutions as well as evaluate how each solution might be viewed as acceptable—or not—to the various stakeholders involved.

When we reconsider the needs of our adult students, ideas presented in the three *R* model (Chickering, 2006) and the funds of knowledge approach (Moll et al., 1992) are directly applicable to nontraditional student employment. Just as orientation programs have created specialized introduction to college courses for nontraditional undergraduates, student employment coordinators could also create specialized student employment orientations for adult student employees where the life experiences, work experiences, social practices, and funds of knowledge adults bring to campus can be acknowledged and purposefully positioned as value-added for the departments in which they work. Perhaps the adult students themselves might offer their own perspective as to what they bring to the campus job and to their peer students, identifying ways they see themselves contributing to the department overall. Likewise, student employment practitioners have the opportunity to help these nontraditional students see themselves as enthusiastic learners of new information and ideas, through new experiences.

Learning Outcomes

To this point, we have discussed several theories of cognitive development and the ways in which student employment practitioners can apply these theories in the context of campus jobs. As stated earlier, traditional views of learning focus on the teacher and student, the textbook and classroom. Yet higher education has many nonteacher stakeholders who add value to the student learning experience every day. The literature is filled with studies about the ways in which the out-of-classroom experiences contribute to student development and learning (Kuh, 1995, 2008). *Learning Reconsidered* (Keeling, 2004) argued passionately for better integration of campus stakeholders in support of student success. It called for academic affairs and student affairs practitioners to collaborate and take joint responsibility for ensuring that students were meeting common educational goals: engaged citizenship, career planning, ethics, leadership, emotional intelligence, critical thinking, informed decision-making, teamwork, conflict resolution, crosscultural understanding, and tolerance for ambiguity (Keeling, 2004).

Learning Reconsidered II (Keeling, 2006) detailed seven broad learning outcomes, or competencies, for all college graduates, presented here with their connection to student employment:

1. *Cognitive complexity*—includes intellectual reasoning, problem-solving, and decision-making. As discussed, student employees can develop intellectually as they confront complex and ill-defined problems.

2. *Knowledge acquisition, integration, and application*—the resourcefulness with which students gather information and their ability to connect knowledge they gain in one setting to a completely different setting. A student employee may have the opportunity to apply the knowledge she is gaining in her accounting class to her job in student activities, where

she is responsible for an event budget. Later in this chapter we address experiential learning theory and its applications to campus employment.

3. *Humanitarianism*—understanding and appreciating differences, and valuing others. Student employees who work with and for persons different from themselves—in terms of gender, ethnicity, race, religion, sexual orientation, culture, language, hometown, family, social class, educational and work experiences, and so forth—are better positioned to incorporate diverse perspectives in their thinking, learning, and actions. They also have a greater understanding of the communities that they may encounter, work with and for, and join.

4. *Civic engagement*—a sense of civic responsibility and willingness to get involved as an advocate and change maker. Students often acquire competency in civic engagement through community service and leadership, but student employees whose work involves service and civic functions also benefit.

5. *Interpersonal and intrapersonal competence*—a sense of self, of personal agency when students feel confident in their abilities to work independently and as a member of a team. Student employees develop their intrapersonal competence as they perform tasks, get feedback on performance, and achieve task and project objectives. Interpersonal competence develops through teamwork.

6. *Practical competence*—applies to any type of campus job and focuses on the student's ability to acquire and hone specific skills relevant to the job and general competencies like communication skills and project management skills that can be transferred to a new work environment. Gaining practical competence also helps students focus on their strengths relative to their future career aspirations and professional development interests.

7. *Persistence and academic achievement*—working on campus has been shown to contribute to student persistence; we explore this topic in depth in chapter 5. Student employees gain skills at work that can contribute to academic achievement, such as time management, the understanding and use of campus resources, and the ability to set goals, stay on track, and achieve them.

A campus job clearly can provide great opportunities for students to learn and develop the competencies they need for success in their futures. At about the same time that NASPA and ACPA were working on the learning outcomes just reviewed, a related higher education organization, the Association of American Colleges & Universities (AAC&U) was also working on outcomes of a college education. In this next segment, we outline the essential learning outcomes of a twenty-first-century college education as defined by Liberal Education and America's Promise (LEAP), a nationwide project sponsored by the AAC&U.

The Essential Learning Outcomes of a Twenty-First-Century College Education

The AAC&U was founded in 1915 by academic leaders of small colleges intent upon preserving and ensuring the quality in the liberal education of undergraduates. Today its membership is far more diverse, but its focus on undergraduate education remains. In 2005 the AAC&U initiated LEAP, a "national public advocacy and campus action network" (Association of American Colleges & Universities, 2014) to clarify the outcomes of a liberal education in the twenty-first century and help institutions reexamine their strategies for undergraduate education in light of these outcomes.

As part of LEAP, a series of benchmarks for excellence in higher education were created. A *liberal education* refers to "an approach to college learning that seeks to empower individuals and prepare them to deal with complexity, diversity, and change" (Association of American Colleges & Universities, 2011, p. 3). Invariably, this approach and the need to focus on the outcomes for each student's college experience serve as a beacon for everyone involved in undergraduate education. Because the AAC&U identified these benchmarks as the essential learning outcomes of a twenty-first-century college education, they have been adopted by several hundred campuses and by more than 10 state systems comprising both public and private higher education institutional collaborations. Following are four essential learning outcomes of LEAP:

1. *Knowledge of human cultures and the physical and natural world*—study of the arts and humanities, social and natural sciences, and history
2. *Intellectual and practical skills*—problem-solving, quantitative and information literacy, oral and written communication skills, and critical thinking
3. *Personal and civic responsibility*—ethical reasoning, intercultural competence, and active involvement in diverse communities to solve local and global problems
4. *Integrative and applied learning*—the ability to synthesize knowledge and apply skills in a diverse range of settings and depth of issues (Association of American Colleges & Universities, 2014)

The LEAP initiative has prompted colleges and universities across the country to give more careful thought to these outcomes, and to refine and structure educational experiences that enhance the ability of college graduates to apply their knowledge and skill to increasingly global and complex societal, economic, political, and human problems. Graduation itself is no longer the defining outcome for success. The LEAP Campus Action Network includes more than 300 institutions making a commitment to improving undergraduate education by collaborating and sharing best practices (Albertine, 2011).

At this point you may be wondering why these outcomes are positioned as exclusively undergraduate outcomes when they obviously would also be appropriate for graduate students. The AAC&U has historically focused on undergraduate education, not graduate education. Moreover, if undergraduates are completing bachelor's degrees and can demonstrate that they have achieved these essential learning outcomes, then graduate-level educators may therefore focus on other outcomes, which are likely discipline specific and at a higher level. Yet LEAP has had influence among graduate educators who are examining the extent to which high-impact practices are being utilized to improve graduate student success (Denecke, Feaster, Okahana, Allum, & Stone, 2016; Gaff, 2002). We review the high-impact practices in greater detail later in this chapter.

Value of LEAP to Student Employment

Why should student employment practitioners know about LEAP and these essential learning outcomes? Although we have a unique niche to fill in the lives of our students as coordinators, supervisors, mentors, and perhaps teachers, our role in the overall educational process is also very important. As you have read in this book, student employment practitioners are instrumental in students' learning and development. On a practical level, student employment embodies the applied learning piece of the essential learning outcomes. We are uniquely positioned to provide a real-world applied learning experience—the campus job—that gives students opportunities to create knowledge, advance their thinking, hone skills, and refine abilities that will enable them to function effectively as citizens, workers, entrepreneurs, and family members in a rapidly changing, complex world. We are not, however, expected to operate exactly like off-campus employers as our students are not simply employees; they are also students.

High-Impact Practices

A set of best practices has emerged from LEAP that applies to in-class and out-of-class experiences. These high-impact practices have been shown through research to have a positive effect on student performance and learning gains (Kuh, 2008). Presently there are 10 high-impact practices: first-year seminars, common intellectual experiences/core curriculum, learning communities, writing-intensive courses, collaborative assignments, global learning, research, internships, service-learning, and capstone projects. Student employment is not presently included in the list of high-impact practices, yet as intimated in the foreword to this book, campus employment could very well be the next recognized high-impact practice (Kuh, 2016).

What makes high-impact practices so effective, and how can we advocate for the inclusion of campus jobs as a high-impact practice in the future? According to Kuh (2008), high-impact practices share the following common elements:

- *Time on task*—investing time and effort in "educationally purposeful activities" (Kuh, 2008, p. 14), through which students gain competence and confidence, and deepen their commitment to learning. Time on task is about practice, just as athletes and musicians hone their skills with significant investment of time with feedback from coaches and teachers. Student employee supervisors might think of time on task as the opportunity to give students time to try; to give them feedback on their progress; and then to give them more time to try again, review, revise, and redraft their work product.
- *Interaction with faculty and peers*—enables students to develop professional relationships, learn how to communicate with faculty mentors and peers, give and receive feedback, and solve problems collectively. Students learn about professional communication in various work settings and receive feedback on performance. Through relationships with faculty and staff, students develop a deeper understanding of the issues professionals in the field face in their jobs.
- *Diversity*—because exposure to difference is paramount for learning and development—be that difference in personal characteristics, such as ethnicity, race, gender, sexual orientation, personality, family background, culture, or socioeconomic status; values; religious or political views; or ways of knowing, thinking, and decision-making. Student employment practitioners can structure work to increase exposure to diversity and the learning that results from interactions with diverse others.
- *Structured teamwork*—not simply applicable to group projects for class, but to a variety of on-the-job situations where students work as a member of a peer team and perhaps even an intergenerational team.
- *Authentic problem-solving*—applies to academic as well as workplace settings, as the opportunity for students to work on real-world problems in an authentic environment helps them connect in-class with out-of-class learning in both directions. Supervisors of student employees can also benefit by putting students to work on real problems because students can generate real solutions.

- *Feedback on performance*—student employees need clarity of expectations, in addition to how well they are meeting those expectations.
Open and honest communication about student performance is
imperative to their learning. Feedback should be specific and timely, for
both constructive purposes and praise. With regular feedback, students
can refine their work product, adjust their styles, bolster their learning,
and improve performance.

Aspects of these practices that make experiences high impact could apply to
the classroom and to work. Note that three of the established high-impact
practices—research, internships, and community-based service-learning—
often take place outside the classroom (Association of American Colleges &
Universities, 2011). These activities are commonly referred to as *experiential*
or *applied learning* experiences. Experiential learning affords students the
opportunity to learn as they work, applying what they have learned through
coursework to authentic situations and real-world problems (King, 2014).
We present theories of experiential learning later in this chapter.

Writing Learning Outcomes for Student Employees

Keeling and Underhile (2007) differentiate outcomes from actions. Chapter
6 addresses best practices for developing job descriptions focused on actions
and responsibilities. Learning outcomes focus on what the student will know
and know how to do, as well as how the student will think, feel, or be different as a result of the experience (Keeling & Underhile, 2007). Pairing
this idea with a common acronym widely used in goal setting, SMART—
specific, measurable, attainable, realistic, and timely (Mind Tools, n.d.)—can
be helpful to supervisors in developing learning goals for student employees.
Here are a few institutional examples.

Stony Brook University (n.d.a) created its Student Employment Learning Outcomes (SELO) program in 2010 using the AAC&U's essential learning outcomes and supported by student development theory. Its student
employee learning outcomes are connected to the essential learning outcomes as follows:

- *Knowledge of human cultures*—The student employee demonstrates
sensitivity to differences.
- *Intellectual and practical skills*—The student employee is able to
gather, evaluate, and apply information to solve work problems.
- *Personal and social responsibility*—The student employee observes
principles of confidentiality.

- *Integrative learning*—The student employee is able to describe her or his role in the organization and how that role fulfills the mission of the department.
- *Career development*—The student employee understands the concept of transferrable skills and how it applies to his or her own career development. (This learning outcome was added by Stony Brook.)

More detail about the SELO process, outcomes, and examples are available from Stony Brook University (n.d.).

Winston-Salem State University (2017) offers good examples of learning outcomes for student employees in a variety of campus jobs. As you read each of the following descriptions, think about prefacing it with, "As a result of this work experience, my student employees will know how to. . . ."

- Finance assistant: Classify, record, and summarize numerical and financial data.
- Fitness assistant: Observe participants and inform them of corrective measures necessary for skill improvement.
- Graphic artist/illustrator: Create designs, concepts, and sample layouts based on knowledge of layout principles and aesthetic design concepts.
- Printing/binding assistant: Inspect and examine printed products for print clarity, color accuracy, conformance to specifications, and external defects.
- Security/facilities attendant: Write reports of daily activities and irregularities such as equipment or property damage, theft, presence of unauthorized persons, or unusual occurrences.

More examples are available from the career services website at Winston-Salem State University (2017).

Inasmuch as the aforementioned examples are great starting points, student employment practitioners should expect to create several learning outcomes for each position, not just a few overall outcomes or just one per student. For example, consider a campus job in the Office of Public and Media Relations. Learning outcomes could be created that range from basic to complex:

- Name the key media outlets that the college pursues for story placement.
- Operate a news camera and cut footage.

- Analyze social media placement statistics and prepare briefs for the staff.
- Create high-quality content using photos and videos to increase online engagement.

Moreover, the National Institute for Learning Outcomes Assessment (NILOA) website (n.d.) encourages developers of learning outcomes to use action verbs aligned with Bloom's taxonomy. Action verbs are suggested because they represent what student employees can do as a result of their campus job, which also aligns with Keeling and Underhile's (2007) framework. Several resources are available on the NILOA website (n.d.) to help practitioners design and assess learning outcomes.

We address assessment in more detail in chapter 6. Next, we focus on the composition and development of good learning outcomes. Table 4.2 provides dozens of verb choices that align with the increasing levels of Bloom's taxonomy.

Finally, the AAC&U offers a selection of sample rubrics created by teams of faculty across the country as part of the Valid Assessment of Learning in Undergraduate Education (VALUE) project (Association of American Colleges & Universities, n.d.). Among the rubrics, several would be particularly helpful to student employment practitioners: ethical reasoning, teamwork, written communication, oral communication, problem-solving, work ethic, intercultural knowledge, and foundations and skills for lifelong learning. These rubrics are available for free download from the AAC&U website (Association of American Colleges & Universities, n.d.).

Experiential Learning

According to the National Society for Experiential Education, *experiential education* refers to learning activities that involve the learner in the process of active engagement with and critical reflection about phenomena being studied" (Ross & Sheehan, 2014, p. 53). Through experiential education, students gain skills, develop self-awareness, learn workplace etiquette, and enhance their professional network (Hart Research Associates, 2006; King, 2014). Among the high-impact practices, global learning, research, internships, and service-learning are inherently experiential. Let's review the seminal theory of experiential learning: Kolb's theory.

Kolb's Theory of Experiential Learning

The preeminent theorist in experiential education is social psychologist David Kolb, who defined *learning* (1984) as "a process whereby knowledge

TABLE 4.2
Action Verbs Related to Learning

Action Verb List: Suggested Verbs to Use in Each Level of Thinking Skills					
Knowledge	Compre-hension	Application	Analysis	Synthesis	Evaluation
Count	Associate	Add	Analyze	Categorize	Appraise
Define	Compute	Apply	Arrange	Combine	Assess
Describe	Convert	Calculate	Breakdown	Compile	Compare
Draw	Defend	Change	Combine	Compose	Conclude
Identify	Discuss	Classify	Design	Crate	Contrast
Label	Distinguish	Complete	Detect	Drive	Criticize
List	Estimate	Demonstrate	Develop	Devise	Critique
Match	Explain	Discover	Diagram	Explain	Determine
Name	Extend	Divide	Differentiate	Group	Grade
Outline	Extrapolate	Examine	Discriminate	Integrate	Interpret
Point	Generalize	Graph	Illustrate	Organize	Judge
Quote	Give examples	Interpolate	Outline	Plan	Justify
Read	Infer	Manipulate	Relate	Prescribe	Measure
Recall	Paraphrase	Modify	Select	Propose	Rank
Recite	Predict	Operate	Separate	Rearrange	Rate
Recognize	Rewrite	Prepare	Subdivide	Reconstruct	Support
Record	Summarize	Produce		Relate	Test
Repeat		Show		Reorganize	
Reproduce		Solve		Revise	
Select		Subtract		Transform	
State		Translate		Specify	
Write		Use			

Source. Kansas State University Office of Assessment (2016), www.k-tate.edu/assessment/toolkit/outcomes/action.html

is created through the transformation of experience" (p. 38). Kolb (1984) believed that learning takes place while individuals interact with their environment and that learning is always influenced by past experience:

All learning is relearning. How easy and tempting it is in designing a course to think of the learner's mind as being as blank as the paper on which we scratch our outline. Yet this is not the case. Everyone enters every learning situation with more or less articulate ideas about the topic at hand. (p. 28)

As with most theoretical models, Kolb's model of experiential learning was shaped by the work of others. Theorists upon whom Kolb built include Jean Piaget, Kurt Lewin, and John Dewey. Kolb's theory of experiential learning defines four modes of learning derived from two domains: ways of perceiving (by doing or observing) and ways of processing (using thinking or feeling). The model, known as the Kolb cycle, appears in Figure 4.2.

Kolb's two ways of perceiving information are:

1. *active experimentation*, which involves doing something that produces information and knowledge through the interaction of person with the environment; and
2. *reflective observation*, which involves deep thinking to ascertain the meaning of ideas and situations, approaching different situations from different points of view.

The two ways of processing information are:

1. *concrete experience*, involving active engagement with other people, or an open-minded approach to acquiring information from others with a focus on feelings; and
2. *abstract conceptualization*, involving thinking about systems and analyzing ideas theoretically.

Figure 4.2. Kolb's cycle of experiential learning.

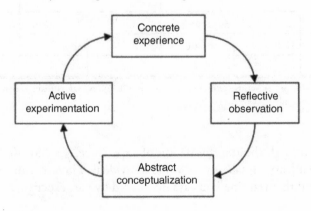

Kolb (1976) explained that there is no right or wrong, no better or worse preference relative to the ways of perceiving and processing. Most people, however, have a natural style or preferred ways of perceiving and processing. Following are the four possible combinations of perception and processing that define four experiential learning styles:

1. *Assimilating* (reflective observation + abstract conceptualization) combines reflection and thinking. This learning style focuses on concepts and ideas. Information is perceived abstractly and processed through reflection and inductive reasoning. These learners tend to create theoretical models without immediately concerning themselves about practical application. Kolb connected this learning style with individuals who gravitate to academic disciplines in the natural sciences and mathematics.
2. *Converging* (abstract conceptualization + active experimentation) combines thinking and doing. This learning style focuses on practical and technical aspects of information acquisition and processing, using deductive reasoning. Kolb connected this learning style to engineering fields, but that is not to say that all engineers have converging learning styles.
3. *Accommodating* (active experimentation + concrete experience) combines doing and feeling. This learning style is about experimentation with people and learning through action with others and the interchange that occurs through it. Kolb connected this learning style with the social and psychological sciences and business.
4. *Diverging* (concrete experience + reflective observation) combines relationship-based experiences with reflection, focused on people and ideas. This learning style involves use of the imagination, creativity, and idea generation using multiple views of a situation. Academic specialties of divergent learners tend to include more humanists and social scientists.

Applying Experiential Learning Theory to Student Employment

Student employment professionals can use the Kolb cycle and the four learning styles with student employees. First, remember that this cycle is about learning experientially. It would be helpful for student employees to understand their natural preferences for perceiving and processing information. Understanding one's own preferences is a great starting point. A student employee who understands her own learning style can then be more aware of learning opportunities that align with her preferred style and those that may stretch her thinking. Second, understanding learning style preferences allows us to better understand our peers and may therefore advance teamwork.

Consider the case of Lucia, a new student employee in the community engagement office who was tasked with recruiting students to participate in a weekend community service project. Lucia's preferred style is assimilating, meaning that she prefers to observe and analyze a situation before she jumps in and acts. Lucia's first task was to meet with the student who coordinated this activity the previous year. She asked questions about the previous year's process, took notes, then met with her supervisor to discuss what she had understood about the process and asked about the supervisor's perspective on the success of the previous year's recruitment. Lucia collected her notes, reviewed them, and reflected on ways in which she might change the process for the coming year. She then developed her own plan and presented it to her supervisor for feedback. Only after this step was she ready to implement the plan.

Kolb (1976) believed that individuals who could better understand their own learning-style preferences would become better learners because they would understand the various learning style preferences and be able to adapt and use their less-preferred styles when engaged in problem-solving. Experiential learning is influenced by internal factors such as learning-style preferences and emotions, as well as by external factors such as context, environments, and relationships. Experiences can prompt new learning as a way to connect current learning to previous experience (Merriam et al., 2007). Student employment practitioners can catalyze problem-solving using multiple ways of perceiving and processing, and as coaches help student employees analyze their learning styles as part of the experience (Merriam et al., 2007).

Reflection

> Reflection is a cognitive process. We can think about our experience—news, review, and so on—but to reflect critically, we must also examine the underlying beliefs and assumptions that affect how we make sense of the experience. (Merriam et al., 2007, p. 145)

Merriam and colleagues (2007) extended the work of industrial organizational psychologist Donald Schön and described a process called *reflection on action*, an after-the-fact review and analysis of an experience or situation. Student employees can use journaling or ePortfolios to assist their reflective process, but the important piece is "framing of critical observations and questions as part of the reflection on action process" (Merriam et al., 2007, p. 176). Conversely, they describe *reflection in action* as happening during an experience, such that a reflective process is used to address a surprise unanticipated event that requires us to change, adapt, or restructure the activity.

Experiential learning includes four dimensions: academic, personal, professional, and civic (King & Sweitzer, 2014). The academic dimension refers to increasing the depth of knowledge in a discipline and applying classroom learning to an authentic, real-world environment. The personal dimension allows for the development of deeper self-awareness, values, confidence, and self-concept. The professional dimension speaks to the immersion into a real environment within a profession, acknowledging the personalities of the professionals within that environment and the behaviors that are endorsed and rewarded in that profession. The civic dimension enables a student to reflect upon the societal impact of the experience and overall civic engagement. We are cautioned, however, to avoid the temptation to silo these dimensions; although they represent different aspects of experiential learning, they are part of a whole person and should be considered holistically (King & Sweitzer, 2014).

The 4R *Model of Reflective Thinking*

Ryan and Ryan (2013) adapted the Bain 5R model of reflective thinking into a 4R model, asserting that reflective thinking has levels that occur over time and should be taken into account when structuring reflections for college students. The model includes four steps: reporting/responding, relating, reasoning, and reconstructing. It is a process of analyzing a situation by understanding the people involved and the actions taken, then linking the situation to existing knowledge, making meaning of the situation, and integrating the new learning into the existing ways of knowing.

Structuring Reflection Activities for Student Employees

To be most effective, reflection should include introspective contemplation and deliberate efforts to change thinking and ways of interpreting the world, both on individual and societal levels (King & Kitchener, 2004). Larkin and Beatson (2014) developed a guide for using the 4R model to process a specific experience reflectively:

1. *Report*—Tell the story in detail. What happened? What was your role? Who was involved? How did you feel about it?
2. *Relate*—Connect the situation to what you know through previous experience. Compare the situations and look for patterns, difference, and impact.

3. *Reason*—Consider reasons why the situation occurred. Consider the different perspectives of each person involved. Look for alternative explanations and consider the ethics involved as well.

4. *Reconstruct*—Consider how you might react differently to this situation or behave differently if it were to happen again.

These questions could be answered as part of a learning journal in written format, or they can become part of a small group conversation among peers, or perhaps in an individual meeting with a supervisor or mentor.

"Reflection," say King and Sweitzer (2014), "is not to be saved for the end of the experience, but to be integrated from the beginning" (p. 12). In fact, student employment practitioners can set students up for success by introducing the concept of reflection, its domains, and the methods through which it occurs before the work experience begins (Sykes & Dean, 2012). King and Sweitzer (2014) called this a *preplacement workshop*, but this could just as easily be part of an orientation and onboarding process. We consider it a *pre-flection*. Ideally reflection takes place throughout the work learning experience and can focus on any and all of the four dimensions of learning: academic, personal, professional, and civic.

Additionally, students should also be invited to reflect on the difference between an experience or single event versus general experience—that is, the accumulation of multiple learning occurrences, many of which are likely unscripted and informal. This could include reflections on the organization's mission and how that mission is or is not being achieved, or it could include the individuals within the organization, their work styles, attitudes, and communication styles, even the extent to which they appear to live the values of the organization through their everyday work. Students could also interrogate their own feelings about the work environment, their personal work and learning styles, their peers, and how their views and the assumptions underlying them are influenced by and through the work (King & Sweitzer, 2014; Ryan & Ryan, 2013).

Henderson, Berlin, Freeman, and Fuller (2002) studied the practice of reflection in medical education in the United Kingdom. They asked students to make connections between the present and their own past experiences. Recall from earlier in this chapter the funds of knowledge approach. By asking students to make connections between the present and the past, you can help them situate the new experience and make meaning of it. In addition affirming feelings and reactions as valid and worthy is critically important to the reflection process (Henderson et al., 2002).

Work-Integrated Learning

We have just reviewed theories and models of reflection that can be used to help students process applied learning experiences and integrate the knowledge they bring to that experience with new learning taking place at academic, personal, professional, and civic levels. A specialized form of experiential learning is called *work-integrated learning*, which traditionally occurs off campus and involves a partnership among employer, educational institution, and student. The term *work-integrated learning* is more popular in Europe, the United Kingdom, and Australia than in the United States. Work-integrated learning in college has been shown to be a prime opportunity for students to integrate traditional educational experiences with work-based learning experiences, better preparing them as lifelong learners (Billett & Choy, 2011). In the United States, this off-campus, paid, work-integrated learning is called *cooperative education (co-op)*. Consider a co-op a paid internship with an off-campus organization. Co-ops are always paid, are always connected to the curriculum, and specifically require learning outcomes that integrate knowledge gained in the classroom with work-based projects on site (Zegwaard & Coll, 2011).

Student employment practitioners can learn a lot from cooperative education and work-integrated learning programs, which have long-standing histories of successfully linking college students with learning-while-earning experiences and contributing to student success. In fact, the authors could make a very strong case for a campus version of these off-campus learning experiences if a campus job were structured for learning just like a co-op or internship. Savoca (2016) sought to extend the high-impact practices framework to include on-campus student employment. She analyzed GPAs and persistence rates of undergraduates from two institutions whose campus jobs were purposefully configured as high impact. Although the results of that study were inconclusive, the investigator suggested that future studies of campus jobs be undertaken to identify which elements of high-impact practices are present in which campus jobs and whether those jobs can be shown to positively contribute to student success.

Recall that earlier in this chapter we reviewed elements of high-impact practices that make them so successful: time on task, exposure to diversity, meaningful relationships with faculty/staff, opportunity to solve real-world problems, structured team-based projects, and regular feedback on performance. The greater the extent to which student employment practitioners can incorporate these quality markers into our student employment programs, the more likely it is that we may find relationships between participation in campus jobs and student success. The authors hope the learning that happens at work, whether it is called *student employment, work-integrated learning,* or *cooperative education,* will benefit the student's persistence; overall learning; academic success; and personal, career, and professional development.

Perhaps the perspective of off-campus employers could be informative. Employers provide work-integrated learning experiences in the form of internships and co-ops. When done well, these experiences enhance student learning and professional development. We need to know how employers plan and structure these applied learning experiences, what they want from college candidates, and what they hope to achieve through these programs.

What Employers Want

Put yourselves in the shoes of a hiring manager. When you set out to hire someone, be that an experienced professional, an entry-level hire, or perhaps a student, you will likely be thinking about the skills and qualities that your new hire will need to perform the job successfully. You might begin by considering the specific technical skills required for the job; for example, if you need someone to collect and analyze data, you might look for candidates with applicable skills and experience. You may also give careful thought to the level of skill you require: Would a candidate with basic skills suffice, or do you require someone with advanced technical skills who can perform high-level duties? Undoubtedly you will also be thinking about the broad-based qualities that you need for the team, perhaps someone with strong communication skills, a candidate who has good interpersonal abilities and customer service skills, or a candidate with experience working with diverse populations. Because the work of your department likely changes regularly (as noted in chapter 3, change is constant in the twenty-first-century workplace), you might be looking for candidates who can demonstrate flexibility and be comfortable with uncertainty. Altogether you will draw a picture of an ideal candidate who possesses the unique mix of technical skills and broad-based competencies.

This process of identifying the skills and qualities needed by new hires is common to employers of all types: corporate, nonprofit, government, even start-ups. For many years, surveys of employers who regularly sourced candidates from colleges have shown a surprisingly consistent group of broad-based skills necessary for workplace entry, regardless of industry or job-specific technical knowledge (National Association of Colleges and Employers, 2015b). Two highly respected surveys of employers of college graduates come from the National Association of Colleges and Employers (NACE), which has been surveying employers for decades, and Hart Research Associates, which has been conducting surveys of employers for the AAC&U LEAP Initiative since 2006 (Hart Research Associates, 2015, 2013, 2006).

Each year NACE's annual survey of its employer membership usually draws several hundred responses and results in a list of the top 10 skills and qualities that most college graduates need (National Association of Colleges and Employers, 2016, 2015a). By and large, over several years the skills have remained the same, occasionally flipping order. In 2015 NACE launched a new effort to define a set of competencies that college graduates would need for smooth career entry. Their survey of more than 600 employers representing a diversity of industries and company sizes yielded seven competencies, presented as *career readiness competencies* (National Association of Colleges and Employers, 2015a): critical thinking/problem-solving, oral/written communication skills, teamwork/collaboration, IT application, leadership, professionalism/work ethic, and career management. Employers expect students will bring these skills to work, meaning they expect students to learn these competencies during college. Moreover, employers overwhelmingly favor real-world applications of these skills through internships.

We argue throughout this book that a campus job can provide equal opportunity for real-world application of skills and knowledge. What is missing from the NACE surveys, however, is a skill that we believe will provide a competitive advantage for students entering the job market: the ability to articulate competencies in light of employer requirements. This competitive advantage is more than oral communication skills. It involves a careful examination of the position requirements, the elements of the job description, an understanding of the industry, knowledge of the employers, and the ability to describe experiences and competencies that would directly contribute to employer needs. Student employment practitioners can help student employees reflect upon their learning on the job so that they can express themselves appropriately in context. As suggested in previous chapters, use your campus resources, particularly your career center, to help your students research employers of choice and practice describing their competencies in light of employer requirements.

Hart Research Associates (2015, 2013, 2006) was commissioned by the AAC&U for three major research studies as part of LEAP. More than 300 companies were surveyed each time about the skills and competencies they valued as important for college graduates to have in order to be competitive in the hiring process. Table 4.3 displays the competencies from both the NACE and Hart Research surveys.

Notice the consistency between the two surveys. You may also recall the AAC&U essential learning outcomes covered earlier in this chapter. These

TABLE 4.3
Career Competencies That College Graduates Need

NACE	Hart Research
Critical thinking	Apply critical thinking and analytical reasoning skills
	Analyze and solve complex problems
Professionalism/ work ethic	Use ethical judgment in decision-making
	Apply knowledge and skills in real-world settings
Teamwork	Work on a team and collaborate with others in a diverse setting
Oral/written communications	Effectively communicate orally and in writing
Information technology application	Stay current on technologies and applications to the workplace
	Work with numbers and understand statistics
Leadership	Locate, organize, and evaluate information from multiple sources
Career management	Innovate and be creative

competencies align well with the four essential learning outcomes: intellectual and practical skills, knowledge of human cultures, personal and social responsibility, and integrative learning. What this tells us in a very practical and fundamental way is that the outcomes of a college education are in fact quite similar to the competencies that employers representing a wide range of industries and sizes are looking for in college graduates. Inasmuch as these broad-based skills are clearly necessary for college graduate success, the authors would be remiss if we did not acknowledge the need for job-specific technical skills. Our graduates need breadth, but they also need depth.

The T-Shaped Professional

Human capital experts at IDEO Designs and IBM coined the term *T-shaped professional* in the 1990s (Collegiate Employment Research Institute, 2016). Later it was embraced and further developed by Phil Gardner, director of the Collegiate Employment Research Institute (CERI) at Michigan State University. CERI has conducted college labor market studies for more than 25 years.

The *T* describes the new type of professional, one with both depth and breadth of knowledge (see Figure 4.3). However, a T-shaped professional is not simply depth and breadth. A T-shaped professional starts with deep

Figure 4.3. T-shaped professional.

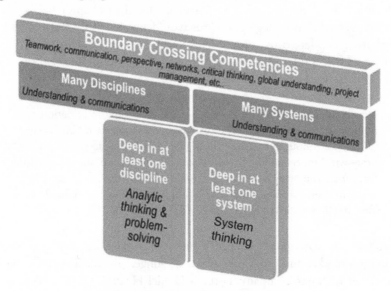

Source: Spohrer, Gardner, and Gross (2015). Reprinted with permission.

knowledge in at least one discipline or system. In addition to academic disciplines, systems could include sectors like energy, transportation, finance, public policy, education, or engineering (Spohrer, 2015). That's the vertical. With depth comes the ability to define discipline-specific problems, acquire data and evidence, and engage in the appropriate analysis to solve those disciplinary or single-system problems. The horizontal part of the T refers to broad-based knowledge of multiple disciplines and systems and crosscutting, or boundary-crossing, competencies. Through the horizontal part of the T, professionals acquire and interpret information from multiple disciplines and systems; develop relationships across organizational units; listen, understand, and communicate with professionals with deep expertise in different disciplines; and come together to solve complex multidisciplinary problems (Spohrer, Gardner, & Gross, 2015).

When applied to the college student population, imagine that the vertical portion of the T includes the depth of knowledge students acquire through their academic major and minor. The top of the T is knowledge that students gain through general education coursework and experiential learning activities. Boundary-spanning competencies include some of the crosscutting skills named in both the NACE (2015b) and Hart Research Associates (2015) studies: communication, teamwork, problem-solving, global perspective, understanding of organizational culture, and project management skills. Another boundary-spanning competency would be emotional intelligence, which we cover in detail in chapter 5. T-experts have suggested that college graduates would not be "fully formed Ts . . . but have a slender trunk with several budding limbs" (Gardner & Perry, 2011, p. 316). Student employment professionals are perfectly positioned to help these limbs bud.

> Upon graduation, students should be able to handle information from multiple sources, advance professional relationships across different organizations, contribute innovatively to organizational practices, and communicate with understanding across social, cultural, economic and scientific disciplines. Tomorrow's workers will build their careers in a globally interconnected and constantly changing world with smarter technologies in an effort to effect positive global change. (T-Summit, 2016)

T-students, or emerging T-shaped professionals, have an advantage in the future job market and economy, which no longer provide a stable, progressive career with one company. Futurist Daniel H. Pink (2000) theorized at the turn of the century that our students' future would be one of independent contracting, talent for opportunity, and the gig economy. More recently, thought leaders in the talent development space have suggested that jobs of the future will require advanced boundary-spanning skills, such as data science analytics, sustainability, and cybersecurity (Business-Higher Education Forum, 2014). Pointing to thousands of jobs that now go unfilled in these high-need, emerging, and interdisciplinary fields, leaders in the Business-Higher Education Forum have called for more meaningful dialogue between the business community and college and university leadership to discuss emerging job trends and new competencies needed in the workforce. "Signaling mechanisms between business and higher education is neither rapid nor nuanced enough to ensure adequate development among potential employees of the competencies needed by business" (Business-Higher Education Forum, 2013, p. 5). While these conversations may be taking place at the highest levels of leadership, student employment professionals can focus on helping those T-shaped limbs bud and structure opportunities at work to help students learn and hone those key career competencies needed by all graduates.

Applicability for Student Employment Practitioners

Given that the T crosscutting skills and competencies needed for career entry compare well to the essential learning outcomes, student employment practitioners may wish to structure purposeful opportunities for student employees to gain these competencies through work. For example, earlier in this chapter we introduced Angelo, an undergraduate working for the alumni relations office. As a history major with a specialization in American history, Angelo has developed strong competencies in reading and critical analysis of historical accounts of major national events as well as the historical figures who played key roles in the development of our nation. If we were to use T-terminology, Angelo's depth would be in his discipline, American history. Working in alumni relations, Angelo may naturally gravitate toward historical accounts of alumni experiences. Assignments related to gathering oral histories from the oldest alumni would further enhance his depth of knowledge. However, if his supervisor considered Angelo as a budding T-shaped professional, she might create assignments for him that would help him acquire knowledge and skills from other disciplines and systems, such as an oral history focused on alumni career paths that could be used to support student career development. Angelo's supervisor may also wish to plan for him to develop horizontal competencies such as project management and teamwork, giving him responsibility to manage the alumni participation in one of the college admissions events. Perhaps she might also invite him to hone his data analysis skills by asking him to review trend data collected about alumni who volunteered at previous admissions events.

In another example, we might consider Hakeem, also introduced earlier in this chapter, who works for the IT department at his university. If Hakeem majored in information systems, you would likely acknowledge the disciplinary depth in technology that he gained from both his academic project and his campus job. You might suggest that his supervisor assign projects that could help him build his boundary-spanning competencies in communication skills and professional networks. Or the supervisor could present opportunities for him to learn more about IT applications in various systems, such as enrollment management, career services, or research labs. But what if Hakeem were a French major? How might you assess his T-development? If you were Hakeem's supervisor in the IT department, how might you proceed? Invariably, supervisors could make some assumptions about depth and breadth based on academic major, previous experience, and so forth. Yet, as we consider developing learning outcomes for our student employees based on the experiences they could have while working, we also want to make sure that we involve the students and invite them to express their views on potential learning goals and stretch assignments. It bears repeating that the authors view these conversations and assignments as solidly linked to the work of the department and to the systems and practices already in place for supervisors to meet with student employees and discuss work assignments.

Institutional Strategies to Promote Learning

More often than not, change starts at the top. Granted there is good reason why the term *grassroots* exists, yet when it comes to student employment on campus, the authors believe that building an organizational culture where learning is an expected outcome of a campus job cannot happen if institutional leadership is not leading. Building a new organizational culture is far more complex and far-reaching than planning a simple program or even a series of programs (Culp & Dungy, 2012). Creating a learning-focused student employment culture on campus requires vision. Hesser and Gotlieb (2014) advise that experiential education broadly cast be built into the mission and values of the institution as a whole. If a culture of learning is to pervade the entire campus, crossing divisions and functional areas, then institutional leadership must invest institutional-level resources and support. Kuk (2009) advocates for organizational models that support the unique mission and characteristics of the institution. She encourages planners to consider not only the institutional mission and goals but also the institution's unique strengths that could be leveraged. For example, if your campus has a particularly strong IT department, then integrating its strengths with the strategic planning for your student employment initiative is a prudent way to leverage institutional assets and experts as well as judiciously and efficiently use resources. Undoubtedly, folks on your campus have already created a learning-focused student employment culture within their functional areas; find those people and bring them in to your effort by creating a leadership team of committed stakeholders and institutional leaders (Busby & Robinson, 2012). The student employment leadership team must be able to marshal internal and external resources for the establishment and sustainability of this initiative.

We can map the learning environment for student employees by defining the specific learning outcomes we want our students to achieve based on their jobs, and moreover, we can leverage the uniqueness of the individual campus and design learning opportunities for that specific environment (Borrego, 2006). Kuh, Kinzie, Schuh, and Whitt (2010) and McNair (2016) remind us that a commitment to learning means a commitment to meeting students where they are. In other words, we must think about inclusive ways to structure our overall learning goals within a transparent learning framework that adapts to individual levels of cognitive development, not just embracing the unique characteristics of a campus or departments.

Another institutional strategy concerns adopting national standards or principles as its foundation. At present there is no nationally accepted standard for campus employment, but the National Society for Experiential Education (NSEE) offers national standards for all experiential education activities. The

Council for the Advancement of Standards in Higher Education (CAS) provides standards for internship programs and undergraduate research programs, two types of experiential learning offered on many campuses. These standards can be adapted to student employment. National standards are explored in greater detail later in this chapter, but for this next segment, we highlight three examples of institutions that have strategically engaged multiple campus stakeholders to create learning-focused student employment programs. The first example describes a start-up effort in which a university created a student employment program from the ground up. The second example describes a campus-wide effort to review, classify, and standardize position descriptions. The third example incorporates a simple and quick reflection conversation that takes place between a supervisor and student employee that adds tremendous value to the learning experience.

Stony Brook University's Student Employment Program

With institutional support, Stony Brook University–State University of New York launched its first student employment office under the auspices of its centralized Career Center in 2015. Its mission is to create "high-impact, transformative on-campus work experiences that prepare students for meaningful and productive careers" (Savoca & Zalewski, 2016, p. 2). A Student Employment Advisory Group was formed with staff from key departments: career services, financial aid services, human resources, and student affairs, and representatives from departments with the largest numbers of student employees: IT, campus recreation, the library, campus dining, and campus residences. In the first year, three goals were defined: (a) set the structure and policies, (b) develop training for students and supervisors, and (c) design assessments of student employee performance and impact of work on career development.

The Student Employment Advisory Group helped craft a process map for campus departments to clarify the administrative actions to initiate and complete the hiring process. Consultations were held with departments to assist them in structuring student work in their areas in alignment with Kuh's (2008) high-impact practices and developing learning-focused position descriptions. A series of training modules for departments and supervisors was developed and offered in person and via webinar. Resources were developed to help departments create learning outcomes, structure assessment, and conduct performance evaluations. A process map for students looking for work was created, as was a mandatory student employee orientation, also offered in person and via webinar. Orientation sessions addressed workplace etiquette, communication skills, ethical decision-making, and practical competence. During the pilot year, feedback was solicited often from departments, supervisors, and students. Program evaluations were positive. In the second year, in progress at the time of this writing, the team is bringing new departments online and continuing consultative work with existing departments and individual supervisors. New in-person and online training modules for undergraduate and graduate student employees have been developed. A digital badging initiative based on the NACE career readiness competencies is being considered for launch in the third year. More information is available on the Stony Brook University Career Center website (Stony Brook University, n.d.b).

Carnegie Mellon University's Position Classification System

In 2015–2016 Carnegie Mellon University's (CMU) student employment unit within its Career and Professional Development Center undertook a massive project to develop a standardized set of job profiles and pay rates for student jobs on campus (Carnegie Mellon University, n.d.). In their first year they described and classified 32 undergraduate job profiles and 24 graduate-level job profiles, each with 4 levels ranging from entry to leadership/advanced, with corresponding skill requirements and pay ranges. They then examined the distribution of hourly rates to see how they fit into the new job classification system, also calculating the standard deviation of actual student wages. Because external compensation market data were not available for student positions, CMU used actual pay rates to design the pay ranges. The minimums represented actual minimum hourly rates, the midpoint of the ranges represented the median of wages within the specified job profiles, and the maximum of the pay range represented one standard deviation away from the mean. The new ranges were implemented, raising any pay rate that would have been below the new minimum, as well as allowing for outliers on the top end of the range, meaning that hourly rates that exceeded the range maximum were not decreased. Over time, as these ranges become more widely used and referenced, outliers will naturally drop off, with the vast majority of hourly rates expected to fall within the new ranges. The job classification codes and the corresponding wage ranges will continue to be evaluated to ensure that they remain competitive while complying with changing federal and state wage laws. Departments are expected to use the classification system when developing their job descriptions, and the increased transparency of the system benefits students as they make their choices. More information is available on the CMU career services website (Carnegie Mellon University, n.d.).

The Iowa GROW Model

In 2009, the Division of Student Life at the University of Iowa sought to transform student campus employment into a high-impact practice.

After consulting with George D. Kuh, the primary authority on the high-impact practices, they designed the Iowa Guided Reflection on Work (Iowa GROW) program. The goal of the program is to make campus jobs educationally purposeful, with structured opportunities for learning and professional development. Departments participating include recreational services, disability services, multicultural initiatives, housing and food services, counseling services, health and wellness, women's resources, and victim advocacy support services. Supervisors are critical to the success of the program and are therefore required to attend a one-hour training session and have a minimum of two structured conversations with their student employees to discuss the students' learning experience, separate and distinct from any conversations about work performance. The conversation involves the following four simple questions (University of Iowa, 2016):

1. How is this job fitting in with your academics?
2. What are you learning here that's helping you in school?
3. What are you learning in class that you can apply here at work?
4. Can you give me a couple of examples of things you've learned here that you think you'll use in your chosen profession?

Results from student surveys in 2016 revealed that program participants were more likely to agree or strongly agree that their campus job helped them achieve the following outcomes of student employment: ability to more effectively work with diverse others; development of communication, time management, problem-solving, and conflict resolution skills; the opportunity to apply knowledge and skills to real-world situations; and the opportunity to connect their work to their academics and career intentions (University of Iowa, 2016). Iowa GROW has been successful within the Division of Student Life, and plans are under way to scale the program to other departments and other divisions (Sarah Hansen, personal communication, September 29, 2016). More information is available at the Iowa GROW website (University of Iowa, 2016).

Roles Within the Student Employee Support Network

Not surprisingly, these three best-practice examples emerged from divisions of student affairs, where the out-of-class curriculum is most frequently situated. However, you may have noted that, throughout this book, the authors have provided examples that touch upon virtually every unit or division within a college or university organizational structure: alumni affairs, advancement, food service, the library, academic departments, enrollment management, research labs, finance and accounting, and technology. Although the departments and cultures within differ across higher education institutions, individual roles remain consistent. Described briefly in the next section, more robust coverage of the special role of student employee supervisor is addressed in chapter 6.

The Role of Student Employment Practitioners

Once we have institutional support and resources to develop learning-oriented student employment strategies, student employment practitioners can use national standards and best-practice examples to develop programmatic goals that align with institutional goals and leverage unique institutional characteristics. How can we, as student employment practitioners, structure our programs, work assignments, training, and ongoing professional development to give students the opportunities to learn, grow, and develop? Our role, as described by Keeling (2006), is one of "learning facilitator" (p. 9), and as such, we are tasked with the exciting opportunity to create dozens of learning laboratories around our campuses.

Facilitating learning is supported by Paulo Freire's philosophy of education as problem-posing and student centered, as opposed to what he deemed a banking education, a teacher-centered philosophy through which the teacher deposits knowledge into a student's bank (Merriam et al., 2007). In this regard, facilitating learning is about inviting students to bring their whole selves—including their ethnic, racial, socioeconomic, sexual orientation, gender, and family identities—along with the funds of knowledge and experience they bring to an open, welcoming environment in which knowledge is cocreated by students and facilitators. So when we consider the progressive nature of learning and its connection to development as well as the various domains in which learning occurs (i.e., academic, social, workplace), what can we really say about what we want our students to be, to know, and to know how to do when they graduate? How can we honor the essential learning outcomes while balancing the need for student employees to learn specific knowledge and behaviors that will enable them to perform their job responsibilities? Here the authors acknowledge that coordinators of student employment programs have much to offer in terms of marshaling institutional resources, setting the direction and strategy for campus-wide student employee learning outcomes, and engaging individual supervisors as student developers and learning facilitators. In chapter 6 we offer best practices in supervision and present the balance between mentored learning and performance evaluation.

The Role of Peers

Coordinators and supervisors play important roles in structuring student employment programs and facilitating learning and development, and peers can also play a vital role in contributing to student employee success. "Peer mentors are valuable to college students and institutions of higher education because their services contribute to students' academic and social support, retention, and academic achievement" (Rieske & Benjamin, 2015, p. 69). Peers have long been utilized in college student support programs, such as orientation, academic support and tutoring services, residence life, careers, health, conduct, social activities, and leadership, as well as with specific populations, such as freshmen, commuters, students of color, students with disabilities, international students, and more recently, first-generation college students (Ender, 1984; Henderson et al., 2002; Rieske & Benjamin, 2015). Students often report feeling that their peers close in age are more easily approachable than professors or professional staff, and peers are believable sources of information and referrals (Ender, 1984; Mentoring Partnership, 2016). In addition to approachability, qualities of successful peer mentors include interpersonal skills, communication skills, leadership, and good academics (Rieske & Benjamin, 2015), as well as listening skills, a desire to support others, and resourcefulness (Mentoring Partnership, 2016).

Peer mentors can play a vital role in the learning and development of student employees. They can serve as coaches, cheerleaders, sounding boards, and problem solvers (Ellinger, 2002; Garringer, Kupersmidt, Rhodes, Stelter, & Tai, 2015; Renn, Steinbauer, Taylor, & Detwiler, 2014). Often they are in the best position to help orient a new student employee to the organizational culture and staff as well as connect peers with social support networks and with campus resources and partners (Rieske & Benjamin, 2015; Renn et al., 2014). Peer mentors may also be utilized as part of the formal training process of new student employees where they serve as trainers and role models and provide shadow opportunities (Holliday & Nordgren, 2005; Manley & Holley, 2014).

From an organizational standpoint, use of peer mentors enables the staff to expand services for student clients, to do so cost-effectively, and to provide added development and leadership experience for the peer mentors themselves, perhaps even introduce them to a potential career path. Mentoring can also motivate both the mentors and the mentees to bring their best to work and to continuously seek to improve their work (Ellinger, 2002). Peer mentor programs may also contribute to students' multicultural awareness and understanding (Hansman, 2002) and conflict resolution skills (Mentoring Partnership, 2016).

The National Mentoring Partnership has developed and refined the following set of seven core principles of youth mentoring relationships and program delivery:

1. Promote the welfare and safety of the young person.
2. Be trustworthy and responsible.
3. Act with integrity.
4. Promote justice for young people.
5. Respect the young person's rights and dignity.
6. Honor youth and family voice in designing and delivering services.
7. Strive for equity, cultural responsiveness, and positive social change. (Garringer et al., 2015)

Although the focus of the National Mentoring Partnership is to recruit adult mentors for youth, their principles are absolutely transferable to a college-level peer mentoring program.

In terms of recruitment, Garringer and colleagues (2015) recommend that mentors be screened for their suitability to serve as mentors, not simply to select those students who have a year of experience or more. Peer mentors should want to make a commitment to the support and development of their peers. It is also recommended that a structured training program be developed for peer mentors (Holliday & Nordgren, 2005) and that resources are provided to help the mentors establish and sustain trusting, positive, and encouraging relationships with their mentee (Mentoring Partnership, 2016). In a case study of library peers, Manley and Holley (2014) found that a peer mentor job description clarified the mentor role. Training could include a mix of in-person group work and also independent self-paced online interactive modules.

One more important thing to remember about mentoring: It works! In a landmark study of 30,000 college graduates, the Gallup Purdue Index report uncovered startling evidence that only 20% of respondents reported having a mentor at all in college (Busteed, 2014). However, evidence in this study also showed that graduates were 1.9 times more likely to agree that their college education was worth the cost if they had a mentor who encouraged their hopes and dreams. In the same study, the odds of thriving in all areas of well-being were 1.7 times higher if graduates had a mentor who encouraged them.

Recent graduates who strongly agree with any of three items measuring supportive relationships with professors or mentors are almost twice as likely to strongly agree that their education was worth the cost. These relationships hold even when controlling for personality characteristics and other variables such as student loan debt and employment status that could also be related to graduates' perceptions that college was worth it. (Gallup Organization, 2014)

These data show that, at the very least, if our student employees feel that a professor or mentor during college cares about them as people and encourages their dreams, they will be more likely to succeed in life after college. Although the benefits of utilizing peer mentors is clear, peer mentors have never been meant to replace full-time staff and should not be expected to do so (Ender, 1984).

Ensuring Quality

Like traditional experiential learning programs such as internships, co-op, and research, student employment programs can be purposefully designed for quality. Earlier in this chapter, national standards were mentioned. The CAS Standards for Internship Programs were codeveloped by the NSEE, a national leader in experiential education theory and practice since its founding in 1971. NSEE created the following eight principles of good practice in experiential learning. These principles have served as the foundation for many experiential programs around the country (National Society for Experiential Education, 1998):

1. *Intention*—Investing purposeful thought in designing experiential learning activities for both specific and holistic knowledge acquisition.
2. *Preparedness and planning*—Developing a program or series of experiences to ensure that students are prepared and ready to engage in experiential learning.
3. *Authenticity*—Ensuring that the experience has a real-world context, application, and meaning.
4. *Reflection*—Fostering testing of assumptions and hypotheses about the outcomes of decisions taken, then weighing the outcomes against past learning and future implications.
5. *Orientation and training*—Acknowledging that students may be bringing different levels of knowledge and preparation to the experience. Providing orientation and training levels the field and clarifies expectations. Chapter 6 delves more deeply into orientation and training.
6. *Monitoring and continuous improvement*—Paying attention through observation and review of performance against goals to allow for changes to the plans and the work, ensuring the best possible learning experience for the student.
7. *Assessment and evaluation*—Beyond monitoring for course corrections, planning for the analysis of the program and the extent to which learning

outcomes were achieved begins at the beginning. Assessment of student employee learning outcomes is covered in chapter 6.

8. *Acknowledgment*—Recognizing and celebrating accomplishments is essential to long-term success.

Just as faculty and employers use the eight NSEE principles to guide their planning of internships, co-ops, and other forms of experiential learning, so can student employment practitioners for learning-focused student employment programs.

In addition to following the NSEE principles, recall these six elements of quality high-impact practices: time on task; meaningful relationships with faculty, staff, and peers; engagement with difference and diversity; frequent and timely feedback on performance; opportunity to apply learning in authentic situations; and structured reflection (O'Neill, 2010). We also know that several experiences that have been shown through National Survey of Student Engagement (NSSE) surveys to positively contribute to student learning can be applied in a student employment environment (NSSE, 2014). Examples of experiential learning activities that can be applied to a student employment environment include making a presentation, preparing two or more drafts of an assignment before turning it in, working on a team project, tutoring another student (mentoring), using e-mail to communicate with an instructor (or supervisor), talking about career plans with an adviser (or supervisor), discussing an assignment with an instructor (or supervisor), and receiving prompt feedback (Kuh, 2003). As has just been described, the quality markers are there; it is just a matter of incorporating them into our student employment programs.

Peter T. Ewell, a scholar with decades of experience researching and writing about institutional effectiveness and student success, suggested the following six items for educators to revise so that instructional practices are focused on the learner, not the teacher. These six items are entirely applicable to student employment and are presented here with our added connection to student employment (Ewell, 1997):

1. Emphasize application and experience (experiential education).
2. Model the learning process and behaviors expected (role modeling).
3. Ask students to link their new learning to established concepts (reflection).
4. Emphasize interpersonal collaboration (high impact).
5. Provide rich and frequent feedback on performance (high impact).
6. Clarify a limited set of clearly identified, cross-disciplinary skills that are priorities (T-shaped professional).

So there you have it: NSEE's eight principles of good practice in experiential learning, the quality indicators of high-impact practices, and Ewell's six big-ticket items to transform a teacher-centered approach into a learner-centered approach. Combining these guides enables student employment practitioners to develop structures and supports that have been shown to add great value to student learning and development.

One caveat: Just designing student employment programs with these quality elements in mind is not enough. You must also build in assessment to validate the practices as providing a quality experience and to change course if elements of the program are not meeting expectations or contributing in measurable ways to student employee learning outcomes. Ultimately we want to develop our own feedback loop for learning and adjustment. As mentioned previously, assessment of student employment programs and student employee learning outcomes will be covered in chapter 6.

Conclusion

In the spirit of reflective learning practice, let us reflect on what we have gained from this chapter. As a result of reading this chapter, hopefully you now can describe the various theories of learning presented and incorporate these theories into your practice with student employees. We hope that you can explain the Kolb cycle and use it to help students clarify their learning-style preferences. We expect that you will have concluded that the skills and qualities employers seek are similar to the essential outcomes of a liberal education in the twenty-first century. We also anticipate that you will be able to devise a plan to give your student employees a chance to grow their limbs as future T-shaped professionals, using NSEE's principles of good practice, the quality markers of high-impact practices, and Ewell's big-ticket items as guides.

The authors trust that the examples we have shared describing different approaches that institutions have taken to advance their student employment efforts will inspire you to consider your own institutional strategies while being mindful of institutional assets and quality indicators. At this point in the book we hope you are feeling energized to spend the time, recruit the partners, and acquire and use the resources to design and implement your unique transformative student employee learning experiences.

5

STUDENT EMPLOYMENT ON CAMPUS AS A VEHICLE FOR STUDENT RETENTION, PERSISTENCE, AND SUCCESS

S tudent persistence, retention, and success are crucial to higher education institutions around the globe. This chapter explores the connection between retention theory and practice, focusing specifically on elements related to the retention and success of student employees throughout varying institutional types and positions. Simply put, how can college employment serve to support student success during college, strengthen student graduation numbers, and ultimately enhance postgraduation success?

At the outset of the discussion, we need to be specific regarding our meaning when using the terms *persistence, retention,* and *student success*. Hagedorn (2005), citing the National Center for Education Statistics (NCES), distinguishes between persistence and retention in a way we find clear, helpful, and succinct: *Retention* is an institution-centric measure of degree completion, and *persistence* is a student-centric measure. Defining *student success* is much more complex and has been the focus of journals, books, articles, and webinars for years. The authors use Kuh, Kinzie, Buckley, Bridges, and Hayek's (2006) definition, as we find it to be the most holistic and all encompassing. They define *student success* as "academic achievement, engagement in educationally purposeful activities, satisfaction, acquisition of desired knowledge, skills and competencies, persistence, attainment of educational objectives, and post-college performance" (p. 7) and emphasize that student success requires faculty, administrators, staff, policymakers, and students to all own and hone their individual pieces of the pie.

Dating back to the 1930s, when undergraduate student retention in the United States was referred to as *student mortality* and discussion focused on the need for universities to repair students' problems, the concept of dropping out from postsecondary institutions has dominated the landscape of theory and practice. The discourse of access, choice, and affordability that dominated much of the conversation in the 1970s through 1990s has now shifted to include a much greater emphasis on persistence, retention, and ultimately time-to-degree-completion, placing these elements of student success at the forefront of public policy, funding formulas, and measures of institutional effectiveness. One in three college students in the United States do not graduate from the university where study began (ACT, 2013). Public and private four-year institutions surveyed in 2012 reported less than 65% of students were retained at their initial institution from freshman to sophomore year (ACT, 2013).

Universities and government entities experiment with various structures, programs, and interventions aimed at increasing student persistence and ultimately graduation with fairly modest results to show for their efforts.

> To retain students, colleges have provided programs for underrepresented students, programs and services for students with disabilities, women, and older adults returning to college or beginning college for the first time . . . . The U.S. and state governments have made financial aid more readily available to a wider range of students. . . . In spite of these programs and services, retention from first to second year has not improved over time. (Seidman, 2005, p. xii)

Astin (1975) explains the macro impact of student retention and the continued need for research focusing on potential predictors of a student's ability to navigate transitions, demographic and social barriers, and academic preparedness, in addition to ways that faculty and administrators can help students remain and ultimately be successful at their institution:

> In four-year institutions, any change that deters students from dropping out can affect three classes of students at once, whereas any change in recruiting practices can affect only one class in a given year. From this viewpoint, investing resources to prevent dropping out may be more cost effective than applying the same resources to more vigorous recruitment. (p. 2)

Degree completion is important not only as a matter of mission but also as a matter of sound financial management. Sans the potential fee and tuition increases over a student's time at a university, according to Hossler and Bean (1990), a student who is retained at an institution for four years will generate the same income as four new students who leave after one year.

This chapter begins with a discussion of factors influencing student retention, then explores the theories and models informing persistence and retention work. Next, the potential connections between student success and campus employment are addressed. We then follow with a focus on the vital role that supervisors of student employees can play, and we finish by offering concluding thoughts.

Factors Influencing Retention and Persistence

Researchers have spent decades hypothesizing about why nearly 50% of students leave their institution of higher education before completing a degree (Swail, 2004). Vincent Tinto's (1975, 1993, 1999) research illuminated barriers to degree completion, including demographic characteristics, prior academic preparation, family educational attainment, socioeconomic status (SES), and motivation. Tinto argues that the degree to which students adjust to campus through social and academic engagement is critical to the likelihood that they will remain at the university through graduation. The literature of higher education also identifies a number of other factors related to likelihood of degree completion. Campus culture, cultural and identity matches (or lack thereof) with those of the institution, first-generation status, gender, academic performance, and part-time versus full-time student status are among these other factors (Pascarella & Terenzini, 2015).

This array of influences, partial though the list may be, illuminates the complexity of addressing retention and persistence. In the next section, we review several models that inform this work and guide higher education practitioners to build processes, programs, and comprehensive plans.

Theories of Persistence and Retention

With decades devoted to research on retention, the literature is rich with varying models and methods for understanding and addressing student completion. Readers are encouraged to seek out any of the outstanding books on the subject for more comprehensive and detailed information. This section provides a description of several theories and models that the authors believe can be particularly helpful when considering student employment as a tool for encouraging retention and persistence:

- Maslow's hierarchy of needs
- Astin's student involvement and input-environment-output theories
- Tinto's model of student departure

- Schlossberg's transitions theory and theory of mattering and marginality
- Vroom's expectancy theory
- Bourdieu's construct of cultural capital

These theories can be helpful in a wide array of forms and aspects of higher education, and the authors find them to be especially applicable to the experiences of student employment practitioners. This section also addresses the concept of emotional intelligence (EI) as an overarching attribute that promotes student persistence and can be honed and developed through student employment.

Maslow's Hierarchy of Needs

Abraham Maslow's (1943) hierarchy of needs is a foundational psychological theory. Applicable to higher education, Maslow's theory can inform the psychological development of students as well as persistence and retention throughout their academic career. He uses the following organizing topics based on a set of human needs ranked in order of salience—physiological, safety, belongingness and love, esteem, self-actualization, and self-transcendence—to detail the pattern by which human beings' motivations and needs progress. Readers have likely seen these needs organized as a pyramid with the most salient and fundamental need at the bottom of the pyramid, and secondary and tertiary, and so on, moving up the pyramid. According to Maslow, the needs can only be met in order of salience. A secondary need cannot be satisfied until the primary needs are met, and so on.

In the context of higher education, Maslow's (1943) theory can help us understand the way students adapt to and continue through their university. At the basic level, students, like all humans, need general items to survive—food, water, and shelter. Universities must provide an environment where students feel safe and secure both inside and outside the classroom. With these needs met, students can begin to feel a sense of belonging with their peer groups, faculty, staff, and physical surroundings as a whole. After such a time that these positive, connecting feelings arise, students have the space, place, and optimism to intake and learn at greater levels, to become more involved, and to be recognized for such. Finally, in Maslow's (1943) theory, these more self-confident and whole students reach levels of fulfillment with themselves, their major, their potential career opportunities, and their university overall.

At the most basic foundational need, students require food, water, and shelter. Many of today's college students are responsible for meeting this need on their own. To that end, 41% of full-time students and 80% of part-time students ages 16 to 24 are employed while taking classes at a college or university (National Center for Education Statistics, 2008). Student employment professionals can help student employees learn to budget money, gain a functional balance of needs versus wants, and financially plan for future semesters.

An added qualitative value to this employment satisfies remaining elements of Maslow's hierarchy. Campus employment can increase students' connection to their university; foster a sense of belonging and the feeling of having a safety net; and increase levels of self-esteem with the completion of projects, positive praise, and relationship building with professional staff supervisors.

As such, it is critical for supervisors to remain engaged with their student employees. How can we develop ways to positively reward and recognize student employees? Perhaps your career services office develops an institution-wide award for the student employee(s) of the year, or on a smaller level, your department honors each student employee at an annual or semester-based luncheon or features student employees on social media accounts or websites. Beyond recognition, the authors stress the connection between student employment and the feeling of belonging to something. In this case, it could be a department, a student leadership team, a larger division, or the university as a whole.

Students can also use on-campus employment to inform new and continuing passions, develop additional skills, articulate potential career avenues, and ultimately find fulfillment. Supervisors can use a wide array of techniques to help students create this meaning-making. These could include spending one-on-one time with student employees listening to reflections, asking probing questions, and helping them tie classroom learning to employment experiences. It could also include administering interest, skill, and personality questionnaires to help student employees identify potential majors to pursue and future career directions and decisions.

Astin's Student Involvement Theory

Alexander Astin's (1984) student involvement theory argues that the development of self-support systems and strategies correlates directly to campus engagement. Campus involvement can include student clubs and organizations, attendance at leadership retreats, interactions with educational lecturers, and student employment on campus. Astin's theory is based upon five basic assumptions related to student engagement in academic and cocurricular programs that he posits create this feeling of belonging. First, involvement requires a student to invest psychosocial and physical energy. Second, involvement exists on a continuum, as does the amount of energy, and both vary from student to student. Third, student involvement may be qualitative or quantitative or both. Fourth, and arguably most important, the student benefits from being involved, and that benefit is directly correlated to the amount of time and the quality of the involvement. Fifth, academic performance increases with a student's engagement with campus.

Like Maslow's (1943) hierarchy of needs, Astin's (1984) student involvement theory correlates directly to campus employment. Meeting the primary element of Astin's theory, physical and psychological energy devotion, an on-campus job requires a student to invest time and mental presence to achieve tasks at hand and serve constituents. However, we can all probably think about student employees who just did not seem to be invested in their position.

Take Mike, who was hired as an intern to do marketing and social media for the student activities department. He interviewed very well and seemed to really make the connection between his academic program and the internship. However, once he began the work, he did not follow through well, and he did not accomplish half of his tasks. The professional staff member responsible for supervising Mike's internship shared a developmental conversation with him. The discussion began with a reminder of his great interview followed by concerns about his lack of motivation and disengagement. Through the conversation it became clear that Mike was just not involved to the level he wanted to be, could be, and needed to be to remain committed to his institution. The staff member discussed Mike's passions and learned that Mike was interested in the fashion industry and using social media as an engine to feature all aspects of fashion. Mike lit up with enthusiasm when discussing the ins and outs of this topic. Seeing this interest in how to do social media and marketing, Mike's supervisor saw an opportunity to tap into his creativity and to get him more engaged with his internship for the student activities office. The two brainstormed several ideas that would help Mike be more involved—for example, he could develop and market a fashion show on exercise apparel to be included as a part of a monthlong focus on being a physically active student in conjunction with the campus recreation and wellness program. Another suggestion was to develop an online training piece to help student organizations market their events utilizing the fashion industry as the example.

Although the work accompanying each campus job varies, involvement in the position can have both quantitative and qualitative outcomes for students. On the developmental continuum, we learned in previous chapters that a campus job can produce student learning and personal enrichment and responsibility. Teaching proportional elements of quality and quantity of involvement falls on the supervisor, where in it can produce the sense of belonging, respect, and engagement a student needs to be invested and retained.

Astin's Input-Environment-Outcome Model

Astin's (1993) input-environment-outcome (I-E-O) model underscores the intersections among a student's background and associated needs, the nature and climate of the institution where a student chooses to study, and the subsequent knowledge and qualities they possess when they leave the university. The core concepts of Astin's I-E-O theory are organized into three elements: inputs—student demographics, background, and educational history; environment—the sum of the student experiences while on a college campus; and outputs—the knowledge, skills, values, beliefs, and attitudes a student has after graduating from the university.

Astin identified 146 characteristics of inputs, including gender, race, ethnicity, socioeconomic class, and family education attainment, that all students possesses differently upon entry to university. Environment includes 192 variables that span eight generalized classifications: institutional characteristics, peer group characteristics, faculty characteristics, curriculum, financial aid, major field choice, place of residence, and student involvement. The last component, output, includes tangible elements such as academic achievement, retention, and graduation, to more abstract components, including skills, behaviors, and knowledge that higher education professionals aim to develop within their students. Utilizing these three components, the theory argues that student outputs are influenced by their historical inputs and the college environment with related experiences. Simultaneously, students' experiences and their feelings and attitudes after the fact are also influenced by their backgrounds.

At the most basic level, Astin's I-E-O model accounts for the education of the whole person—specifically, the understanding that no two students are alike and that each person brings something different to the academic journey. It is therefore incumbent upon the university to create an environment where each student feels a connection, has a sense of belonging, and can thrive as a learner inside and outside the classroom. Universities have the most control over this environmental aspect of the model (Pistilli & Gardner, 2015).

Astin's (1993) I-E-O model has been adopted in various realms of higher education with direct application to retention and career readiness. This theory requires an institution to build an environment that is welcoming and accepting of all students as they arrive with a myriad of input variables, is conducive to learning inside and outside the classroom, fosters belief systems and attitudes, assists students in articulating career pathways, and promotes the development of associated skills and competencies.

One of the ways a university can create this environment is through offering on-campus jobs where students can develop their skill sets, beliefs, and passions in a safe and developmental way. In addition to aiding in student development, these positions increase the effectiveness of the institution, enhancing the university environment and increasing student retention, thereby creating a circular, mutually beneficial relationship. As we think about how student employment practitioners can have impact in this arena, the authors offer the following as one way to conceptualize I-E-O. As supervisors, we do not necessarily control the *I*, although we can set requirements for positions. We can influence the *O* in student employment positions, but we cannot control what skills, values, or beliefs our students hold after they graduate. However, we can, and should, focus on the *E*: That's where the power lies! It is up to us to create an open, engaged, respectful, safe, and caring environment where our students can learn, develop, and thrive.

Tinto's Model of Student Departure

One important aspect of the high-school-to-college transition is the departure from previous peer groups and the process of navigating membership to potential new groups. Vincent Tinto's (1993) model of student departure, which was based on the work of Van Gennep's (1960) model of cultural rites of passage, focuses on this aspect of the transition. Tinto adopted Van Gennep's model, believing that students must separate themselves from their formerly associated groups (e.g., high school peers or family), undergo a transition because of it, and then incorporate and adopt the behaviors of a new group (Kuh et al., 2006). During these developmental transitions that occur during an undergraduate education, Tinto postulates three major reasons that students leave college: academic difficulties, inability to resolve educational and occupational goals, and the failure to become or remain engaged in the institution's intellectual and social life (Kuh et al., 2006). Tinto argues that academic and social integration are complementary processes that occur independently and lead to greater commitment to the university and to graduation.

The authors acknowledge the critiques of Tinto's model, notably Braxton's (2000) review that called for the "abandonment of the construct of academic integration from further research" (p. 23). Braxton concluded that Tinto's theory of student departure mainly applied to residential institutions and primarily a White population. Critiques of Tinto's theory have been widely published, but we note the holistic nature of his theory for integration in this section.

Tinto (1993) recommends that colleges and universities integrate students deliberately into the academic, social, and intellectual environment and culture of the institution. Equally, a required element of his theory is for universities to create opportunities for cocurricular activities, informal student interactions, and a myriad of opportunities for faculty-student and staff-student interactions in order for students to succeed and be retained.

Student-faculty and student-staff engagement opportunities are the intersections of Tinto's (1993) theory and its application to student employment, as well as one of the many by-products of on-campus jobs. Dependent upon the type of on-campus employment, academic and social integration can occur concurrently and be manifested by recurring and intentional student-staff and student-faculty interactions. On-campus employment may also mitigate one of Tinto's (1993) three main causes of student departure— the inability to resolve educational and occupational goals. We have all likely worked with students who question their choice of major and career path— one of the leading causes of student attrition. However, when students are employed on campus and have the opportunity to discuss their career concerns (and other matters) with a caring student employment practitioner, they are more likely to remain engaged with their institution and graduate.

Angela, for example, was a returning adult student who spent two decades in a previous career and enrolled in a local university in her mid-40s to change careers and also show her three teenage sons that they could achieve whatever they set their mind to. She entered as an elementary education major. While working at a campus job she loved, she began to think about a career working with college students and became disengaged with her courses. Ready to drop out of her degree program for a full-time secretarial position to work in higher education, she came to talk to her supervisor because they had forged a significant relationship. The two discussed higher education career pathways, and her supervisor referred her to an academic adviser who helped her find a major that would take all of her completed courses and helped her set out a plan to apply for graduate programs while being able to work to support her family. Utilizing her on-campus position and her relationship with her supervisor, Angela reconnected to the university and her academic endeavors and was able to resolve the educational and occupational struggle she was experiencing. Moreover, her student employment position helped her through the transition back to school, through a major change, and ultimately into graduate courses.

As we see in this example, an on-campus position may not directly align with a student's potential career path. However, these positions serve as a laboratory setting for student employees to develop and enhance job- and life-related skill sets such as critical thinking, problem-solving, communication, and conflict resolution. On-campus jobs can also satisfy a variety of student expectations as they relate to transitioning through and remaining integrated and engaged in university life and ultimately retaining and graduating from the same institution.

Schlossberg's Transition Theory

Nancy Schlossberg's (Goodman, Schlossberg, & Anderson, 2006) transition theory, although specifically modeled for adult students in transition, can be applied to the multiple transitions college students face. Schlossberg defines a *transition* as any event or nonevent that changes one's relationships, roles, habits, and assumptions—as only the individual experiencing this event or nonevent can determine.

We have all had students experience the beginning or end of an intimate relationship, a fight with a roommate, a failing midterm grade, moving to a new residence, or a death in the family, to name a few. Sometimes these events or nonevents can be expected, and others are unanticipated. All are events or transition points in the lives of our students that can cause a myriad of reactions and alter one's daily life as a student.

Schlossberg's research identified four factors that influence coping with such transitions—situation, self, support, and strategies—sometimes called the 4 Ss. *Situation* refers to the timing, scope of control over, duration, and person's role in the transition. The second S, *self*, is characterized by Schlossberg as the personal and demographic characteristics (gender, age, health, ethnicity, stage of life, etc.) and psychological components (commitment, value systems, ego development, and outlook). These aspects of self are accompanied by the third S, *support*, defined as intimate relationships, friends, family, community, and formal and informal institutional systems. The fourth S is *strategies*, also referred to as *coping resources*, that control the problem, assist in stress management, and have the ability to change the event or nonevent at hand.

Chickering and Schlossberg (1995) partnered to describe the college student transition as having three phases: moving in, moving through, and moving out. This cycle applies as students enter higher education, ascend from freshman to sophomore and so on, and ultimately graduate. It also applies as they change majors, move into different places of residence, start an on-campus job, or move from one student employment position to the next. It should be apparent from even this short description that students may be engaged in more than one transition at any given time, and they may be in different phases for each transition they are experiencing. For example, an entering first-year student is moving out of high school but moving into the college experience simultaneously. Therefore, it is critical for supervisors to build relationships with their student employees, make themselves available to listen and notice when a student may be in transition, and most importantly, make referrals to appropriate campus and community resources when the student employee seems to be struggling through an impactful event or nonevent. Likewise, student employment professionals are uniquely positioned to be able to coach the development of the four Ss prior to, during, and after a transition.

Schlossberg's Theory of Mattering and Marginality

Building on Rosenberg and McCullough (1981), Schlossberg's (1989) theory of mattering and marginality details the feelings associated with transitions, new environments, and new positions. She asserts that these feelings can represent a permanent or temporary condition and are greatly influenced by their environment and the people in it. Schlossberg contends that there are five aspects of mattering: attention, importance, ego extension, dependence, and appreciation.

These elements offer the perfect intersection with student employment on campus. As we have all seen on our campuses, selection for a student employment position is a great way for students to know that they are seen or noticed on campus (attention). A word or two letting student employees know how much the project in which they are involved means to the office conveys importance. Sharing pride in student employees for an accomplishment in or out of the workplace can help them have a sense of ego extension; the student might feel, *My supervisor is invested in me and sees my success.* The last two components of Schlossberg's (1989) theory, dependence and appreciation, are wrapped up into the same aspect of mattering when student employees feel needed in their position and are celebrated and appreciated for their efforts.

In this theory and others discussed throughout this book, the supervisor clearly plays a crucial role in this relationship and can assist students through various transitions to and through the institution, in specific on-campus positions, and ultimately through their final transition to a career after graduation. A student employee who has a sense of mattering in the workplace is more likely to persist there and at the institution; a student employee who feels invisible or engaged in meaningless busy work may feel marginalized and less inclined to stick with either the employment position or the university.

Vroom's Expectancy Theory

Victor Vroom's (1964) expectancy theory seeks to identify the elements of motivation. Vroom defines *motivation* as making a choice among varying forms of voluntary activities for the purpose of maximizing pleasure and minimizing pain. Vroom suggests that motivation is a function of the interaction of the following three factors:

1. *Valence*—the importance an individual places on an expected outcome. For valence to be positive, the outcome must be clear in the student's mind, and the student must want it more than not having it. Vroom refers to these outcome qualities as *clarity* and *salience.*

2. *Expectancy*—the belief that additional effort will lead to better performance. In the case of students, they must see and understand a pathway that will lead to the desired outcome.
3. *Instrumentality*—the belief that positive performance equals valued outcome. Simply put, students must believe that they can do what it takes to complete the pathway to the outcome.

Vroom's theory postulates that individuals can be motivated, regardless of goals, if they believe the following:

- Their efforts are positively correlated with their performance.
- Positive performance will result in a desirable reward for said performance.
- The reward will satisfy an important need.
- The desire to attain the need will make the effort worthwhile. (Vroom, 1964)

Although it is not a traditional retention or student success theory, Vroom's theory can be readily applied to retention, persistence, and on-campus student employment. For example, consider a student who is financing her own education (valence/outcome). In order to ensure she has enough money to pay for weekly groceries (need), she must work while attending school full-time. She knows that she must keep her job to have enough money for food, so she must perform the assigned tasks to the best of her ability and show up to work on time (expectance/ability). This student also knows that if she performs well, is punctual, and fulfills her supervisor's expectations, she will take home the necessary amount of money to live comfortably (instrumentality/pathway). Therefore, she does everything her supervisor asks her to and does so well, creating a positive relationship between her and her supervisor, resulting in increased and sustaining motivation to continue to perform. Think back to Mike, the student in an earlier example, who has an interest in social media and fashion. Vroom's theory offers another way to frame and address Mike's performance. By realigning the projects Mike would work on in his internship, the pathway of his employment was better aligned with both an outcome about which he cared and his own sense of his abilities.

Bourdieu's Construct of Cultural Capital

The intersectionality of motivation, expectation setting, social involvement, academic engagement, and the necessity for student needs to be met are what makes up the whole student who walks into our universities. As can be seen at institutions across the country, the student body is a fluid, ever-changing environment that will continue to grow in diversity. The National Center for

Education Statistics (2016) offered the following overview and forecast of this changing student population:

- Enrollment of White students will increase 4%, compared to the exponential increase of Hispanic students at 42% and a 25% increase of Black students.
- Enrollment of traditional-age students, 18 to 24 years old, will increase about 10%, and enrollment of returning adult students will grow at twice that rate, while the population of students 35 and older will increase 25%.
- Part-time enrollment will grow at roughly 18% compared to 14% for full-time students.
- Enrollment of women will continue to grow at a faster pace than men—18% versus 10%, respectively.

Swail (2002) said, "Our capacity to conceptualize and understand the impact of impending demographic change at the national and international levels is crucial to our ability to mold responsible higher education policies as a nation" (p. 23). Due to these shifts on our campuses, it is critical to note theories related to cultural immersion and the retention of non-White-identifying students.

Tierney (1999) provides a foundation on which we can build cultural considerations relative to retention, persistence, and student success.

> A cultural view of issues of college access and retention interprets the world differently from those notions which contend that an individual's success or failure in college is dependent upon singular variables such as financial need. Rather than view the academic world as a place into which students need to fit and assimilate or face intellectual suicide, this explanation views the academy as ripe for reinterpretation and restructuring. Not only must students fit into the academic culture, but educational organizations must also accommodate for and honor students' cultural differences. (p. 83)

With this notion of mutual responsibility at the forefront, the authors highlight Bourdieu's (1984) concept of *cultural capital*. Bourdieu (1984) observed that people enter into a social milieu, such as higher education institutions, with knowledge born of their own culture and life experiences. The social setting has embedded in it structures and systems that reflect the cultural capital of the majority or dominant group in that setting. If the person entering into the setting is not of that majority or dominant group, the person has an inherent disadvantage with regard to pursuing the available opportunities.

Connections can also be made between cultural capital and student employment. Students who are first generation, for example, are learning job-based skills within their campus jobs while getting the opportunity to experience situations, people, and environments they may not have previously encountered. These experiences not only offer some financial assistance but foster a deeper connection to the institution.

In addition, Kuh and Love (2004) illustrate the importance of minority students making formal and informal cultural connections within their campus as a critical factor in persistence. Universities can afford these intentional and informal connections through cultural student organizations, residence halls, Greek systems, and employment opportunities, to name a few. Likewise, on the university side, Tierney (2004) and Pidgeon (2008) stress the necessity of validating the opinions, worldviews, and experiences of cultural minorities, especially on campuses dominated by majority cultures. Jensen (2011) summed up this intersectionality, saying that "[in order] to promote the integration and retention of minority students, higher education institutions could recognize and honor the cultural capital of minority students" (p. 1).

Student Employment and Student Success

As noted at the onset of this chapter, student success is distinct from (although related to) retention and persistence. In addition to the ways student employment opportunities can support retention and persistence, these opportunities can also assist students in being successful in college and beyond. This section focuses on that connection, highlighting the ways in which student employment can foster intelligence and the skills requisite for success. In particular, the potential of EI theory for fostering student success in student employment settings is explored.

Emotional Intelligence

Modeling of effective leadership, behaviors, communication, and work habits is our responsibility as student employment practitioners, and the holistic development it affords our student employees will prepare them to be successful wherever they go after graduation. How do we effectively do so and ensure they are developing the necessary skills as they grow? There are certainly cognitive factors and measures of academic preparedness, or in Astin's (1993) terms, *inputs*, such as cumulative high school GPA, standardized test scores, class rank, and a student's intelligence quotient (IQ), that have been used as predictors of success. However, dating back to the early 1990s, a new intelligence was identified, one that has been labeled as being a greater indicator of success than a student's IQ: EI (Nasir & Masrur, 2010).

EI was introduced by Salovey and Mayer (1990), and it became popular with Goleman's (1995) publication *Emotional Intelligence*. Bar-On (1997) defines *emotional intelligence* as "a set of emotional and social skills that influence the way we perceive and express ourselves, develop and maintain social relationships, cope with challenges, and use emotional information in an effective and meaningful way" (cited in Stein, Book, & Kanoy, 2013, p. 4). EI involves a set of skills that can be learned and developed in a laboratory setting like on-campus student employment. Although there are numerous theories, lists of attributes, behaviors, and skills that encompass EI, most can be organized into the five foundational and leading framework elements as developed by Goleman (1995):

1. self-awareness
2. self-regulation
3. motivation
4. empathy
5. social skills

A strength of EI for use in higher education is its applicability to student development, work functions, leadership behaviors, relationships, health issues, psychological well-being, and many other facets of human performance. In fact, there is almost no area of life where EI does not apply (Stein et al., 2013). Another strength is that EI is cross-cultural; EI is not only a Western notion. Emotional management, regulation, and sensing are foundational aspects to one's cultural intelligence and are behind many definitions of *leadership* inside and outside of the higher education sector.

Emotional Intelligence and Student Employment

Expanding upon Goleman's (1995) five categories, Stein and colleagues (2013) articulate key employment and leadership skills as the student's ability to

- recognize and effectively manage one's emotions,
- leverage emotions to solve real-world problems,
- communicate effectively in emotionally charged situations,
- make good decisions,
- build effective relationships, and
- manage stress.

Student employees can develop these emotionally intelligent leadership skills by learning, shadowing supervisors, and participating in on-the-job training. These skill sets honed in meaningful on-campus jobs not only enhance student employment but are crucial in professional settings regardless of field.

Michael Coomes adds an important leadership and EI skill that students learn through on-campus employment: integrity. "The effective student employee will take the job seriously, will recognize the value of work, and will come to appreciate the need for collaboration as a means of accomplishing goals. All of these values and many others can be learned through student work" (Coomes, cited in Noel-Levitz, 2010, p. 3). In addition to the development of integrity, Baxter Magolda (1992) states that the most important part about on-campus employment is that students learn to work with diverse people and situations, thus learning about themselves and how they work to help others—all aspects of EI.

> Ultimately, a positive work-study experience will result in a student having gained valuable job skills and a high degree of self-confidence, as well as the motivation to continue to perform at the highest level after leaving the institution and entering the world of work. In addition, the network of relationships developed through on-campus employment continues to serve the student as he or she graduates, as supervisors provide references for students applying to graduate school or full-time jobs, thereby helping students make that critical first step in launching their careers. (Noel-Levitz, 2010, p. 3)

Student Employment and Student Success

Research has found a link between EI and academic performance in college and career success and fulfillment.

> As EI involves such skills as motivation and determination, it can play an important role in achieving goals in various fields of life thereby leading to success. Studies conducted in multiple areas like education . . . indicate that [EI] is related with different aspects of success in life. (Nasir & Masrur, 2010, p. 40)

The literature also includes studies focused on EI and student leadership behaviors and decisions (Kanoy, 2011). Campus employment can have positive impact on the development of leadership skills and on the various elements of EI (Noel-Levitz, 2010): "On-campus jobs can provide a supportive and non-threatening environment where students learn to interface comfortably with the public, understand the value of teamwork, develop time management and computer skills, and build self-esteem as they are recognized for their accomplishments" (p. 3).

Campus employment can also help prepare students for success after college (see chapter 3 for an extended discussion of student employment and career development). The National Association of Colleges and Employers publishes an annual report of the top five skills employers most desire in college graduates. Relatively unchanged for the last decade (National Association of Colleges and Employers, 2015b), the top five in 2010 included the following:

1. communication skills (assertiveness, emotional expression)—EI related
2. analytical abilities (problem-solving)—EI related
3. teamwork (social responsibility, interpersonal relationship)—EI related
4. technical skills
5. strong work ethic (self-actualization, self-regard, impulse control)—EI related

The remaining 5 of the top 10 include interpersonal skills, flexibility and adaptability, honesty and integrity, motivation, and organization—all EI related.

Promoting Postgraduation Success

When we think about students in transition, our thoughts normally turn to incoming freshmen, perhaps those changing majors, or students returning to good academic standing from a semester on probation. What we tend to forget is the importance of the transition *out* of the university. This is an arena where on-campus student employment can serve as a life-changing catalyst. After all, retention is all about getting students across the stage at graduation, and student success includes aspects of helping students achieve career-based goals.

As you may recall from chapter 3, on-campus jobs can be excellent catalysts for student career development. As Luzzo and Ward (1995) state, "Earning while learning provides the student with both financial assistance to help meet college expenses and practical experience which may lead to enhanced opportunities for employment after college graduation" (p. 307).

Gleason (1993) found that students who worked consistently in college were more successful in terms of earnings and employment rates in their first year or two after graduation. Pascarella and Terenzini's (2015) review of research, in *How College Affects Students*, suggests that working during college has a positive impact on career choice, career attainment, and level of professional responsibility attained early in one's career, particularly if that campus employment is related to major or career aspirations.

According to Kincaid (1996), employers agree. Citing a survey of United Parcel Service (UPS) human resources professionals, there is a "strong bias" when hiring entry-level staff who had student employment experience during college. Put in terms of career-related skill sets, Kincaid (1996) expands this notion, stating that part-time jobs are more important than academic success because former student employees exhibit the following behaviors consistently more than peers who did not hold an on-campus job:

- produce better work
- accept supervision better
- are better time managers
- have better team skills
- make a more rapid transition
- have more realistic expectations

Not only do on-campus positions help students acquire these skills, but they lead to a greater chance of full-time employment upon graduation. According to Casella and Brougham (in Kincaid, 1996), "Job/intern/volunteer experience as an undergraduate is the runaway number-one factor in finding postgraduate employment . . . and it was perceived as more important than high GPA, major, job search skills, personality, and knowing someone"(p. 5).

Much research has been dedicated to these skills and the eventual development of career maturity. Simply, career maturity details a student's ability to make age-appropriate decisions as he or she evaluates and weighs potential career options and steps to get there (Patton & Creed, 2001). Results from similar studies show that the impact of employment experiences on students' career decisions depends, in some degree, on the extent of congruity or similarity between the job and the students' career goals (Luzzo, 1995; Luzzo & Ward, 1995). Again, in this aspect of student employment, the supervisor is critical in helping students find and articulate these connections and remembering they, in many·cases, are serving in the role of mentor and coach.

Supervising student employees in terms of mentoring and connecting them to career readiness and skills is one of the most critical pieces, and sometimes one of the most difficult aspects, of the student-supervisor relationship. Due to a variety of aspects, including incongruence between staff and student, supervisor's schedule and lack of time to properly transition and train a student worker, and nature of the working environment and projects to be completed, supervisors may lack the time and ability to help students connect the dots between their academic, work, and future career aspirations. In an effort to strengthen this critical element, Noel-Levitz (2010) suggests the following eight ways for supervisors to best help student employees:

1. *Communicate clear expectations.* Communicate job standards and expectations to your student employees. Written process documentation is the best reference.
2. *Be firm and fair.* Maintain high standards and expectations, while recognizing that your workers are students first and campus employees second.
3. *Give frequent feedback.* Frequent, positive communication boosts morale and improves performance. Feedback about errors framed positively and with clear direction on how to prevent future errors is essential.
4. *Provide training.* Focus training on essential skills and standard processes of the department. Engage students in identifying desirable work habits and how to measure performance. Offer scripts for common transactions.
5. *Share the vision.* Coach students on how their work fits into the function of the department and the mission of the institution.
6. *Promote team spirit.* Work to develop and nurture the unique contributions of each team member, while stressing the common mission. Involve student workers in staff meetings and discuss roles and responsibilities inherent in effective teams.
7. *Give recognition.* Catch your student employees doing things right and recognize them for their positive performance.
8. *Set an example.* Student employees take their cue from you. By exhibiting efficient, diligent work habits, you model behavior for students to emulate. Get the best out of student employees by being the best.

With these important practices at the forefront, it is critical that supervisors provide a solid foundation and environment for students to thrive both in their employment and on the campus at large. Modeling effective leadership is one of the best things we can teach student employees as they persist and are successful in college and beyond.

Fostering Emotional Intelligence in Student Employees

Although there are numerous critical elements of workplace success, Bradberry and Greaves (2009) write, "[EI] is the single biggest predictor of performance in the workplace and the strongest driver of leadership and personal excellence" (para. 8). Bradberry and Greaves (2009), in their research study of people at individual places of employment, found 90% of the top performers were also high in EI, compared to only 20% of the bottom performers. Likewise, a higher degree of EI is directly correlated to earnings:

> You can be a top performer without emotional intelligence, but the chances are slim. Naturally, people with a high degree of emotional intelligence

make more money—an average of $29,000 more per year than people with a low degree of emotional intelligence. The link between emotional intelligence and earnings is so direct that every point increase in emotional intelligence adds $1,300 to an annual salary. These findings hold true for people in all industries, at all levels, in every region of the world. We haven't yet been able to find a job in which performance and pay aren't tied closely to emotional intelligence. (Bradberry & Greaves, 2009, para. 9)

Clearly there is no better venue for the development of EI than an on-campus job—putting a more prepared, emotionally intelligent graduate into the workforce and positioning that person for future career success.

So, how can supervisors help student employees develop EI? Utilizing foundational points from Bradberry and Greaves (2009) and McKee (2015) and adapting aspects from Fatum (2013), the following represent specific ways on-campus jobs can help students develop greater EI.

Creating a Sense of Self

Fatum (2013) organizes eight EI competencies into three macro areas: know yourself, choose yourself, give yourself. She adds the eight micro areas to those as follows:

1. *Know yourself.* Enhance emotional literacy and recognize patterns.
2. *Choose yourself.* Think consequentially, navigate emotions, possess intrinsic motivation, be optimistic.
3. *Give yourself.* Increase empathy and pursue noble goals.

Helping students know and articulate self-concept assists in supporting them as they manage emotions, pursue their goals, sharpen critical thinking tools, and cultivate motivation.

Intentional Change: Personal Vision and Ways of Operating

Richard Boyatzis's (2006) intentional change theory (ICT) illustrates the process of undergoing a desired and viable change in behavior, attitudes, thoughts, and perceptions. For students at various places along the continuum of development, an on-campus job can be and is the place where this intentional change begins. Supervisors can help students find and define a personal vision of their own future that begins the process of intentional change. McKee (2015) articulates this part of the process of change as helping an employee—in our case, a student employee—find a dream, discover what is important in life, and craft a clear and compelling vision for the future. The second stage is determining the student's current EI level, uncovering what is really going on in that student's life, and building trust along the way. You can help a student move through these stages by engaging in strengths finding; administering an EI assessment; using SMART goal setting (as reviewed in chapter 4); connecting student leaders with professional networks in their chosen career field; and having honest, real conversations about professional tact and leadership skill building.

The next and most crucial step in developing EI and intentional change is helping students identify how their current operational procedures need to be amended in order to realize the future they have just articulated (McKee, 2015). To do so, supervisors can help students establish learning goals and plans for self-assessment that ultimately lead to change. Does your student need to develop greater empathy so as to not trample people on the way to achieving a goal? Is there a need to focus on developing grit to avoid being derailed in the face of setbacks and challenges? Or is the missing piece the ability to offer and receive constructive criticism and to use it to develop greater proficiencies? At this juncture, it is critical that trust has been established and that the supervisor possesses enough EI and ability to communicate effectively with this student employee.

Fostering Emotional Intelligence in Supervisors

Knowing the elements of EI and being able to practice them as supervisors as well as assist student leaders in developing them are often two different things. It is important as a first step in developing EI that supervisors are able to articulate and understand the eight basic emotional sectors and the intensity by which human beings experience emotions.

Ni (2014) presents six keys, or abilities, to increasing EI.

Ability to Reduce Negative Emotions
Reducing negative emotions sounds quite simple, yet it can be one of the hardest concepts to master because negative interactions occur even in the best environments. In an effort to reduce negative reactions, Ni (2014) suggests changing the way one thinks about the situation. Take, for example, your feeling after leaving a contentious meeting. Do you return to your office filled with frustration and vent to a colleague? Supervisors must ask themselves, *Who is watching and listening? Are student employees in earshot as we model ineffective ways of dealing with negative emotions?* Rather, if you attempt to depersonalize the situation, realizing someone in that meeting did what they did because of them, not you, you can begin to see things from a different perspective and reduce the likelihood of a negative interaction.

Ability to Stay Cool and Manage Stress
Similar to reducing negative emotions, staying cool in stressful situations is one of the key aspects of EI (Ni, 2014). Everyone experiences stress differently

and has varying triggers that cause angst and anxiety to rise. Supervisors should strike a balance between not clouding reality and overdramatizing due to one's feelings. Ni (2014) suggests finding coping mechanisms when you are experiencing triggers—applying cold water to your face and neck, putting your body into motion by leaving the stressful situation for a period of time, and knowing when you are triggered and need to find a healthier outlet for stress.

Ability to Be Assertive and Express Difficult Emotions

Ni (2014) emphasizes the need to set boundaries appropriately, exercising your right to agree or disagree, being able to say no when your plate is too full, setting your own priorities, and protecting yourself from additional duress and harm as the ways to deal with difficult emotions. Setting boundaries is perhaps the most challenging aspect of EI development, as daily life is often full of hard times. Ni (2014) suggests using the XYZ technique when discussing difficult emotions you may be experiencing while in the workplace: "I feel X when you do Y in situation Z." You can easily model this approach for student employees in meetings, group settings, and one-on-one interactions.

Ability to Stay Proactive, Not Reactive, in the Face of a Difficult Person

Similar to modeling expressing difficult emotions, working on self in an effort to be less reactive is a critical element of EI. People with high EI can defuse situations, inclusive of their own emotions, and communicate proactively once the level of stress has been reduced. In doing so, it is important for supervisors to once again depersonalize the situation, trying to understand that person X is acting in this way because of his- or herself and exercising the ability to count to 10, take a deep breath, and reapproach the situation when emotions have subsided. Ni (2014) also suggests setting consequences:

> The ability to identify and assert consequence(s) is one of the most important skills you can use to 'stand down' a difficult person. Effectively articulated, consequence gives pause to the difficult individual, and compels her or him to shift from violation to respect. (para. 14)

Ability to Bounce Back From Adversity

Sometimes it is not just a difficult person affecting your attitude, but a host of setbacks and general adversity. Many are familiar with basketball icon Michael Jordan's response to adversity: "I've missed more than 9,000 shots in my career. I've lost almost 300 games. Twenty-six times I've been trusted to take the game-winning shot and missed. I've failed over and over and over again in my life. And that is why I succeed" (Brainyquote, 2017). EI is honed in that same spirit. It is your reaction to setbacks, feeling hope instead of prolonged despair in the face of challenges and optimism instead of frustration (Ni, 2014). If supervisors can show their employees how to ask quality questions and think outside the box to find new sets of answers, students will be able to see the qualities of grit and perseverance and emulate those abilities.

Ability to Express Intimate Emotions in Close, Personal Relationships

The ability to express intimate emotions is not just reserved for romantic relationships. Instead, being able to share true feelings of appreciation verbally and nonverbally is key to healthy workplace relationships between staff members and students. These behaviors can be as simple as asking people how they are doing; saying, "Thank you" or "I appreciate you"; maintaining positive eye contact; and smiling. These expressions of emotions, and exercising control thereof, are important aspects of EI.

Supervisors as Catalysts for Retention and Success

Research conducted by Noel-Levitz (2010) indicates that 21% of first-year undergraduates planned to work 1 to 10 hours per week; 29%, 11 to 20 hours per week, and 26% more than 20 hours per week while going to school (Noel-Levitz, 2010). These data call for additional attention to be paid to student employees immediately upon their transition to higher education. With over 75% of incoming freshmen planning to seek employment, on-campus positions are at a premium as campuses work to help students through the difficult transition from high school to college. Nearly 18 million students entered college in 2008, with almost 34% stopping out after the first year due to overconfidence, underpreparedness, and unrealistic expectations about university life (Harke, 2010). Juxtapose the need for students to seek employment and the difficulty of the transition to higher education, and the results can be dangerous.

However, there is research that demonstrates on-campus employment can help students perform better academically (Gleason, 1993) and that this part-time employment helps students engage and integrate into their new environment sooner than nonworking peers (Cuccaro-Alamin & Choy, 1998 as cited in Kincaid, 1996). Dennis's findings in a survey of financial aid administrators across the country uncovered that working during the freshman year has a

> positive impact on first-year students because it provides students with an inside view of the school . . . . Working involves students with the activities of the university and provides social contact. Employment also teaches students how to better manage their time and can, at some schools, provide career-related job experiences. (in Kincaid, 1996, pp. 32–33)

As student employment practitioners, we can be one of the reasons these students perform better academically and are retained on campus.

> Students working in a particular department often develop a feeling of connectedness as they make friends with staff members and fellow student workers and take pride in their inside knowledge of the institution. Capable and trusted staff members who take an interest in students' academic progress and general wellbeing—but, unlike faculty members, are not involved in evaluating their course work—often become supportive mentors or even surrogate parents for students who work with them. In many cases, staff members create relationships that nurture ongoing ties to the institution. (Noel-Levitz, 2010, p. 3)

These relationships between student employees and their supervisors are crucial aspects to creating a sense of belonging and increased involvement.

Supervisors serve an immense role in forming relationships that positively impact retention through this engagement to campus. Kincaid (1996) describes staff and faculty supervisors' roles as "retention agents," saying,

> Campus work supervisors are ideally positioned to be highly effective "retention agents" for the students who work with them. In fact, students often say it is their work supervisor who knows them best—better than any teacher or adviser on campus. The best-of-the-best supervisors become proxy "moms and dads" to dozens of students (and over the years, to hundreds and even thousands of them). For many students this relationship prominently figures in their decision to return to campus each fall. (p. 32)

In addition to developing positive relationships with student employees, supervisors can empower their departments to have an impact on the success, belonging, involvement, and retention of their student employees. The Human Resource Services office at Brigham Young University (BYU) provides great insight into how departments can keep student employees within their unit as well as at the university (Brigham Young University, 2014). In order to do so, BYU suggests that departments do the following:

- *Add value.* Students who feel valued tend to stay. One way to do this is to provide an open atmosphere where they can offer opinions without worrying that their job is on the line. Using students' ideas shows respect for them, and they will show respect in return. Treating everyone equally and fairly is another way to cultivate respect and to show students they are valued.

- *Adjust pay scale.* For some students, the possibility of pay increases gives them incentive to stay. Establishing a pay scale that rewards longevity can increase employee retention. Other pay scales can be put in place that reward performance. As students demonstrate they have successfully learned new skills or programs, they can be rewarded with a raise.
- *Create purpose.* Student employees need to have a sense of purpose. They enjoy understanding how their work is helping the university. They want to know what is going on in their department and how the activities they are doing will help. Students also desire clear knowledge of how their job will benefit them in the future.
- *Promote training and growth.* A university education is much more than going to class and doing homework. For many students, the skills they learn and develop in a student job give them the experience they need to find a job after graduation. Employers should provide positive mentoring opportunities that will benefit the student whenever possible. Students want responsibilities that challenge them and keep them busy. Such variety and challenge may alleviate the trapped feeling that accompanies a boring or static job. Providing teamwork opportunities is a good way to promote friendships and training.
- *Be flexible.* Students with a heavy workload and a string of midterms or projects can feel overly stressed and may want to quit work to keep up their studies. When possible, employers can give students a needed break by reducing their hours or allowing them to take a leave. Other arrangements specific to the situation may also be appropriate. Being flexible will help students feel a sense of value and appreciation that will help keep them around.
- *Provide recognition.* Recognition for a job well done can be a key factor in retaining students at work. Offering praise and performance feedback are easy ways to recognize employees. Other programs such as employee of the month are more public and often very effective ways to recognize employees. Nominating your outstanding students for student employee of the year is another way to show appreciation. Promoting students to supervisory roles and giving them specific or special projects shows them you appreciate their hard work.
- *Have fun.* Students who enjoy their work are more likely to stay and excel in their jobs. Allowing music, jokes, or contests can increase everyone's morale. Having periodic departmental parties or departmental lunches and treats gives everyone something fun and social to look forward to. The sky's the limit with ways to have fun at work.

Through supervisor dedication and departmental focus on employees, campuses can leverage student employment to ease the transition for students, increase their engagement with the university and ultimately strengthen retention.

We must also do our due diligence to ensure that student employees are navigating transitions and building positive experiences and are integrated into the campus environment, beyond building relationships with us. To ensure student success, student employment experiences need to be assessed formally and informally. One example is the 2015 Student Employee Survey of undergraduate student employees in work-study and hourly positions at Indiana University–Purdue University Indianapolis (IUPUI). The student employees surveyed reported the following (IUPUI Office of Student Employment, 2015):

- 87.5% of respondents agree or strongly agree that being a student employee at IUPUI has positively impacted their overall college experience.
- 44% of respondents agree or strongly agree that being able to work on campus while attending IUPUI influenced their decision to stay enrolled at IUPUI.

At IUPUI, approximately 75% of students work while attending classes, with roughly 3,000 students working on-campus each semester. These students work among 17 schools and 140 individual departments on campus and have an average 3.19 GPA.

The best-sought outcome would be for students' responses on satisfaction surveys to match the reasons they sought an on-campus position. The NESEA/Cornell survey (as cited in Kincaid, 1996) did just that by asking students why they work. After paying college bills and earning money for expenses, the top reasons cited were as follows:

- career exploration
- enjoyable/fulfilling
- career contacts
- enriches academics
- social interaction
- learn time management (in Kincaid, 1996, p. 4)

Student responses at IUPUI, according to the 2015 Student Employee Survey of undergraduate student employees in work-study and hourly positions (IUPUI Office of Student Employment, 2015), aligned with the NESEA results:

- 75.7% of respondents agree or strongly agree that their on-campus job has helped them understand workplace expectations and professionalism.
- 69.8% of respondents agree or strongly agree their job has helped them plan and prepare for their future career.
- 59% of respondents agree or strongly agree that their job is directly related to their major and/or career interests.
- 87.9% of respondents agree or strongly agree that their on-campus job has helped them develop skills or learn new skills.

Not only do these concepts arise in satisfaction surveys, but student employees develop a sense that they matter to their supervisor, department, peer group, and institution.

Conclusion

From supervisor to graduate student to administrator to faculty member, we all play an important role in supporting and retaining students at all junctures of their college education. As this chapter illustrated, for many students, an identity in that journey is as a student employee on our campuses—a crucial time and place for us to aid in these students' development, learning, and success. Kincaid (1996) said it best:

> Student employment is more than financial aid—it provides students with the social benefits, with the opportunity for involvement, and with the inherent pressure to better manage their time. In the long run it provides students not only with experience, but also with increased confidence in their ability to tackle significant tasks and relate well to many different types of people in the world of work after graduation. (p. 34)

We must not forget that student development, well-being, and success are at the forefront of our supervisor-student employee relationship. "In the long run, on-campus employment can dramatically bolster the experience for students and yield benefits for the institution. At the center of all of this is the student employment professional, serving a pivotal and invaluable role both in the lives of the students and in the success of the institution" (Kincaid, 1996, p. 34).

6

THE IMPORTANCE OF INTENTIONAL MANAGEMENT AND SUPERVISION IN STUDENT EMPLOYMENT

T hroughout the previous five chapters we have presented the history of student employment; its critical ties to student development, learning, and retention; and the important role student employment practitioners play in mentoring and coaching. We now turn our attention to specific ways student employment practitioners can effectively manage, supervise, and lead student employees. Perozzi (2009) said it best:

> Yes, any program is better than none—even if the only thing it accomplishes is offering students a way to earn money while they are going to school. But if given the chance to make the program more than this—to make it educational, rewarding, preparatory, and grounded in theory—this approach is beneficial to both employer . . . and employee. (p. 163)

This chapter provides a functional overview for student employment practitioners to build effective recruitment, selection, supervision, and evaluation strategies.

Elements of a Successful Student Employment Program

Perozzi (2009) details the following as elements of successful student employment programs and depicts them in a circular model informing the next stage:

- orientation
- area-specific training
- shared input and recognition
- evaluation
- recruitment and hiring

The authors offer an expanded model of successful student employment programs that incorporates the elements identified by Perozzi (2009) but also includes knowledge and application of theories of student development, learning, and retention/persistence/success as well as student employment legal issues. Figure 6.1 shows that expanded model.

Whether you are a first-time student employee supervisor, a graduate student in a higher education preparation program, or a senior administrator working to develop a comprehensive student employment program, these elements are vital to the success of students and your overall program.

Structuring a Student Employment Program

Now that you are convinced that a successful job for student employees is one that provides for growth, development, and learning, as well as contributes

Figure 6.1. Elements of a successful student employment program.

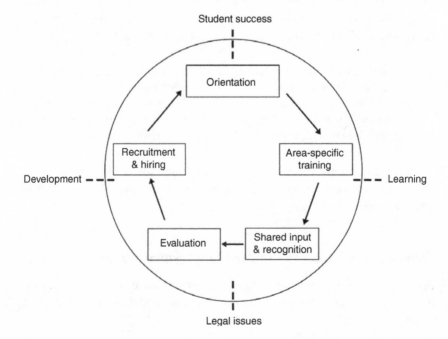

to retention, persistence, and success, your next step is to consider how your student employment program will fit in with your organizational structure and function.

The authors recommend that each department, or each unit within larger departments, creates an overall strategy for student employment as part of its strategic goals, incorporating student employees into as many aspects of the department's work as could provide a learning opportunity, assuming available funding. Involving all members of the team in the planning process gives each person a voice while including as many perspectives and ideas as possible. A needs assessment exercise can reveal several tasks and projects that the staff need help with, or that the staff would love to implement if they had help.

For example, a conferences and special events office may design a student employment program that would align student employees with each line of business, such as marketing and sales, event planning services, operations, technology and audiovisual services, catering, and accounting. A library staff may create a student employment program aligned with specific collections, data management services, community library services, or special functions such as book preservation and cataloguing. A student health center may structure a health outreach and prevention component that students could coordinate and execute. The project management office could use some extra help in general and may be interested in helping students develop the project management skillset while they support large-scale projects in administration.

A conversation about budgeting must be part of the planning process. The federal minimum wage is rising, but do not let that constrain your planning; the authors recommend that you begin your brainstorming session without regard to budget constraints. Later, when you develop your resource allocation plan as you likely do each year, the projections you make for student employees can be incorporated into the resource proposal process. Using round numbers as an example, a student employee who earns $10 per hour and works 15 hours per week for 15 weeks each semester will cost $4,500 annually. Once your strategy and resource plans have been approved, planning for the recruitment cycle can begin.

Recruitment and Hiring Practices

Recruitment and hiring practices are essential to a successful student employee experience. To that end, NACE provides the following six guidelines (Mackes, 2017). Although NACE focuses primarily on the interactions between off-campus employers and career services offices, the authors find relevance and application in the following guidelines to student employment on campus.

1. All candidates should have the opportunity for open and free selection of employment opportunities consistent with their personal objectives and optimum use of their talents.
2. Colleges and employers should both support informed and responsible decision-making by candidates.
3. All aspects of the recruiting process should be fair and equitable to candidates and employing organizations.
4. Career services professionals and faculty involved in recruiting will provide generally comparable services to all employers, regardless of whether the employers contribute services, gifts, or financial support to the educational institution or office and regardless of the level of such support.
5. As required by the Family Educational Rights and Privacy Act (FERPA) of 1974, any disclosure of student information outside of the educational institution will be with prior consent of the student unless health and/ or safety considerations necessitate the dissemination of such information. Sound judgment and fairness will be exercised in maintaining the confidentiality of student information, regardless of the source, including written records, reports, and computer databases.
6. When employment professionals conduct recruitment activities through student associations or academic departments, such activities will be conducted in accordance with the policies of the career services office and accepted ethical and legal practices.

Throughout this section of the chapter, we unpack these pieces as they relate to creating an inclusive environment, and the management and supervision of student employees.

The Job Description

In your planning process you have likely identified some areas of responsibility that student employees could fill, or you may have existing student employees already performing some of those tasks. Whether you are starting fresh or continuing a previously established hiring plan, it is good practice to review and reassess the job descriptions for each student position.

Writing a good job description begins with a job title. "Student assistant," "work-study," and "student helper" may be common, but these titles do not communicate anything at all about the position. Consider devising a job title that is more descriptive of the role or function, such as "A/V technician," "peer tutor," "marketing assistant," "special collections library associate," "event planner," "tour guide," "accounting assistant," "business analyst," "project management trainee," and so forth. After the title, describe the duties and responsibilities. In your first draft it may be easier for you to create a running list of every possible task a student employee in that job title might perform. The authors recommend that you then edit the draft for brevity, keeping your descriptions short and listing only the most important responsibilities or priority projects for that position during the term or year.

Next, reflect upon the responsibilities and consider the minimum skills and qualifications you need students to bring with them to the job. Remember that your goal is to make student employment an opportunity for learning and development, so give careful thought to the skills you will train for as well as the skills the student employee can learn on the job; recall the section of the learning chapter (chapter 4) on student employee learning outcomes.

Next, determine the number of hours per week or an acceptable range of work hours this role would require, along with the pay rate and any other benefits you may wish to include. With respect to hours, remember the caution from the previous chapter to not overload employees' schedules as they are students first. Also there may be institutional restrictions on the total number of hours students can work on campus; check with your human resources department to ensure compliance. With respect to benefits, a resident assistant is often paid a stipend and receives a portion of or full bed waiver as compensation. Sometimes a position in campus dining might include free meals for student employees who work a certain number of shifts per week. One career center not far from New York City provides a paid student membership in a professional association related to the student employee's work function (e.g., marketing students are offered membership in the American Marketing Association or New York Women in Communications).

Last, determine the method of application. Requiring a résumé for on-campus jobs is becoming more common; however, this requirement may exclude good candidates. Think broadly and inclusively about the students you will be recruiting, especially if they are first-year students. You might create a simple application that students can complete online or in person. If your department hires many students at one time, such as for IT, dining, and residence life, you might also offer information sessions where students can learn about the opportunities and apply on the spot.

At this point you have created a meaningful job title, a brief description of the work that emphasizes priority projects and tasks, basic requirements, learning outcomes, a range of hours needed, pay rate, benefits, and preferred application method. The next step is to convert all of this information into an appealing advertisement. Avoid the temptation of simply posting the description as is, and also avoid anyone who suggests that your advertisement is not important. Like any other demand for students' time, a job ad needs to be attractive and inviting.

Transforming the Description into an Advertisement

In a LinkedIn Talent blog about advertising job opportunities to millennials, Reilly (2014) strongly advocates for simplicity. She recommends keeping the advertisement short and brief, using bullet points and white space while personalizing the message in a fun and conversational tone. She also suggests writing for the mobile world, expecting that your ad will be viewed on a mobile device and as such, not be too wordy. Key elements of a successful ad include a compelling personal introduction using "you" statements that address the candidates directly, a simple explanation of major duties and projects (not a laundry list of every single task that might be performed), and the attributes of top performers. Box 6.1 is an example from Trinity University in Washington, DC, of how a traditional job description might be transformed into an exciting advertisement for an admissions assistant role (adapted from Trinity University, 2016).

Box 6.1.
Admissions assistant (traditional job description)

DUTIES: Prepare all admissions packets. Answer telephones. Take student ID photos. Tour students. Scan transcripts. Assist with front desk. File. Make appointments. Other duties as assigned.

QUALIFICATIONS: Typing. Good people skills. Alphabetizing. Good computer skills. Good organizational skills.

APPLY: Complete application form and fax to (xxx) xxx-xxxx or drop off in person at the admissions office.

Using Reilly's (2014) principles, Box 6.2 is a more appealing way to present the same information.

Box 6.2.
Admissions assistant (transformed advertisement)

- Do you want to share your love of Trinity with future classmates?
- Do you enjoy speaking in front of people?
- Can you walk and talk at the same time?
- Can you answer the phone, type an e-mail, and greet a visitor at the same time?
- Do you want to learn professional-level sales skills that will set you apart in the next job?

If you answered "YES" to these questions, then the admissions office wants you to join our team! The admissions office will teach you how to conduct tours with enthusiasm, organize materials for marketing research and social media outreach, and use several software platforms to execute office duties.

Benefits include formal software training, professional work experience, and mentorship! Work shifts vary from Monday through Friday between 9:00 a.m. and 7:00 p.m. and Saturday between 8:00 a.m. and 2:00 p.m. Students may work up to 15 hours per week. E-mail your résumé and the hours you will be available to work to xxxx.

Clearly the transformed position is far more engaging and appealing than the traditional job description presented. Box 6.3 is an excerpt from an advertisement that focuses exclusively on the learning benefits for student employees.

Box 6.3.
ESPN3 production/camera operation (basketball)

If you have an interest in gaining valuable television production and broadcast experience, this is your opportunity. Stony Brook University students will have a hands-on, immersion-based look into the world of sports broadcast production, and a top-flight experience to add to any résumé. Production assistants will play integral roles in the ESPN3 broadcasts, including operation of on-screen graphics, replays, cameras, and audio boards. Prior experience in broadcast production is NOT required. Students will be provided training for these roles. The ability to work night and weekend games is required. (Stony Brook University, 2016)

Some of you reading this section may be concerned that the online system used at your institution is not flexible enough to add attractive photos or accommodate a creative display. You may face constraints based on the formatting and fields required in your institutional human resources information system. Although limiting, these conditions should not preclude you from using a compelling personalized introduction that captures a viewer's attention and describes the work priorities, learning outcomes, and benefits in an attractive, appealing manner.

Once you are confident that the position descriptions and advertisements are ready, the next step is promotion. Many institutions have a centralized posting system for student job opportunities. These systems could be managed by one or more of several departments, including human resources, financial aid, career services, or a standalone student employment office. Use your resources and find out what promotional opportunities exist on campus. Some institutions coordinate a campus job fair exclusively for part-time student employment, where your department can represent in person to recruit applicants. Additionally, do not forget about the power of social media to post available positions and involving faculty partners to spread the word in their classrooms and online environments.

The Interview Process

The interview process is both evaluative and educative. Student employment practitioners, department heads, and supervisors use the interview process as a way to evaluate potential candidates and assess training needs; that is the *evaluative* part. However, also consider that you will simultaneously be giving students an opportunity to practice talking about themselves and discussing their qualifications in light of job requirements; this is the *educative* part. Your interview process should be designed to fit the nature and level of the position, but a welcoming, educative mind-set on the part of the interviewer will actually benefit you as well as the student. At the very basic level, you want to understand your candidates' motivations for work and the skills and attitudes they bring with them to the job. You may find that some of your candidates have never held a job of any kind. Give them a fair chance by inviting them to describe their school experiences and interests and talk about their goals and how they see their future unfolding. Dezube (2016) suggests that it could be more difficult to get a sense of job-relevant skills from candidates who have had no job experience.

Putting your candidates at ease will help them feel more comfortable with the conversation, thereby making them more apt to speak freely and earnestly rather than recite canned responses they may believe you wish to hear. An interview could start with a warm-up like the following:

Hello, Jean-Claude. It's a pleasure to meet you. I'm glad that you've applied for the XYZ position here in our department. To help make this interview go smoothly, I would like for us to think of this as just a conversation, more so than a formal interview. Now I do have some questions for you, but really what I am hoping for is to learn more about you—what you're studying here in college, if you have some ideas about your future. I'd like to hear you talk about some of the experiences you have had until this point and how those experiences have helped you become who you are today. And I want you to feel free to ask me questions as we go along as well. Does that sound like a good way for us to begin our conversation?

Your goal is to relax your candidates so that they present you with their true selves. After the warm-up you may want to describe the position and the type of person who would be successful in the role. An emphasis on the training and the opportunities students can have on the job will put your candidates at ease. Think about the progression of your interview as a series of questions that relate to each aspect of the job. You could begin with specific responsibilities or start with skills and qualities needed overall. Regardless of how you frame your interview, be consistent and give each of your candidates the same opportunity to answer the same questions and describe their skills, qualities, attitudes, and experiences.

Recall the admissions assistant example described earlier in this section. After describing the role of speaking in front of people, giving tours, and sharing stories, you might suggest that while people who are naturally outgoing tend to do well in the admissions assistant role, you have had many successful students who began the job feeling a little shy about public speaking. You might ask your candidates how they feel about learning to do public speaking and if they have had any experience speaking in front of anyone—a class, a group, a club, their friends, and others. You could ask your candidates if they remember their own tour of the campus or other tours they have taken, and what qualities stood out in their memory about those tours and the tour guides.

In keeping with the rest of the admissions assistant job responsibilities, you could ask some questions about the candidates' use of social media, both as a consumer of social media and as a community builder/user. You might ask the candidates to share their opinions about which social media channels they use most frequently and which they would recommend your team use for future outreach to potential new students. You could ask the candidates what their favorite place is to study on campus, or eat, or the best spot for private meditation. You can then gauge their body language and verbal responses to determine if they are truly enthusiastic and love the place, or if they appear to simply be responding to questions.

Finally you could ask about the intangibles: work ethic, time management, integrity, resourcefulness, communication style, teamwork, service orientation, willingness to learn, how they deal with personality conflicts, how they receive critiques, and how they recover from mistakes. Do these attributes sound familiar? Several of these are named in chapter 5 as qualities employers seek in college graduates and are part of EI.

Most entry-level interviews take about 20 to 30 minutes, so be sure to give the candidates time to ask questions. Close the interview by describing the next steps in the process, giving the candidates a sense of when you will be making a decision.

Here is a list of some basic interview questions and prompts and what to look for that you might choose to incorporate into your interviewing plan:

- Tell me about something you accomplished recently. (skills/actions they are proud of)
- Share two of your strengths and one thing you want to improve. (self-awareness)
- What does good customer service look like for you? (service-oriented)
- Tell me about a time when you went above and beyond what was expected of you—at home, at school, at work, or in the community. (high standards, interest in exceeding expectations)
- How do you know when someone is listening to you attentively? (knowledge of what it takes to listen respectively and actively)
- Have you ever had a disagreement with someone? Friend? Classmate? How did you resolve it? (problem-solving, communication)
- In your opinion, what are the pros and cons of group work or teamwork? (teamwork)
- How do you manage your time and stay organized? (time management, organization)
- Did you ever miss a deadline? What happened? (learning from experiences)
- Tell me about a time when you had to be creative to find a solution to a problem. (resourcefulness)
- What motivates you to do your best? (motivation)
- What do you hope to gain from this job? (fit with future, self-awareness)
- How do you see this position fitting in with your future goals? (fit with future, learning orientation)

Student employment practitioners and supervisors may use these questions as a starting point; the specific nature of the position will likely require you to create customized questions to help you discern the applicants' abilities and potential for your specific position. For example, the Office of Institutional Research and Planning might be hiring students to work on mid-level data analyses, requiring exposure to Statistical Package for Social Sciences (SPSS) and advanced Excel skills. In this case, the interviewer may wish to ask candidates to provide tangible examples of the ways in which they have used SPSS and Excel to analyze data in the past. They may also consider giving the candidates a quick simulation exercise to see how they solve a data problem. Similarly, a student interviewing for a graphic design position may be asked to bring to the interview samples of her past work, perhaps a portfolio, so that she can show her creativity and skill in using Adobe Illustrator. If Illustrator were a required skill, you might give candidates some time during the interview to demonstrate what they know how to do. As a final example, a candidate for a position developing software applications might be asked to write a few lines of code.

To summarize the recruitment process, begin with the articulation of needs, and from those needs construct a concise position description that highlights key responsibilities and requirements. The position description is then transformed into an attractive job advertisement and posted using whatever institutional resources exist to get out the word. The application and interview process should be inclusive and welcoming, emphasizing training and learning opportunities. Interview questions are aligned with the qualities sought, and the process may include demonstration, simulation, or quizlike activity. If you have any questions about developing a good interview protocol, use your institutional resources. Career services in particular would be your go-to department as they are the professionals on campus who teach students how to prepare for and ace interviews for corporate internships and full-time positions. You could also reach out to colleagues in your field for additional suggestions.

Onboarding and Developing Student Employees

Congratulations! You've successfully hired your student employees for the semester. Now the fun really begins. *Onboarding* is "the process of helping new hires adjust to social and performance aspects of their new jobs quickly and smoothly" (Bauer, 2010, p. 1). The term *onboarding* tends to be more commonly used in industry, but it represents a transition process for any new hire and is entirely applicable for student employees in a university setting.

Consider the parallels between employee onboarding and new student orientation: Both involve acculturating to a new environment.

The onboarding process involves four steps, referred to as the four Cs of onboarding: compliance, clarification, culture, and connection (Bauer, 2010). Let's review these steps in the context of student hires:

1. *Compliance* refers to the hiring paperwork, identity documents, timesheets, and payroll system, as well as sharing policies and procedures. For example, reviewing the departmental policy on confidentiality of student records and having the student employee sign would be part of this basic step. The dress code, distribution of uniform, or job-relevant badging would also fall under compliance.

2. *Clarification* is a review of the actual job responsibilities with the student, giving the student a clear picture of the tasks to be performed, the expectations of that performance, and the ways in which the performance will be judged. In fact, the supervisor may have tweaked the job as a result of serendipity—finding a candidate who presented a unique skill set that can be useful in the department. This step is the time to review priorities and potential projects, work hours, shift responsibilities, how often the students will meet with the supervisor, and the best way to communicate if there are questions or problems.

3. *Culture* describes that intangible way things work around the place. What are the organization's values and priorities? How do the student employee's work responsibilities fit into the overall structure of the department? What are the peak times and priority activities that many of the staff members engage in as a team? What are the buzzwords or acronyms that are most often used? Is there a flexible, open-door, drop-in way of meeting, or are electronic meeting requests or some other protocol preferred?

4. *Connection* is about social integration and refers to the relationships you want your student employee to build with others, including full-time staff and peers. When will your student employees get to meet the entire staff, even if their particular job is working within a specific smaller unit? At this stage, informal group coffees or lunches can be effective in helping new student employees get to know people and get known by others. Networking and social time, especially at the beginning, can help your new student employees feel more integrated and more like members of the larger team. Recall the retention theories from chapter 5 that speak to the value of feeling included. In this stage, a few social icebreakers could be helpful to encourage networking. If you are not familiar with social icebreakers, be sure to engage your

student activities or residence life staff, who tend to be most experienced in this area. Once again, use the resources of your campus to help you.

But let's pause for a moment. We have just reviewed the onboarding process, and in keeping with the obvious airline analogy, let us regress for a moment and discuss preboarding activities. Preboarding is part of your planning and should occur before the student employees arrive for the first day of work. Suggestions for preboarding are as follows:

- Post student employees' photos, names, and job titles in advance so that staff can study them.
- Send summer updates about the department mailed to the home addresses of your new student employees. Yes, use snail mail, which will be a welcome surprise for most social-savvy Facebook, Instagram, and Twitter users (that is, if you completed your hiring cycle in the spring for the following fall).
- Get the workspaces ready—supplies, computers, telephones, and so forth.
- Order badges, shirts, uniforms, and whatever swag will be needed.
- Prepare the office policy manual and student employee handbook.

Effective onboarding has been shown to improve an employee's transition and adjustment to the new work environment and decrease time to productivity (Bauer, 2010). Sometimes organizations assign an experienced peer as a buddy during the onboarding and orienting process. As we saw in chapter 4, peers can be a terrific support system for new student employees. If you choose to involve experienced peers in the onboarding process, make sure that they are afforded a similar opportunity to train as a trainer, process their learning as future trainers and peer mentors, and get support when they need it.

Technology and Social Media in the Workplace

At this point the authors wish to discuss briefly the use of social media and technology at work. Our student employees have been and will continue to be digital natives, where technology has been integrated into most every aspect of their lives since their first days. Technology is not just a tool for these students; it is who they are and part of their everyday lives. Technology has become part of our lives as well. Colleges and universities routinely use social media platforms to connect and communicate with future students, current students, and alumni using global platforms like

Facebook and Twitter, as well as closed groups, such as Yammer. Undoubtedly over time new technologies will influence our work lives and home lives. Therefore it is critical to include social media usage (and misusage) when onboarding student employees. Is it okay for your student employees to have Facebook open on their computer or phone while working? What do your student employees need to know about balancing working for the institution and free speech on social media? We review the legal aspects of this difficult balancing act later in this chapter.

For now, remember that social media and Internet usage are parts of our students' and our daily lives. In fact one of the more recent disruptive ideas about the proliferation of technology in everyday lives is the Internet of Things (IoT), which describes a future in which every single thing, including products, objects, animals, and even people, is assigned an electronic marker, is connected to the cloud, and both gathers and transmits sensory information to other things (Barrett, 2012). We already see and use some of these concepts in our daily lives: Our phones are smart, our fitness bracelets track our steps and measure our heart rates, and we ask Siri for directions and Alexa to play music during dinner. Driverless trains already exist in countries like Singapore, France, Denmark, and India, as well as in the United States in New York City's AirTrain, West Virginia's Personal Rapid Transit, and portions of Washington, DC's Metro System (Jaffe, 2015; Iqbal, 2016). The IoT ushers in a "completely new way of interacting with the world" (Barrett, 2012, 6:18). IoT will change what we do and how we do it, and we must remain attentive and open to practical uses of new technology in our work. Students are likely to be the ones to help us identify those new applications.

Given the ubiquitous nature of constant connectivity to others and instant communications, what can student employment practitioners do to help our student employees utilize technologies effectively while simultaneously realizing when personal interaction might be more effective? Besides remaining vigilant for opportunities to incorporate technology into our work, we also want to review our organizational policies around use of e-mail and social media for personal use, as well as for use on behalf of the organization. Your institution may already have policies like this, which helps you; as the authors have stated many times in the chapter, use the resources available to you. If there is no institutional policy, or perhaps the policy does not quite fit your work environment, consider developing something simple that all of your employees, staff, and students can abide by and understand.

Handman (2013) suggests that these social media policies at their core, are about mutual respect. He created the acronym RESPECT to help with remembering the principles:

- *Responsibility*—Employees must be acutely aware of their responsibility to the organization and to their audience when making posts.
- *Etiquette*—Social media and university e-mail should not become a person's private vehicle to demean, threaten, or harass another person or group.
- *Selectivity*—Staff should hold back before acting on emotional or knee-jerk reactions to another's posting or behavior.
- *Privacy*—Social media should not be used at work to identify personal information.
- *Efficiency*—Suggest that employees limit their social media time, even those for whom the majority of their work could be social media marketing. Disconnecting from devices is healthy!
- *Confidentiality*—Confidential and personal information must be kept confidential.
- *Transparency*—Clear policies and clear communication about their purpose are equally important.

Using the RESPECT model helps us clarify expectations so that students can meet the standards when promoting services, recruiting candidates, blogging about department-related topics, or interacting with communities online.

The Society for Human Resource Management's (SHRM) guidelines for social networking policies align nicely with the RESPECT model, referring to codes of conduct for employees using social media as part of their work responsibilities and as part of their personal social engagement, which SHRM (2016) suggests is unavoidable.

Regardless of how your policies are ultimately shaped, most important to remember is our opportunity—and frankly, our obligation—to guide our student employees in the most respectful, ethical, and responsible use of technology and social media in the workplace. As a result, our student employees will be well positioned to make a smooth and professional transition to their future work environments.

Training and Talent Development

Training was touched on earlier in the book, but let us now fully define *training* as a structured learning opportunity. The length, timing, and content of training depend upon the position description and the time your student employees need to be functional at work. Many organizations have moved away from the term *training*, which implies a one-time lesson, and are moving toward the terms *talent development* or *professional development*, which signify a learning effort or process that takes place over time. As you read in chapters 2 and 3, development does not occur in one day or over the course of a weekend retreat. In fact, the premier professional association of workplace trainers has changed its name from the American Society of Training and Development (ASTD) to the Association of Talent Development (ATD). For the purpose of this next section, we use both terms—*training* and *talent development*—with the understanding that training is actually part of the larger talent development approach.

As we have come to know, student employment practitioners are in the business of student development and learning. Kuh and colleagues (2010) suggest an overall student learning and development philosophy to working with student employees:

- *Know your students.* For supervisors to set appropriate learning and developmental goals, they need to get to know their students. Get to know your student employees as whole persons—their family backgrounds, cultures, traditions, and nonacademic interests, as well as their talents, academic interests, and career goals. Your knowledge of your students will enable you to assess their level of cognitive development and learning styles, giving you more information to use in designing learning and performance goals.
- *Establish high expectations.* If you have hired well, your student employees will aspire to meet these expectations. Do not be afraid to stretch your students by giving them responsibilities that may feel slightly intimidating. Structure the assignment, provide the resources, and give students a chance to try. Pay attention and coach them through any difficulties, but keep your expectations high.
- *Set reasonable and attainable performance standards.* Keep these standards consistent with their level of preparation and skill, and give them time to practice.
- *Provide frequent and specific feedback on performance.* This requires strong communication skills on the part of the supervisor and may require demonstration and resources for additional support. Help students understand how to accept and act upon constructive feedback.
- *Balance challenge with support.*
- *Ensure that diverse perspectives are represented and students feel included.*
- *Encourage collaboration across reporting lines and between the campus and the community.*
- *Leverage the expertise and resources of others on campus.* This is particularly important in the era of strained resources and shared services. Kuk (2009) invites practitioners to reflect upon the

organization's strengths and incorporate those as often as possible. For example, if your institution has a particularly strong teaching and learning division or a highly sophisticated talent management and training department, use staff and resources from those areas in your training program.

Timing

With these ideas in mind, let us attend to the planning of the first part of your talent development program: the initial training. First, consider when the program should begin by determining your department's peak cycles. Resident assistants (RAs), for example, must be trained before residents move in at the beginning of each semester. RAs must have the knowledge and skills needed to support their residents from day one. The same can be said for dining services. Dining services staff must also be ready to go when students arrive for their first meals on campus as does IT services, which needs to be ready to help students set up their networks and devices after they have unpacked and settled into their residence halls. Other departments may operate on a different schedule. Admissions tour guides will likely do the bulk of their training during the first few weeks of school as the fall recruitment season heats up for visiting high school students and their families. Academic support tutors may not need to be ready for tutoring on the first day as their potential clients may need a week or two to get their course schedules settled and experience being in class and digesting the course material before they request tutoring services. Laboratory assistants would also have a week or two before labs begin. The telefund, the accounting department, and student financial services may also have lead time to train students after the semester begins.

Content

After you have made decisions about when your student employees need to be minimally ready to function on the job, you then can focus on what exactly your students need to know and be able to do to perform their jobs adequately and perhaps even exceptionally. Recall our review of student employee learning outcomes in chapter 4; this process is similar. Begin with the job description and think about each task or responsibility as a learning outcome. Then consider what intervention or type of training you could prepare that will help the student employee develop competence in that area. For example, one of the responsibilities of a peer career consultant at a career center is to help student clients use the online recruitment system to look for jobs and internships. In order for the peer career consultants to be able to perform that task well, they need to have experience themselves in using the system—understanding all of its features, how to search, how to upload a résumé, how the job application feature works, and so forth. Accordingly the supervisor could design a session in which the system is demonstrated, then the student employees are given time to play with the system and practice using the features themselves, with the supervisor standing by to answer any questions that arise.

Continue with each responsibility outlined in the job description. As you consider the type of intervention or training modality, consider also structuring a variety of activities and methods to accommodate varying learning styles and intellectual development stages (Scrogham & McGuire, 2009). You may wish to use Kolb's learning styles, which were reviewed in chapter 4. Do not forget about the need to train student employees about ethics. Use the theories of ethical and moral development reviewed in chapter 2, and if you need more help, use your campus resources. Who on your campus already has a strong student employee training program? It is likely that residence life, orientation programs, and the career center have highly developed training curricula you could borrow from and professionals who can provide advice and support. You might also consider getting help from the instructional design team that helps graduate students and faculty structure their syllabi and incorporate active learning strategies in the classroom. You could perform outreach to professionals at other universities who do what you do or contact the National Student Employment Association for referrals. Find those resources already available to you.

Before you finalize your plan, note that your training program is not simply a curriculum compiled of disparate exercises and sessions planned for individual task performance. The best training program begins with a big-picture overview of the organization, the department, and the roles within them (Scrogham & McGuire, 2009). At Stony Brook University, the career center director gives this big-picture session for two reasons: (a) to have some time with the 25 to 30 student employees who begin work with three days of presemester training in August and (b) to explain the larger context of career services, and how the department relates to other student services, as well as with academic departments and administrative units. In fact that piece of training is called "Stony Brook as a Corporation." Key cabinet-level positions are reviewed and compared to corporate counterparts (e.g., chief executive officer correlates with president; chief operating officer correlates with provost; chief human resources officer and chief information officer correlate with vice presidents). Students are often unaware of what a provost is or does. They may not know what a registrar or a bursar is. Explaining how the business of the university gets done helps students understand the bigger picture. An abbreviated organizational chart is displayed and reviewed so that student employees can see literally where departments fit into the larger organizational chart of the university. A focus on divisions outside academic affairs gives students a sense of their role as employees for the university as opposed to their role as students.

Consider including the following content elements for your initial training:

- overview of the university as employer
- overview of your division's vice president or cabinet-level executive
- your department—its mission and goals, practice areas, staff and their roles, student employees and their roles, particular challenges expected this year, policies
- opportunities for student employees and staff to get to know each other as people more than just job titles
- workplace skills and knowledge that all students will need who work in your department
- specialized skills and knowledge that each student employee needs for their work

Who Can Assist With Content?

The supervisor does not have to go it alone. Enlist members of your staff, including past student employees, to help you construct a plan for initial training. You could approach colleagues in other departments to assist with general training that does not require intimate knowledge of your operation. Consider a quick review of the literature; several good articles are available, for example, on student employee training in libraries.

Delivery Models

The next step is to determine the modes of delivery of initial training. You may recall from Kolb's experiential learning theory described in chapter 4 that individuals have different learning styles. To accommodate for this variety, consider using different delivery modes for your initial training that could include independent work, in-person group work, and individual coaching. You might consider the use of observation or shadowing, role-play, simulations, online tutorials, videos, or webinar-style sessions. Consider managing initial training through your course management system. Provide each student employee with a print guide and assign independent reading from it, and offer an online version for those who prefer to access the material using their mobile devices or computers. Look into creating a training wiki or blog page where student employees could post questions or ideas and have other student employees respond. Over time the blog posts could be used to refine training curriculum.

Who Can Assist With Delivery Models?
Your campus likely has experts who can help you design and develop a multimodal delivery system for your initial training. Consider enlisting support from instructional design professionals in your teaching and learning unit, the career center, IT department, or perhaps any faculty who may have expertise in training and organizational development. You might also secure the services of a student who can take your in-person workshop and translate it into a webinar.

Trainers or Facilitators
Give careful thought to who will conduct or facilitate the in-person training. In some instances, departments handle all the training themselves, based on the nature of the work (i.e., laboratory assistants), the supervisor's expertise and interest, or the amount of training funds available or lack thereof. In other instances, departments look for external staff to facilitate portions of their training curriculum. Following are some examples of how departments might leverage the talent and expertise of other departments in their student employee training:

- The career center could lead a session on professional presentation skills.
- A representative from your bookstore or dining services corporate partner could lead customer service training.
- Your disability support staff can help student employees develop a better awareness of issues students with disabilities may bring and how best to support them.
- The counseling center staff and faculty from the communications department can work with RAs to hone their conflict resolution skills.
- The business librarian can review all online databases for company research with career peer advisers.
- The building and grounds staff might be invited to have a session with the student activities' student facilities management team.
- The conferences and special events staff might assist the student event planners with best practices in event management.
- The alumni affairs staff can lead training for the admissions team on networking and touring.
- The conduct team or a faculty member from your philosophy department could lead training on moral and ethical decision-making.
- Your secretarial staff can demonstrate professional telephone etiquette and help students practice their telephone skills.
- The career center staff can train library and IT help desk student employees in the use of their résumé recruitment system.

- Your writing center could lead a session on writing effective business e-mails.
- Your multicultural affairs staff could lead a session on diversity in the workplace.
- Staff in your academic advising center can facilitate a time management workshop.
- The student activities or leadership staff can lead teambuilding sessions.
- Your IT security team can help student employees learn about data ethics.
- You could even involve alumni volunteers to lead a session on EI in the workplace.

The preceding examples largely involve basic workplace competencies—such as customer service, ethics, teamwork, time management, presentation skills, writing, and EI—that many student employees need in their daily work. However, the department itself will also need to structure department-specific and job-specific training for student employees. Here you might engage your graduate students or your experienced undergraduate students to facilitate portions of training. As noted in chapter 4, involving peers in the learning process can be helpful for the learner as well as for the peer facilitator. Peers can help with demonstrations, coaching, and even role-plays of different scenarios that a new student employee might encounter on the job.

Student employment practitioners who incorporate online learning modules may also wish to assign experienced peer coaches to check in with the new student employees after a certain number of modules have been completed to review the material, clarify any confusion, or simply have a discussion about how that material comes to life while students are on the job. If there are no peers then the supervisor would want to process the outcomes of the online modules with the student employees.

Timing Redux

New York Yankees player and manager Yogi Berra once said, "It ain't over till it's over" (Ulin, 2015). That phrase says it all when it comes to the end of training. It really is not the end because training is never over. The bulk of it may be over, but remember our commitment to talent development—to developing our student employees over time. For most institutions, each semester has about 14 to 15 weeks (for those working at institutions on quarterly schedules, obviously your timeline will be different). If we are to take the talent development view, then we must consider how we will continue to develop our student talent over the 15 weeks. Much like a faculty member creates a course syllabus with learning objectives that are met through a series of in-class activities and homework, the later assignments are likely more complex and build upon knowledge gained in the early part of the term; so, too, student employment practitioners might think about structuring the student employees' learning experience. Yes, after initial training the student employees will learn as they go, improve their competence and confidence as they complete work assignments, hone their skills, and accomplish increasingly challenging tasks. However, that does not preclude us from planning a syllabus-like professional development program that student employees can participate in regularly.

Ongoing Professional Development
You could plan a weekly student employee staff meeting, no different from a professional staff meeting, where some of the time might be spent addressing issues that cropped up that week. Some of the meeting time could also be dedicated to professional development activities. Examples of talent development during staff meetings include career-building activities such as writing résumés, working with LinkedIn profiles, developing ePortfolios, and completing personality inventories like the Myers Briggs Type Indicator (MBTI) or those from the VIA Institute on character. You could dedicate sessions to diversity, ethical dilemmas, presentation skills, or the latest research on student success. Alternatively, you could create a journal club, inviting students to select journal articles the group would read and then lead a discussion about the article and the topic. If your department is more business focused, you could engage students in a discussion about the latest news or professional trends in the field. You could invite alumni professionals for a group informational interview depending on the department, the work, and the students' professional interests. If you are unsure how to identify professionals, your career center or alumni relations office will have a long list of alumni from which to choose. Often these offices also coordinate student-alumni mentoring programs, which you could present as an extra opportunity for your student employees. Last you might also wish to consider offering your student employees an opportunity to engage in professional development activities that are often reserved for professional staff, such as webinars, conferences, industry meetings, or even online courses relevant to the work they do (Komives & Carpenter, 2009). Don't be afraid to get creative.

Komives and Carpenter (2009) wrote for higher education professionals, but their wisdom applies to student employees as well; they encourage "the skills of being effective beginners" (p. 371) as a way to frame the importance of having a learning mind-set and being open to continuously refining what we think we know. They offer a neat acronym, PREPARE, as a guide for us to use when crafting a professional development plan:

- Purposeful, intentional, and goal related
- Research, theory, and data based
- Experience based
- Peer reviewed
- Assessed
- Reflected on and reflected in practice
- Evaluated

Notice that the second *R* in their model stands for *reflection*. As you may recall, reflection was discussed in chapter 4. You may wish to consider incorporating the 4*R* method of reflection (Ryan & Ryan, 2013) during initial training as well as for part of the ongoing professional development activities throughout the semester.

To summarize this chapter thus far, we have taken you through the process of planning for your student employment program, and you have theoretically developed learning-oriented position descriptions, created a hiring strategy, constructed onboarding and preemployment training programs, and forged a plan for ongoing professional development throughout the semester. Your student employees are now ready to launch. This next segment focuses on the heart of the student employee's daily experience: supervision.

Supervision

Chapter 4 outlined the important role student employment practitioners play in facilitating learning and development. The crux of that role lies with the supervisor, whose responsibilities range from trainer and learning facilitator to coach, role model, mentor, assessor, and performance evaluator (Borin, 2001). Not unlike a good professor who creates a positive and open atmosphere for learning and support, yet also provides critiques and assigns a grade, a good supervisor can set the tone for a positive work-learning experience with the understanding that evaluation is part of the learning. What makes a good supervisor? Is a degree in management or supervision needed to be effective? How can student employment practitioners develop good supervisory skills themselves and advance those skills in others?

Recall the elements of high-impact practices that make them so effective: opportunity to apply learning to real-world situations, time on task, exposure to diversity, opportunity to work in a team, feedback on performance, and reflection (Kuh, 2008). The supervisor's role is ultimately about structuring those opportunities for student employees to apply their learning to real-world problems, to practice, to develop team skills by collaborating with diverse partners, and then to provide supportive feedback and encourage reflection (Lewis, 2008).

Setting the Tone/Creating the Office Milieu

Supervisors are well positioned to create an inclusive department milieu that supports the learning and development of all student employees. Inclusivity relates to all forms of diversity: racial and ethnic backgrounds, learning styles, ability/disability, gender, sexual orientation, religion, political affiliation, socioeconomic status, career intentions, and so forth. The goal is to ensure that, from their first contacts with your department, student employees feel valued for all dimensions of their identities. Student employment practitioners can set the right tone by creating a work environment that affirms all identities and prizes personal and professional integrity, supports learning and personal development, encourages creativity and teamwork, allows for risk-taking and small failures, promotes flexibility and resilience, and acknowledges efforts and accomplishments (Jackson, Moneta, & Nelson, 2009).

Clarifying Expectations Through Communication

Once the tone is set and the department is ready to engage the student employees, the best way to galvanize your student employees is to set clear expectations for the work (Jackson et al., 2009; Slagell & Langendorfer, 2003). Granted, expectations should have been clarified through the position description, the interview, the hiring, and delivering of onboarding and training. However, communicating your specific expectations can never be overstated.

Communication style and frequency can also be clarified so that the student employee knows the preferred way to communicate with the supervisor (e.g., pop in to the office or workspace, instant message, or e-mail), and how often progress reports are expected. Depending on the work and the structure of the organization, the authors strongly recommend at least one weekly check-in between supervisor and student employee. A new trend in small businesses and large companies is the morning huddle, where teams gather daily for a quick status update from each team member (Buchanan, 2007; Vrable, 2014). Vrable (2014) suggests that huddles can be used to keep team members informed of team progress, individual priorities, and any positive recognition or requests for help. Buchanan (2007) emphasizes the purpose of huddling as quick information briefings, not problem-solving meetings. How might a huddle work in a student employee environment? Daily huddles are unrealistic given that students don't all work full-time or, likely, the same shift; however, the idea of a quick regular meeting can keep student employees in tune with overall departmental accomplishments, challenges, and priorities; acknowledge individual contributions; and keep everyone connected.

The Day-to-Day

Finding the right level of responsibility for each student employee and the right amount of communication and feedback only happens on the job and requires attention, reflection, and adjustment (Inkster & Ross, 1995). Once the work begins, the first weeks are critically important; in that time, your students will demonstrate their understanding of expectations and competence in the work, their ability to complete tasks and assignments on time, and the extent to which they have integrated into the organizational culture (Slagell & Langendorfer, 2003). A supervisor should schedule extra time during the first weeks to observe the student employee in action, respond to questions while they engage in their work assignments, provide role modeling and coaching where needed, and continue to clarify standards of performance. Supervisors need to understand that new employees need time to adjust to their new roles and responsibilities, and as a result their peak performance will likely not occur in the first weeks. As such, it should not be an expectation (Borin, 2001).

While the semester progresses, a supervisor will delegate new tasks, role-model ethical behavior and decision-making, coach for new skills, provide feedback, and evaluate performance. Occasionally a student employee handles tasks with ease and is ready to accept increased responsibility not originally listed in the job description. When these exciting discoveries occur, supervisors may wish to invite those student employees to give input into the type of projects they may want to initiate, or any problems they have discovered on which they would like to work. Conversely, in other occasions, student employees do not meet expectations for performance, which may warrant supervisory conversations, reclarification of expectations, specific and substantive constructive feedback, additional training, or all of the preceding.

At some points during the semester, even your star employees may question their abilities, lose focus, feel insecure or frustrated, have conflicts with peers or staff, and experience failure or a general malaise because the work and the work environment are not what they expected (King & Sweitzer, 2014). Supervisors should be watchful, and if they notice that something seems off with an employee, they need to meet with that student and discuss it, supportively. In fact, a supervisor might consider the roles they play in mentoring student employees.

Mentoring as a Supervisory Strategy

While student employment practitioners are working with department staff to create a welcoming and open workplace milieu for a positive and productive student employment experience, they are reinforcing the role of departmental staff and supervisors in particular as facilitators of learning on the job. In addition, as you may recall from chapter 5, Kincaid (1996) described the supervisor's role as a retention agent, which speaks directly to the notion of supervisor as mentor.

One may argue that mentors do not conduct formal performance evaluations, which is often true, but the roles of a mentor are strikingly similar to the roles of a supervisor. The literature on mentoring is quite clear about the importance of quickly establishing a trusting relationship (Ellinger, 2002; Schlee, 2000). Mentors get to know their mentees personally, including their background, values, talents, interests, and goals. Mentors are good listeners and provide personal encouragement and support; they share their experiences and knowledge, their insight into the work world and their particular organizational and professional culture, while being honest about where they have made mistakes or were faced with failure. Mentors also often provide honest and constructive feedback to foster learning and development (D'Abate & Eddy, 2008; Ellinger, 2002; Manley & Holley, 2014; Schlee, 2000).

Benefits to the Mentor

Note that mentees are not the only ones who benefit from the mentoring relationship. Research has shown (Ellinger, 2002; Ernst & Young, 2015) that mentors truly enjoy the opportunity to change the trajectory of mentees' lives, enhancing their own sense of purpose, improving their own communication skills, and increasing their understanding of student needs. Moreover, one could argue that, through mentoring and supervision, we are reinforcing the concept of the T-shaped professional, only this time applied to supervisors. A T-shaped manager has both the deep knowledge of the department or unit and the broad understanding of the different units, functions, and people throughout the organization (Hansen & Oetinger, 2001). This knowledge enables the T-shaped manager to leverage relationships and knowledge across the organization while staying committed to the goals of the specific unit. Hansen and Oetinger (2001) describe a T-shaped manager as "one who connects people in the organization seeking information with those who can help them, effectively serving as human portals in the companywide knowledge web" (p. 16).

T-shaped student employment professionals have the breadth of knowledge and relationships throughout a variety of functional areas, divisions, and departments, and the ability to make the right connections among those often-labeled academic silos to leverage knowledge, talent, and best practices in support of their student employees/mentees.

Giving Feedback

Some people say that mentoring, being supportive and encouraging, is the good part. But when most practitioners hear the word *supervisor*, they think "evaluation" and "critique"; they fear conflict. It's not that bad. Your responsibility as a facilitator of learning is to guide your student employees and help them learn, grow, achieve, accomplish, and be successful. We know from Kuh (2008) that time on task and feedback on performance are vitally important to learning, so let's consider this whole idea of feedback. Some management scholars have focused on the emotional aspect of feedback (Grenny, 2015; Slagell & Langendorfer, 2003; Su, 2015). Supervisors can become more emotionally ready to give feedback by dismissing the notion that feedback is confrontational and negative and embracing the idea of feedback as performance enhancing (Su, 2015). Consider the types of constructive, purposeful, and encouraging feedback you might have received in the past. Perhaps you took guitar lessons and your teacher corrected your finger positions so that you could play a new chord. Or some of you may have enrolled in a language course and your teacher or possibly your peer conversation partner corrected your vocabulary, verb tense, or accent so that you could improve your ability to communicate more effectively in that language. How about athletes? If your basketball coach corrected your free throw technique or your softball coach directed you to take an extra hour of batting practice so that you could improve your view of the ball and your swing, all of that is feedback. These examples demonstrate the positive, growth-oriented, supportive yet critical feedback conversations that take place every day.

Your role as a supervisor is to frame feedback for yourself and your student employees as support for improvement on a regular basis, not just at the midpoint and end of the semester (Chur-hansen & McLean, 2006; Slagell & Langendorfer, 2003). According to Chur-hansen and McLean (2006), formative feedback should be timely in that if a situation occurs where a critique is required, it is best to have that conversation as soon as possible after that situation occurs. A direct approach can be respectful and constructive and focused on specific observable facts and behaviors (Harms & Roebuck, 2010; Su, 2015). Feedback is not simply a redirect; it could also involve a conversation with the employees about their perspective on the situation. Perhaps they were faced with an ethical dilemma; recall from chapter 2 the stages of moral and ethical development and the ways in which you might help your student employees develop higher-level ethical sensitivity, thought process, motivation, and follow-through (Anderson et al., 2005).

The BEAR Model of Giving Feedback

Harms and Roebuck (2010) created a mnemonic, BEAR, to assist supervisors in giving feedback.

- *B* stands for *behavior* and refers to the objective, detailed description of the specific behavior that warrants adjustment.
- *E* refers to the *effects* of the behavior, that is, how that action affected the client, the team, the project, or even the supervisor.
- *A* stands for *alternative*, that is, the alternative behaviors that the supervisor would like to see the employee exhibit.
- *R* represents *result*, which is what the result of the alternative behavior would be.

Consider the following example: Gabriel works as student consultant for the IT help desk in the residential computing center. One evening a client approached him requesting help using a software package for class. The client appeared rushed and anxious and relayed that she was going to be late for class if she didn't get this homework finished in the next 10 minutes. Gabriel was excited to help because he had just reviewed a tutorial on this very software package. As he had learned during training, he initiated a series of questions to diagnose the issue and get a better sense of the client's level of understanding. The client became even more anxious with all the questions and pleaded with Gabriel to just fix it for her. Her anxiety level raised Gabriel's anxiety level, and he acquiesced. He fixed her issue, essentially completing her homework for her. He felt quite proud of himself that he could fix the issue so quickly and that she seemed thankful as she rushed out of the lab.

If the supervisor observed this exchange and were to apply the BEAR model to this situation, it might look something like this. He would invite Gabriel to a private conversation, not in front of other consultants or clients, and suggest that they have a quick meeting about the recent exchange. He could share with Gabriel that he observed how customer-focused Gabriel had been and praise his eagerness to be helpful as well as his knowledge of the software package. However, he must then address his concern about Gabriel's doing the student's homework, describing the effect and, perhaps in this case, asking Gabriel to come up with possible behavioral alternatives that would result in the student learning how to use the software package but not resulting in the consultant doing her homework for her. The supervisor might also process the emotions that were at play in this scenario and consider the extent to which handling anxious and potentially demanding clients was covered in training, and whether to include more practice in handling difficult clients in one of the professional development sessions.

Use of Peers in the Feedback Process

Using peers in the feedback process is a way for students to learn how to both give and receive feedback (Phillips, 2016). Learning to be observant; to use critical thinking skills in evaluating another's performance against standards or benchmarks and to present objective, detailed, and specific examples using BEAR—behavior, effect, alternative, and result—can be beneficial. Duhon, Bushardt, and Daniel (2006) teach students to give feedback by distinguishing among constructive, positive, and negative feedback. They define *positive feedback* as that which reinforces behavior, while *negative feedback* strongly encourages a change in behavior. They also offer a third type of feedback they call *constructive*, described as suggestive, where a giver presents alternatives from which a receiver might choose.

To summarize what we have learned about the feedback process, here is what student employment practitioners need to know. First is the mind-set. A helpful, encouraging, and purposeful mind-set can help even the most reluctant supervisors engage in giving feedback. Positive feedback can reinforce the right behaviors and encourage continued progress. Negative and constructive feedback can be given honestly and objectively with a focus on learning, development, and improvement. It is very important to provide objective, specific, and fact-based descriptions of behavior while avoiding superlatives (e.g., "You always . . .") or generalities (Duhon et al., 2006). Using the BEAR model (Harms & Roebuck, 2010) can help you focus on the behavior and its repercussions.

Teaching Students to Receive Feedback

Inasmuch as we may need to orient our supervisors to the positive outcomes of constructive and even negative feedback, we may also wish to orient our students to the same idea. A session about feedback could be offered during training, where students are invited to reflect upon feedback they have received in the past along with their reactions to it (LeVan & King, 2016). Kruse (2014) offers four ideas:

1. *Actively listen*, even if the feedback is difficult to receive. Remain open and alert to the full message, asking questions if you need clarity, and responding with paraphrasing to show the giver that you have understood.
2. *Never argue*, even if the circumstances do not represent what really happened. Limit defensiveness. Hold back retorts. Assume the good. Accept the feedback and express gratitude for the effort made to help you improve.

3. *Evaluate slowly*, in that you may need a day or two to consider the feedback and its merits to determine whether the feedback has validity and how you might address the issues raised.
4. *Be mindful*, keeping your mind open to observing your own behavior, giving yourself the opportunity to make corrections and feel good about your progress.

Recognition

Lest you think that daily supervision is largely about catching behaviors that need to be changed, supervisors also enjoy the position of catching students doing things well. Positive feedback, specifically delivered, is motivating. For example, "Julia, you're doing a great job," is not as effective as, "Julia, I noticed how quickly you solved that client's problem by asking good questions and using the techniques we taught you in training." This second example is more effective because it describes the specific behaviors and reinforces the learning. Julia would likely feel far more valued knowing her supervisor had observed the work and could specifically describe what she did well. Platitudes are not helpful. Recognizing your student employees' specific accomplishments shows them that you are paying attention and motivating them to continue to excel (Wenger, 2016). Praise can be shared individually, during team huddles or larger staff meetings, or through official recognition events (Inkster & Ross, 1995). Recognition can be fun as well as serious.

Common Issues for Supervisors

Despite effective onboarding and training; a values-based, supportive work environment; a strong professional development curriculum; and good supervision, problems sometimes arise. Interpersonal conflicts could occur. Mistakes happen. Lapses in ethical judgment occur. An unintentional microaggression offends. Personal, health, or academic problems also may arise that affect performance (Inkster & Ross, 1995). What is a student employment practitioner to do?

Above all else, you must accept that no one is perfect; no situation is perfect; and, as learned in chapter 3, uncertainty is certain. That problems arise regularly is guaranteed. A supervisor's job is to solve problems, so expect and reframe them as opportunities to find good solutions. Consider the example of conflict between two employees. Managing conflict may be just as distasteful and just as avoidable as providing feedback. The authors are not suggesting that you can eliminate all feelings of angst when confronted with an interpersonal conflict between students or between students and staff.

However, supervisors have many resources at their disposal to help them work through the conflict management process. You could use Johnson's *5I* format, the ethical decision-making framework we reviewed in chapter 2. The five *I*s begin with identifying and investigating the problem. An interpersonal conflict would require listening to both sides and seeking to understand people's feelings and needs, not just their stated positions. Does the problem stem from unclear communication or differences in communication style? A lack of clarity? An organizational problem? An intergenerational misunderstanding? A lack of sensitivity? An unethical decision? Getting to the root of the problem requires creating an environment where the people involved feel valued, supported, and heard. The next *I*, innovate, gives all parties a chance to generate creative solutions that would reasonably satisfy everyone. Implementation is the action piece where a supervisor would be wise to monitor the extent to which the agreed-upon solution is being implemented and negotiated decisions are explored. Key to successfully managing conflict is the ability to engage in active, deep listening, so that each person feels heard and valued.

Other problems may not seem so daunting. If your student employee is consistently late to work, speak with her to find out why. You might discover that she commutes to campus with public transportation and simply cannot get to work before a certain time. This is an easy fix: Change her hours. You might receive an e-mail from a faculty member who has pointed out a glaring grammatical error in a promotion sent by one of your marketing assistants. Also an easy fix: Respond to the e-mail with grace, thanking the professor for the feedback and assuring him that you will work hard to ensure that all future communications from your department are vetted for grammar and spelling. Separately you can meet with the student employee and talk about the situation. Maybe the student was in a rush and made a mistake, or maybe English is not her first language and she struggles daily with English grammar. You could refer her to resources on campus that can help with her overall writing skills, and you might consider assigning a peer to work with her and review e-mail promotions before they are sent.

Another issue that arises more often in a student employment environment than in a corporate environment is requests for scheduling or shift changes during midterms and finals weeks. The beauty of this issue is that it is by and large preventable. Although supervisors cannot predict when exactly the exams will take place for each of your student employees' courses, you can make some good guesstimates of midterm period and you know with certainty when finals take place. Clarifying expectations for shift change requests or other forms of flexibility can be done early in the term. It is also incumbent upon us to role-model some of that flexibility and adaptability we wish to ingrain in our student employees, and no time for flexibility would be more appreciated than when students are overstressed with multiple academic deadlines and exams.

The essence of this segment is about framing potential problems as opportunities to find good solutions, accepting that problems occur, having the confidence to confront, listening actively and carefully, providing feedback supportively, stepping through the five *I*s to understand the problem and develop ethical solution options. In addition to all these actions, perhaps we might also role-model, demonstrate, and train. Student employment practitioners may wish to develop a series of trainings and professional development sessions specifically to help support supervisors in solving technical and interpersonal problems at the lowest possible levels to avoid further complications.

Evaluation of Student Employees

Utilizing the five *I*s helps the supervisor articulate the problem, find solutions, and learn about and improve the personnel and program in the process. That, in essence, is evaluation—making a decision about someone's or something's characteristics. A good supervisor regularly provides timely, positive, and constructive evaluation or feedback to student employees, but there is also merit in conducting formal performance evaluations. Student employment practitioners who have embraced a learning-focused philosophy of student employment may wonder about the difference between a learning outcomes assessment and a performance evaluation. These two functions seem very similar at times, but there are subtle differences. Assessment of learning outcomes emphasizes the learning process. A performance evaluation emphasizes the judgment, or rating, of performance against a standard. Scholars could argue that the differences are profound, yet the authors urge student employment practitioners not to worry so much about those differences here. In some occasions, the learning and the performance goals are eerily similar. For example, Hakeem, our IT student from chapter 4, must learn to solve IT problems. At the same time, his performance is contingent upon his ability to master the solutions and actually solve the IT problems. In our PR example, we developed learning outcomes that point to skill development in writing; the student employee's performance would certainly be evaluated based on the quality of her writing. Conversely, the business analyst might be invited to learn how to develop strong presentation skills as one of the learning outcomes, yet the evaluation of her performance on the job would be the extent to which she performs her analyses accurately and in a timely manner, not whether she can present in front of an audience.

There is one major similarity: the Assessment of Learning Outcomes Intervention (ALOI) cycle, which is discussed later in this chapter (Makela &

Rooney, 2012). Planning for your performance evaluation is similar to planning your assessment of learning outcomes; in the beginning you determine the job responsibilities and the tasks you would expect your student employee to perform. If you were to use an academic example, think about a class in which the professor gives the final exam questions at the beginning of the semester and expects the students to work toward an *A* throughout. Give your student employees the performance evaluation tool at the beginning and clearly show them your standards for performance. If a new project pops up midsemester, when you are describing the project and the expected deliverables, describe what success looks like so that your student employees can deliver what is expected in a timely fashion and with the necessary level of quality.

Student Self-Evaluation as Part of the Process

Inkster and Ross (1995) suggest that student employees be invited to self-evaluate first, giving them an opportunity to rate their own performance before an evaluation meeting with the supervisor. When you think about the big picture, assuming that the job description and projects were clearly explained and that there has been regular contact between student employee and supervisor that included feedback sessions, a formal performance evaluation should simply be a written confirmation of what the student employee already knows. DePaul University's Student Employment Office uses one document for both the student self-evaluation and the supervisor appraisal. The National Student Employment Association has an electronic mailing list for members through which they can inquire about samples from among their members. Our best advice is for the student employment coordinators to develop a set of baseline professional benchmarks for skills and tasks that cut across a wide variety of positions, such as organization, teamwork, reliability, initiative, and attitude. Remember the career competencies, or broad-based skills that employers are looking for that we reviewed in chapter 4? The University of South Carolina has a great example, as does Georgetown University, and the AAC&U workplace ethic rubric developed by Chattanooga State University offers another good example.

Evaluating the Evaluator and the Program

Student performance is not the only thing that can be evaluated. Student employees should be given the opportunity to evaluate the employer, from initial onboarding to orientation and training, supervision, opportunities structured for them to achieve their learning goals, and their overall experience. Alvin Community College's evaluation is a great example as it asks the employee to rate the supervisor on accessibility, fairness, supportiveness, responsiveness, and effectiveness. One way to achieve this reciprocal evaluation and provide an additional learning experience for employees is to have the supervisor and student employee craft the instruments, sets of questions, and lists of outcomes together. That ensures a clear understanding and foundation to build upon throughout the employment term. Shared clarity and expectations between supervisor and student employment practitioner are not only important when it comes to evaluative methods but also critical and essential to assessing and improving the program for years, and students, to come.

Assessment of Student Employment Programs

Assessment is defined as "the process of collecting and analyzing information to improve the conditions of student life, student learning, or the quality and efficiency of services and programs provided for students" (Blimling, 2013, p. 5). Assessment is no longer new; it is an integral part of asking questions about what we do in higher education (Schuh, 2013). It is a long-term commitment to continuous improvement and accountability to stakeholders. Schuh (2013) uses the term *positive restlessness* (p. 91) to describe the state of mind one has when concerned about continuous improvement. You may recall Gelatt's theory of positive uncertainty from chapter 2, which suggests that we can approach unpredictable and uncertain futures with positivity and enthusiasm. The same can be said for our attitude toward assessment; we can choose to approach the assessment process with positivity and enthusiasm for the future knowledge we will gain about the effectiveness of our programs and interventions by asking questions and engaging in assessment.

Asking questions enables a program to improve and inspires an organization to evolve to higher levels of success. Our positivity helps ensure that employees feel comfortable asking hard questions about why things are done, how things are done, and the extent to which those things are effective. Asking hard questions is paramount if we are to create a learning and growing organization (Marquardt, 2005). According to Marquardt (2005), a questioning culture enables us to look for changing environmental pressures and outside influences as well as to question ourselves, prompting personal introspection and encouraging greater levels of self-awareness, which can lead to new ideas and new ways of solving problems.

We should be asking questions about the extent to which our programs and services are accomplishing their goals. These days, we are expected to use evidence and data from multiple sources to answer those questions, adjust resource allocations, and make policy decisions. Assessment gives us the data we need to make adjustments for improvement and to celebrate our accomplishments. It also gives us the cause and the freedom to stop doing things that are not working.

In addition to the assessment of program outcomes, we are also of course concerned about assessing learning outcomes of our student employees. If we are asking the right questions, what will our student employees know, be, feel, and know how to do as a result of their time working with us? At what levels? How will we know if they learned what we wanted them to learn? When should these questions be asked? We can certainly ask at the end of the term. Summative assessments are the ones higher education professionals tend to know about: the end-of-term measure of achievement, whether that measure is part of a written or performance evaluation. But we may also want to ask during the term, to gauge their progress and whether they are learning what we expect and hope. Formative assessment occurs during the experience for the specific purpose of helping to improve the experience in progress. For example, think about a midterm exam or performance evaluation. Hodges (2011) has shown that students can and should be actively involved in the formative assessment process, starting with the development of specific and individualized learning goals, which in the case of student employees may include general workplace skills, workplace-specific competencies, an understanding of the work culture, the subject matter or populations served, and so on. Essentially we are asking the questions at the end, in the middle, and at the beginning.

Assessment of Learning Outcomes Intervention Cycle

Makela and Rooney (2012) created a model for cyclical assessment of learning outcomes called the ALOI that can be applied to student employment programs. The ALOI cycle has eight steps:

1. *Defining the context.* This step refers to the idea that outcomes must be "tailored to unique environments" (Makela & Rooney, 2012, p. 14). Student employment practitioners can work closely with department coordinators and supervisors to clarify unique and shared aspects of individual work environments to ensure that the learning outcomes are in alignment. For instance, consider a campus job in the college public relations office. Baseline learning outcomes for verbal and written communication skills would be supplemented by more specific learning outcomes for communicating to audiences with whom the public relations office would most often interact, such as the community, the press, alumni, and parents.

2. *Brainstorming outcomes.* This step invites the departmental supervisor to consider as many learning outcomes as possible that could result from working in that specific context. A simple framework for brainstorming

might include this series of questions: What do you hope your student employee will know, be, be able to do, and feel as a result of the work experience in your environment? Consider the continuum of knowledge, skill, and activity, moving from the basic to the more complex. You may have already begun to think about this process if you have developed a job description. If you have not, or need to update the position descriptions, this step is the perfect time to do so. Using our public relations example, a brainstorming session might generate ideas about the type of writing, such as press releases; the tone of writing, perhaps more formal; and the level of verbal communication skills needed to communicate with reporters and possibly angry community members.

3. *Writing outcome statements.* As discussed earlier in this chapter, this step invites the supervisor to describe the outcomes using action verbs that are specific, measurable, and achievable given the time the students have to work (e.g., hours per week) and the resources available to support their learning while working. Using our public relations example, consider this drafted outcomes statement: "As a result of working for the public relations office, the student employee will be able to create effective verbal and written messaging for specific audiences, using language, tone, style, and vehicle appropriate to each audience."

4. *Connecting theories and professional standards.* This step invites program developers to consider how each learning outcome statement they have created is supported by theory and professional standards. These standards could be common standards for general education, such as the essential learning outcomes, or they could be more specific competency standards, such as those associated with industry-relevant practices in the public relations field, health care, chemistry, engineering, project management, student affairs, and so forth. We suggest that supervisors start with the specific outcomes for their environment; then they can seek to connect their outcomes with theory and professional standards—as practitioners will likely feel more comfortable doing so. Revisions or additions would be a natural part of this step. For example, the supervisors may be quite familiar with professional standards set forth by the Public Relations Society of America (PRSA), the premier national organization of public relations executives.

5. *Prioritizing learning outcomes.* In this step the outcomes developed in the brainstorming stage and vetted in the connecting-to-standards stage are reviewed for importance. In this step, supervisors must prioritize. Makela and Rooney (2012) suggest the following questions as prompts:

- What three learning outcomes do you most want to accomplish?
- What three learning outcomes would provide information for improvement?
- What three learning outcomes do your stakeholders care most about?
- Based on these responses, what learning outcomes do you want to pursue?

6. *Evaluating learning outcomes.* This step is an important part of the planning process, in that you must consider what evidence you will collect to demonstrate the extent to which the learning outcomes have been achieved. Who will collect and evaluate the evidence, and when (formative or summative or both?) will the evidence be collected? How will you know, for example, if your student employee is able to write a persuasive appeal letter to place a story about one of your faculty members in the local newspaper? Will you use a rubric to assess that student's competence, and how will the student know what standards exist for a good versus an outstanding press release? Will you survey the students to see how they feel about their learning? Tucker (2014) warns that indirect measures of learning, vis-à-vis asking students to agree or disagree on a Likert-type scale representing how much they believe they have learned as a result of an experience, does not tell us enough. Tucker suggests that direct measures of learning and skill development should be incorporated into the assessment process, perhaps through small quizzes or tests or perhaps direct observation of the student performing a specific task or a review of tangible evidence, such as work product; in our PR example, the supervisor could review drafts of the student employee's press releases. If you are feeling a little uneasy about this step, we recommend that you return to steps 1 and 2 so that you can think more deeply and more specifically about the context, the outcomes, and the levels of knowledge and demonstrated performance that you expect students to achieve.

7. *Reflecting on results.* This step is part of your continuous quality improvement. Once the evidence has been collected, a supervisor or program manager needs to review it to determine what the results actually mean. Did the evidence show that the learning outcomes were achieved? Was anything surprising discovered? This step can be depressing if your results do not support the level of learning you were expecting. But the beauty of this step is that you now have the evidence you need to make changes in your goals, in your training, in the assignments you give to your students, and even in the mentors with whom you connect them.

8. *Continuing the ALOI cycle.* Assessment is an iterative process. The goal of the ALOI cycle is continuous improvement and enhancing the student experience. You might find over time that your assessments show deep learning and great performance on students' behalf. Pat yourself on the back, but continue to ask questions about which students might not be able to access these opportunities, or perhaps determine how structuring a peer experience could add extra value to both the student employee and the peer. You will likely be even more excited to ask more questions and ask different questions as each cycle begins.

The eight-step ALOI cycle is an excellent model to use in designing student employment programs and student employee learning outcomes, but working out the first couple of steps takes time and effort. This is a terrific opportunity to solicit the experts on your campus. Engage your teaching and learning professionals as they work with faculty on a daily basis to develop specific, measurable, and attainable learning outcomes for courses and for programs. You could also consider experts in your region, or even your national network and professional organizations. Check the CAS or take to the Internet, where many schools have posted their learning outcomes and assessment rubrics. The authors highly recommend the National Institute for Learning Outcomes Assessment (n.d.) and the AAC&U Value Rubrics; you do not have to reinvent the wheel.

However, as leaders of student employment programs, you do make a commitment to include assessment as part of the planning process—and being open to less than exciting results. Student employment coordinators are well positioned to help coach individual supervisors to develop context and job-specific learning outcomes, either through training seminars, webinars, or ongoing consultation with respect to learning outcomes creation. Student employment coordinators can also provide a forum on campus for supervisors to discuss their process and challenges, get help from their peers, and celebrate their successes.

ePortfolios

The use of ePortfolios has gained tremendous momentum, with a 2008 study by the Campus Computing Project reporting more than 50% penetration among public and private colleges and universities (Clark & Eynon, 2009). ePortfolios have been described as "a mechanism for curricular development; a cornerstone to academic advising; and a tool for career preparation, the job search, and professional credentialing" (Reese & Levy, 2009, p. 2). Their use cuts across institutional types. ePortfolios are being used by medical students at the University of Michigan's Department of Internal Medicine, at Stanford University to track freshmen learning, at Portland State University in their University Studies Division (Reese & Levy, 2009), and at community colleges (Clark & Eynon, 2009). In fact, by 2009, the Minnesota State University system had come online with more than 100,000 individual users of ePortfolios (Clark & Eynon, 2009). The AAC&U reported the usefulness of ePortfolios in assessing learning outcomes over time: "ePortfolios can facilitate student reflection upon and engagement with learning across multi-year degree programs, across different institutions, and across diverse learning styles while helping students to set and achieve personal learning goals" (Miller & Morgaine, 2009, p. 8).

LaGuardia Community College in New York City was one of the early adopters of the ePortfolio as a tool that students can use creatively to reflect on and represent their learning. Over the years, ePortfolios have become a signature for the campus. Table 6.1 shows a sample rubric from LaGuardia that you can adapt to your specific program.

Washington State University is one institution that purposefully sought to use ePortfolios with student employees. The WSU libraries staff joined the campus's ePortfolio movement and sought to help student employees make better connections between their campus job at the library, their academics, and their career intentions (Reznowski & McManus, 2009). Library staff worked closely with their teaching and learning colleagues to develop a template and with their computing services team to provide training on use of the software. Student employees were required to include these items in their ePortfolios: responses to a set of reflection questions, résumé, job description at the library, links to their academic department and the library websites, and a photo. Student employees were invited to present anything else they wished that would inform a reader about their learning experience. Career services staff coached the students about what employers generally look for, and supervisors met with their employees to review the ePortfolios and determine holistically if they represented the student's work accomplishments. Although not specifically designed to assess learning outcomes, the ePortfolio project was judged to be successful in that it "provided students the opportunity to navigate a tool that balances employability, accountability, and assessment, with self-expression and personal identity" (Reznowski & McManus, 2009, para. 8).

ePortfolios were a best-practice tool adopted by Washington State University, but that may not be the best option for every institution. In fact, that is assessment's beauty. As a supervisor or program coordinator, you can choose what methods work best and make the most sense for your populations. The authors suggest that intentionality coupled with customization for your specific

TABLE 6.1

Evaluation of ePortfolios Rubric

Points / Decisive Factor	Quality of Writing	Reflective Writing	Quality of Design	Quality of Multimedia	Annotation	Ease of Navigation	Completion of Sections	Total Amount
400–500 Excellent	Outstanding control of language, including effective word choice and sentence variety; superior facility with the conventions of standard written English.	All reflections clearly describe the ePortfolio artifacts.	The background, font, color, size, and style of the text permit clear understanding.	Graphics, sound, Flash player, and video components include reflective statements and are appropriate for academic purposes.	All external links are clearly described.	All navigation links work properly and go back to the homepage.	All sections have been completed.	
Note								
300–400 Good	Clear and effective control of language, including word choice and sentence variety; competence with the conventions of standard written English.	Some reflections do not clearly describe the ePortfolio artifacts.	The background, font, color, size, and style of the text permit adequate understanding.	Some of the graphics, sound, Flash player, and video components do not include reflective statements and are not appropriate for academic purposes.	Some external links are not clearly described.	Some navigation links do not work properly.	Some sections have not been completed.	
Note								

Points / Decisive Factor	Quality of Writing	Reflective Writing	Quality of Design	Quality of Multimedia	Annotation	Ease of Navigation	Completion of Sections	Total Amount
200–300 Fair	Intermittent control of language, including word choice and sentence variety; occasional major or frequent minor errors in standard written English.	Many reflections do not clearly describe the ePortfolio artifacts.	The background, font, color, size, and style of the text limit adequate understanding.	Many of the graphics, sound, Flash player, and video components do not include reflective statements and are not appropriate for academic purposes.	Many external links are not clearly described.	Many navigation links do not work properly.	Many sections have not been completed.	
Note								
100–200 Poor	Poor control of language includes problems with word choice and sentence structure; frequent errors in standard written English.	The reflections do not clearly describe the ePortfolio artifacts.	The background, font, color, size, and style of the text are inadequate; understanding is uneven or ineffective.	The graphics, sound, Flash player, and video components do not include reflective statements and are not appropriate for academic purposes.	The external links are not clearly described.	Navigation links do not work properly.	The sections have not been completed.	
Note								

Source. LaGuardia Community College (n.d.).

audience is the best equation. This could and should often take the form of a combination of formal and information assessment measures and purposeful evaluation of the student employees, the program, and you as the supervisor.

Conclusion

We have provided an extensive look into all of the pieces that go into building high-impact practices in recruiting, hiring, training, and supervising student employees. Whether you are a first-time student employee supervisor, a graduate student in a higher education preparation program, or a senior administrator working to develop a comprehensive student employment program, these aspects are critical to the success of students and the overall program. Regardless of whether your campus has a centralized or decentralized administration of the student employment program, you have the ability to affect positive development, learning, retention, and success for every student employee you contact. Thinking about your specific role as it relates to student employment on your campus, we provide a moment for you to stop and ask yourself, first, how will you use the information you garnered from this chapter to improve the student employee recruitment, hiring, and evaluation practices on your campus? Second, reflecting on the steps to writing a good job description, advertising, hiring, training, supervising, and evaluating student employment practitioners, in what areas do you need to develop additional skill sets? Where can you turn for assistance and support in doing so?

As you consider these and other questions and thoughts while putting the pieces of student employment together, we encourage you to not stop here when it comes to your development as a supervisor or student employment coordinator. Instead, talk to your colleagues at your university, in your state, across sister institutions, and within professional associations dedicated to student employment, such as the National Student Employment Association. In what ways do they tie learning outcomes to evaluative processes? Without a doubt, every university and each student employee are different; certainly, there is no one-size-fits-all approach. Instead, we hope you can take aspects from this chapter on supervision and management and infuse them into your daily practice as you continue to support student employees on your campus. As you do so, we invite you to consider the importance of continuous evaluation of self and assessment of program and positional goals and outcomes. The following chapter provides a technical look at how to balance this supervision and management while ensuring legal and ethical standards of practice.

7

LEGAL ISSUES IN STUDENT EMPLOYMENT PROGRAMS ON CAMPUS

S imilar to the concepts of planning, recruitment, hiring, onboarding, training, and supervising student employees, the legal issues governing student employment on our campuses are robust. Equally, mastery of both the legal concepts and the application are critical to the success of collective programs and one-on-one relationships, regardless of in which department or unit the supervisor and student employee(s) reside. Six legal issues, providing a baseline of understanding resources and tools for supervisors, are discussed in this chapter. This list of potential legal issues associated with student employment is not comprehensive, nor is it meant to act as legal advice. Therefore, while we discuss critical aspects to be considered, the authors encourage you to work with your human resources and legal consultants for planning and advising purposes related to these and other potential legal issues.

Fair Labor Standards Act

The Fair Labor Standards Act (FLSA) of 1938 is a federal law that governs minimum wage, overtime pay eligibility, and child labor standards for part- and full-time employees in private and public sectors. Although minimum wages, available work hours, and so on are dictated by the government and can change annually, the intersections of FLSA and on-campus student employees are multiple. Supervisors and managers must have a clear understanding of what is and is not permitted under the law.

The U.S. Department of Labor provides minimal direct information as to when a student worker is considered an employee rather than a volunteer, but the following excerpt from section 10b24 of the *Department of Labor's Field Operations Handbook* dictates when an undergraduate student is entitled to minimum wage and overtime under the FLSA:

> (a) University or college students who participate in activities generally recognized as extracurricular are generally not considered to be employees within the meaning of the Act. In addition to the examples listed in FOH 10b03(e) [which relates to students participating in activities such as drama, musical groups, radio stations, and athletics], students serving as residence hall assistants or dormitory counselors, who are participants in a *bona fide* educational program, and who receive remuneration in the form of reduced room or board charges, free use of telephones, tuition credits, and the like, are not employees under the Act.
>
> (b) On the other hand, an employment relationship will generally exist with regard to students whose duties are not part of an overall educational program and who receive some compensation. Thus, for example, students who work at food service counters or sell programs or usher at athletic events, or who wait on tables or wash dishes in dormitories in anticipation of some compensation (money, meals, etc.) are generally considered employees under the Act. (United States Department of Labor, 2016a, c. 10)

In addition to this definition and explanation of when students should be compensated for their work on campus, the FLSA provides additional guidelines for full-time college students. The Full-Time Student Program, according to the Department of Labor, is for full-time students employed at a college or university that allows the student to be paid no less than 85% of the current minimum wage. Additionally, this program limits a student to no more than eight hours in a day or 20 hours in a week when school is in session and 40 hours per week when there are no classes (United States Department of Labor, 2016b, para. 1). The Department of Labor cautions that there are some limitations to the use of this program and employers must obtain a certificate from the Wage and Hour Division of the U.S. Department of Labor.

Regardless of whether employers apply for this program or are paying a student employee at least the current minimum wage, Pokorny (2011) issues the following cautions for colleges and university supervisors:

- Students, such as research assistants, who perform work that is closely tied to the institution's educational program can often be treated as nonemployees even if they are paid a stipend or receive other compensation, such as tuition credits or reduced room and board charges.
- Titles are not controlling. Students who perform work that does not directly relate to the institution's program of instruction may be

regarded as "employees" and entitled to minimum wage and overtime even if they are classified as nonemployee graduate or undergraduate assistants. As a general rule, the less educational value the job has for the student, the more likely that the student is considered an employee for wage and hour purposes.

- Student assistants who are unionized or who are otherwise recognized as employees by a college or university for other purposes should be treated as such for purposes of minimum wage and overtime compliance.
- Colleges and universities should pay close attention to developments not only in wage and hour law, but also traditional labor law, as the status of student assistants as employees remains in dispute (adapted from para. 7–10).

As supervisors and managers, staying up to date with the current FLSA guidelines for minimum wage, full-time students, overtime hours, and guidelines for hours worked per week is critical for individual student, departmental, and institutional success.

Confidentiality and Student Employees

Knowledge of confidentiality rules and on-campus student employment is also critical. With varying positions come differing degrees of responsibilities for student employees. In many instances—whether working a front desk in an advising center, assisting students with course registration during new student orientation, processing transcripts in the registrar's office, or working as a peer coach—students have access to other student records and private information. Therefore, as discussed in chapter 2, confidentiality is part of ethical behavior and of utmost importance for student employees to understand and supervisors to ensure.

The need for confidentiality is clear, yet not as obvious as the varying degrees of inappropriate utilization of access. Take, for example, a student employee acting in a backup secretarial role for the Office of Student Activities. That student employee has been asked to do grade checks for student organization eligibility. While in the system, he gets the urge to check the GPA of some of his friends who are not club presidents. Although the student has been given access to this system, he has just violated confidentiality because he has no need to search for that information.

What seems like an innocent enough act has just compromised this student employee and the data of his friends. Situations like these illuminate the critical need for student employees to understand as well as agree to confidentiality terms. To address these concerns, a best practice is developing a student acknowledgment-of-confidentiality form that is used campus-wide with department-specific information added where necessary. Many examples of these forms exist in student employment handbooks, running the gamut from a single-paragraph statement to a more detailed list of declarative statements. The College of William and Mary (n.d.) lists the following five points on a form that a student employee must sign and date in the presence of a witness:

1. As a student employee, intern, and/or volunteer in the Dean of Students Office, I understand that I will be working with sensitive and confidential information.
2. I understand that what I learn in this office about University students and University business must remain in this office and is not to be discussed with anyone else, including the student involved. Discussions in the office must be limited to business purposes only.
3. I also understand that I cannot access confidential information for any reason other than for that which I have been asked to do by my supervisor.
4. I understand that alteration or misuse of the University identification cards, records, documents, or computer data is not acceptable and I could be charged with lying and/or stealing under the Honor Code.
5. I understand that I am potentially subjecting the University to litigation for violation of the Family Education Rights and Privacy Act if I break the confidentiality in this office. If I violate any of the above, I will be held accountable by the University Student Conduct system for failure to comply with directions of the College official. I understand that I may be subject to dismissal from my position if I have violated any of the above.

Student employment coordinators would be well served by developing a standardized general confidentiality agreement that would be signed by all student employees, regardless of their particular positions on campus.

The same is true when training and educating a student employee about the Family Educational Rights and Privacy Act (FERPA). A federal law that protects the privacy of student records, FERPA not only controls how much information parents or legal guardians can view or be told but also acts as a blanket law protecting student records in general. Simply put, other than public directory information, FERPA prohibits sharing more personal information (academic standing, health records, disciplinary infractions, etc.) with anyone outside of a need-to-know basis.

Therefore, student employees must completely understand FERPA and, crucially, how it applies to their work on campus. Specifically, student employees need to realize that this law prohibits them from accessing or sharing information outside of the scope directed by their supervisor. In order to train a student employee and protect the university, supervisors can utilize a multitude of FERPA-related tools that the U.S. Department of Education provides or develop in-house pieces. Similar to a general confidentiality form, departments should also have a signed statement from the student employee acknowledging understanding of the tenets of the law, appropriate and inappropriate behavior, and consequences for adverse actions.

At Indiana University–Purdue University Fort Wayne (IPFW), for example, any student employee who will have access to the student information system must complete in-house FERPA training, answer all questions correctly on a seven-question quiz, and sign the FERPA release form prior to being provided login information. The quiz consists of the following yes or no questions:

1. If a student's parent calls asking how a student is doing in a class, can you give out that information?
2. You receive a call from a recruiting firm for names and addresses of students with a GPA of 3.0 or better. They say they have good job information for these students. Can you help these students get jobs by giving out this information?
3. A person comes to the College of Arts and Sciences office with a letter containing a signature that gives consent to release the transcript of a student. Do you give the transcript to them?
4. You receive a phone call from the local police department indicating that they are trying to determine whether a particular student was in attendance on a specific day. Since they are in the middle of an investigation, are you allowed to give them this information?
5. You get a frantic phone call from an individual who says he is a student's father and must get in touch with her immediately because of a family emergency. Can you tell him when and where her next class is today?
6. Is it wrong for professors to leave graded exams, papers, and so forth outside of their office for students to pick up?
7. An unauthorized person retrieves information from a computer screen that was left unattended. Under FERPA, is the institution responsible? (Indiana University–Purdue University Fort Wayne, 2016).

This quiz is certainly not all-encompassing, but it provides an overview of the kinds of situations in which student employees may find themselves and requires them to think through the tenets of the law before providing answers.

Free Speech: When, Where, and How

Similar to FERPA laws and the general notion of confidentiality as it relates to college students and the release of their records, the extent of free speech on public college campuses has been a polarizing topic for generations. Surfacing in *Tinker v. Des Moines Independent School District* (1969), when the administration became aware of a few students' intentions to wear black armbands in protest of the Vietnam War, free speech or free expression has been at the core of lawsuits since. In this case, the families took the suspension of their students all the way to the U.S. Supreme Court, which ruled in its majority opinion that neither students nor teachers lose their constitutional rights when stepping across the threshold of a public school. The same notion was extended to higher education in *Healy v. James* (1972) when Central Connecticut State College refused to recognize a chapter of Students for a Democratic Society. Similar to *Tinker v. Des Moines Independent School District* (1969), the U.S. Supreme Court ruled this as an attempt to block the constitutional rights of these students.

Yet even with additional court cases and progress made toward greater recognition of the expression of beliefs, free speech, or the extent to which free speech is protected, is still a hot topic on college and university campuses. Hall (2002) described this paradox accordingly:

> Free speech at public universities and colleges is at once the most obvious and the most paradoxical of constitutional principles. It is obvious because given the nature of academic inquiry, only an open, robust and critical environment for speech will support the quest for truth. At the same time, universities are at once communities that must balance the requirements of free speech with issues of civility, respect and human dignity. (para. 1)

This delicate balancing act is particularly the case when it comes to student employees who represent campus departments, often wearing university and unit insignias on their apparel and becoming known for their campus affiliation, less for their personal association.

When considering free speech as it directly relates to student employees on public campuses, there is one primary question: Is the person acting as a student or as an employee? The problem in this situation is separating the two. Letzring and Wolff (2009) provide the brief legal history on this matter:

> In the development of First Amendment free speech jurisprudence on public college campuses, which cases and legal theories apply depends on whether the person claiming free speech violations is an employee or a

student. A question not yet answered by the United States Supreme Court as it relates to the public higher education setting is: what if the person is both? (p. 5)

Supervisors and managers must operate from the answer to this question in determining when, where, and in what manner the student is operating as an employee versus *just* a student.

Take, for example, a new student orientation leader who represents the university throughout the summer giving tours to students and family members, assisting students in registration, and helping them get acclimated to their campus environment. This student, while on the clock during orientation, tells a group of students and family members that the university administration is corrupt while utilizing slurs and offensive language. A few of the students and parents complain to the professional staff members. The supervisor decides, after consulting with the student, that because she was acting in paid status and representing the university, she would be terminated for this speech. Is this fair? Although this individual was being compensated for her work at the time of the incident, was she an employee or a student at the time of the utterance?

The same can be true when a student leader runs for a student government office. Take, for example, a candidate for student body president who, while trying to rally a group of peers to vote for him, makes the same accusations about the corrupt administration and pledges to take them down as student government president. Is this student in work status as a candidate for office? Is it the place of the administration to suspend or terminate a candidate's run for student government president? Using a developmental lens, having a tough conversation with this student is certainly warranted. Do you also require the student to make a public statement thereafter if he stays in the race for president? Think through this situation and others that are similar, and have conversations with your colleagues, mentors, and sponsors as to how they would handle such occurrences.

Whether the potential offender was acting as an employee or a student at the time of infraction is critical, but it is not the only factor for supervisors and managers to consider. Consider the developmental theories of moral and ethical behavior in chapter 2. Does this behavior warrant a termination or would a developmental conversation and performance improvement plan serve a better purpose for the student in this situation? How would you have handled this as a supervisor?

These developmental and procedural questions can apply to any situation at a public or private institution. However, what the law says about free speech at these two separate entities is very different. The Foundation for Individual Rights in Education (2016) illustrates the distinct applications at public versus private universities:

> As state agents, all public colleges and universities are legally bound to respect the constitutional rights of their students. That the protections of the First Amendment apply on public campuses is well-settled law.

> . . .

> Private universities are not directly bound by the First Amendment, which limits only government action. **However, the vast majority of private universities have traditionally viewed themselves—and sold themselves—as bastions of free thought and expression.** Accordingly, private colleges and universities should be held to the standard that they themselves establish. If a private college advertises itself as a place where free speech is esteemed and protected—as most of them do—then it should be held to the same standard as a public institution. (para. 2–3, emphasis in original)

Explore and understand your university's stance on student free speech prior to employing students and determine the best way(s) for you to communicate these policies and expectations to potential and current student employees. Do you talk about it in a training handbook, as described earlier in this chapter? Is there a policy in your code of conduct or posted on the dean of students' website that you can reference?

Due Process

As previously discussed, recruiting, hiring, training, and supervising are certainly the more intricate and administrative parts of employing students on campus. When those interactions go wrong, and a student employee is terminated, managers and supervisors need to be aware of the need to grant student employees due process. The Fifth Amendment of the U.S. Constitution applies to public institutions and on-campus student employment in stating that no person shall be "deprived of life, liberty, or property, without due process of the law." Over time, the courts have further defined each of those individual concepts and developed two kinds of due process rights that are prevalent on college and university campuses: substantive and procedural due process.

To bring about a claim violating the right to due process, a student must present a case where life, liberty, or property rights have been damaged and removed as a result of action or inaction on behalf of the institution. These aspects come to bear in a variety of ways on college campuses as described by Pauken (2015):

In higher education, liberty interests are implicated in a wide variety of cases involving student admissions, discipline, academics, degree revocation, and employment. . . . Traditional liberty interests include rights to speech, religion, assembly, and privacy. Yet much of the discussion of liberty interests in due process analysis involves the interest in persons' good names, reputations, honor, and integrity. . . . If the damages were to harm the faculty members' or students' ability to obtain employment or other lucrative opportunities, then the injured parties may have successful due process claims. . . . For students, property interests include the right to an earned benefit such as a course grade or degree or the right to stay in school. (para. 3)

Although termination of student employees must occur at times, supervisors must be aware of the tenets of due process and have a functional understanding of how to grant student employees their due rights under the law. The authors encourage supervisors, when determining the need to terminate a student employee, to remember and practice legal, developmental, and caring conversations and processes.

Tips for Supervisors
Many colleges and universities have appeal processes for students. Specifically for student employees, however, the authors recommend developmental conversations starting at the lowest level possible—hopefully with the student's supervisor and continuing from there when necessary. We highlight and reference Saginaw Valley State University's (SVSU, 2016) procedure that provides a student employee due process in resolving complaints.

- The student and the supervisor meet to discuss the issues in question.
- If the issues are not resolved at this meeting, a written appeal is sent to the Student Employment Coordinator. The Student Employment Coordinator shall submit to both parties, in writing, a suggested resolution to the issue(s).
- If either the student employee or the supervisor rejects the resolution suggested by the Student Employment Coordinator, a hearing will be arranged with the Director of Career Services. The Director shall listen to the presentation of information from each party and examine any pertinent writings submitted by both parties to determine a resolution to the issue. The Director of Career Services shall submit his/her resolution in writing to both parties.
- The student may appeal the Director of Career Services' decision to the Vice President for Student Affairs. Upon review, the decision of the Vice President will be binding upon both the student employee and SVSU. (para. 1)

Having a set process similar to SVSU's, and posting that policy in an easily accessible place for students—perhaps in a student employment handbook or website—will provide student employees and supervisors protections and resources to navigate the process. This is another area where involving experts on campus, perhaps faculty or your dean of students, can aid in developing these processes and materials.

Equal-Opportunity Policies

Similar to ensuring confidentiality, free speech, and due process for student employees, it is essential that supervisors, managers, departments, and student employment coordinators as a whole provide equal opportunity when employing students. The notion of inclusivity and the valuing of differences seem given and easy enough for supervisors; however, these notions should be obvious in practice, not just in thought.

One of the ways to ensure equality is following the hiring practices illustrated at the beginning of this chapter. Additionally, outside of the logistical hiring procedures, supervisors, managers, and departments can set the tone for inclusion; a couple of practices are highlighted here. Supervisors can craft and advertise a nondiscrimination statement in student employment handbooks, during hiring processes, or on career center websites. As an example, a nondiscrimination statement is explicitly stated in the Student Employment Handbook at Northern Michigan University (2016). Their statement follows:

> Northern Michigan University does not unlawfully discriminate on the basis of ancestry, race, color, ethnicity, religion or creed, sex or gender, gender identity, gender expression, genetic information, national origin, age, height, weight, marital status, familial status, handicap/disability, sexual orientation, military or veteran status, or any other characteristic protected by federal or state law in employment or the provision of services. NMU provides, upon request, reasonable accommodation including auxiliary aids and services necessary to afford individuals with disabilities an equal opportunity to participate in all programs and activities. Persons having Civil Rights inquiries may contact the Equal Opportunity Office at (xxx) xxx-xxxx. Students having inquiries regarding the Americans with Disabilities Act (ADA) may contact the Disability Services Coordinator at (xxx) xxx-xxxx. (para. 1)

In contrast to Northern Michigan University's statement, the University of Oregon's human resources department takes a different angle on equal opportunity with respect to student employment:

> The policy of employment of students by the University of Oregon is based on a philosophy which seeks to address and balance two equally important objectives: 1) furnishing valuable work experience for qualifying students (i.e., those who meet stated enrollment criteria) through the performance of necessary jobs on campus, and 2) providing financial assistance to students to help fund their academic studies.
>
> The former gives students the opportunity for experience in the real world of work by performing work important to the university. This work provides students with experience and skills attractive to future employers and complements their academic credentials. Student employment provides financial assistance in the form of on-campus work responsive to the student's class hours and schedule. However, a student's financial need should not override relative merit and qualifications when departments make hiring decisions. In the implementation of the university's student employment policy, no student shall be discriminated against on the basis of race, color, religion, gender, age, disability, national origin, marital or veteran status, sexual orientation, or any other extraneous considerations not directly and substantially related to effective performance (UO Policy Statement 3.600, issued 3/1/85). (University of Oregon, 2016)

Through a mixture of excellent hiring practices and making explicit statements, universities can ensure equal opportunity and nondiscrimination in student employment programs. The authors encourage supervisors and career services personnel to develop additional resources, statements, and procedures using appropriate university-specific language.

Relationships: Sexual Harassment, Intimacy, and Title IX

Similar to the other issues highlighted, understanding the laws, expectations, and resources related to personal relationships, sexual harassment, and Title IX is crucial legally, professionally, and personally. One of the best things we can do to help ourselves and our student employees is to understand the tenets of Title IX in addition to drawing a clear line of sexual harassment and amorous relationships between a supervisor and a student employee.

Sexual harassment can be very tricky and difficult for our student employees. Everyone can have different ways of communicating as well as receiving messages, but the line is clear: When the student employee or supervisor is feeling harassed—whether the other party feels or thinks the same—the interaction has crossed that threshold. However, Kaiser (in Samuels, 2015) notes that it is often very difficult for student employees to tell anyone that they are feeling sexually harassed for a multitude of reasons:

> Since student employees are typically at "the bottom of the ladder," they can often be isolated from the workplace culture and may not have close friends at their job. . . . Student workers are also likely to be targeted when they're perceived as vulnerable. Each of these factors can act as an obstacle to getting the support needed to identify sexual harassment for what it is and to gather the courage to report it. As a result, student employees may sometimes be less informed than non-students about their rights. (para. 8)

Our ethical responsibility as supervisors is thus to include sexual harassment prevention modules and related university policies, as noted earlier in this chapter, in student employee training.

Many ways to communicate university policies regarding sexual harassment are available. We note Northern Michigan University's (2016) excerpt from the Student Employment Handbook in particular for its comprehensive definition, statement of policy, and inclusion of federal law that requires supervisors and all professional staff to report any knowledge of sexual harassment on its campuses:

> Northern Michigan University is committed to creating a work environment for all faculty and staff and a living and learning environment for all students that is fair, humane, and responsible. Such an environment supports, nurtures, and rewards faculty, staff, and students on the basis of ability and work performance in their progress toward career and educational goals. Sexual harassment has no place in this environment.
>
> Harassment on the basis of sex is discrimination in violation of Title VII of the Civil Rights Act of 1964, Title IX of the Educational Amendments of 1972, and the Michigan Elliot-Larsen Civil Rights Act. Federal and state laws prohibit sex discrimination in employment and in the utilization of educational facilities and services. Sexual harassment is considered to be sex discrimination and is therefore illegal.
>
> Supervisors must document any complaints or incidents of sexual harassment in a manner consistent with the Northern Michigan University Sexual Harassment, Consensual Relations Policy. Supervisors are responsible for making employees aware that sexual harassment is defined as unwelcome sexual advances, requests for sexual favors, and other verbal or visual communication or physical conduct of a sexual nature when:

- Submission to such conduct or communication is made a term or condition, either explicitly or implicitly, of obtaining employment, public accommodations or public services, education, or housing.
- Submission to or rejection of such conduct or communication by an individual is used as a factor in decisions affecting such individual's employment, public accommodations or public services, education, or housing.
- Such conduct or communication has the purpose or effect of unreasonably interfering with an individual's employment, public accommodations or public services, education, or housing; or creating an intimidating or hostile environment in employment, public accommodations, public services, education, or housing. (para. 4)

In concluding this last legal aspect within student employment, we want to draw your attention to an excerpt from the preceding Northern Michigan University statement: "Supervisors are responsible for making (student) employees aware. . . ." The statement clearly explains sexual harassment while also indicating in general the importance of ensuring that student employees are knowledgeable about a wide range of legal and developmental issues. It is indeed the supervisor's job to educate student employees on all of their rights and responsibilities. We have no more important job than that!

Conclusion

This chapter has been primarily technical in nature, but we have tried to highlight two important things—first, that these technical and legal aspects are critical to creating and sustaining a comprehensive student employment program, and second, that these technical pieces go hand in hand with learning, development, and student success. Without ensuring proper hiring and supervisory practices or remembering and practicing proper legal procedures, employing students can be potentially dangerous to student, supervisor, and university. However, the authors believe that with new knowledge on best practices in student employment shared throughout this book, student employment programs will be mutually beneficial.

With that in mind, please pause to allow some important space for reflection:

- In what ways can you ensure confidentiality, free speech, and non-discrimination in the student employment program on your campus?
- How can you develop and ensure an environment where the student employment practitioners on your campus are both knowledgeable of their rights and resources and feel safe in consulting professional support when they have a complaint about discrimination, lack of due process, or inappropriate relationships?

Additionally, we suggest that you use your formal and informal networks of colleagues at your institution, in professional associations, and throughout the country to further increase your foundation and working knowledge when it comes to legal issues. Specifically, ask how they address legal aspects of student employment. Whether it is helping student employees learn, develop, or retain at our institutions—or supporting each other as practitioners in the supervision, management, and legal navigation of these programs—let us not forget that we are each other's most important resources.

8

STUDENT EMPLOYMENT AS A HIGH-IMPACT PRACTICE AND HALLMARK OF INSTITUTIONAL EXCELLENCE

The American Council on Education's 1937 Student Personnel Point of View (SPPV) argued,

> One of the basic purposes of higher education is the preservation, transmission, and enrichment of the important elements of culture. . . . It is the task of colleges and universities so to vitalize this and other educational purposes so as to assist the student in developing to the limits of his potentialities. . . . This philosophy imposes upon educational institutions the obligation to consider the student as a whole—his intellectual capacity and achievement, his emotional make-up, his physical condition, his social relationships, his vocational aptitude and skills, his moral and religious values, his economic resources, his aesthetic appreciations. (quoted in Rentz, 1994, pp. 67–68)

Acknowledging the challenges of the gendered language of the times in which the statement was developed, the present volume has been written very much in the spirit of the SPPV argument with regard to the purposes of higher education and the emphasis on the development of the whole student.

The opening chapter focused on the phenomenon of college student employment, with particular emphasis on on-campus employment. While noting and accepting the essential role of college employment in meeting the subsistence needs of students, the chapter also emphasized the importance of student work for use value. The next four chapters held students as the center of the narrative with discussion of the potential impact of campus employment on student development, career development, learning, and retention. The act of supervision or management was at the heart of chapter 6, and chapter 7 addressed several important contemporary ethical and legal issues related to student employment on campus. This eighth and final chapter builds on the preceding chapters but has an institutional-level focus. Here, the central consideration is how institutions might frame their student employment programs in ways that help assure the institutions are fulfilling their highest purposes and in so doing develop these programs' high-impact practices (Watson et al., 2016) as hallmarks of institutional excellence.

Three models that we believe might be particularly helpful to institutions interested in pursuing the question are identified and described in this chapter. As has been the case throughout this book, the conversation includes practical examples to illustrate what success might look like in developing and implementing a campus-wide strategy to maximize the impact of campus student employment. Next we identify broad qualities and strategies essential no matter which model a college or university might select, should the institution wish to move beyond campus employment as merely a matter of institutional convenience and remuneration for students. The chapter and the book conclude with some final thoughts and words of encouragement for student employment practitioners and institutions of higher education.

Three Models for Framing Institutional-Level Efforts

Successfully developing and implementing institutional-level programs requires identification and articulation of a model or framework for the shared effort. The process of selecting and agreeing on a model provides an opportunity for the campus to consider assumptions, beliefs, and aspirations related to the question at hand. Once a model or framework has been identified, it provides a focus for professional development programming in support of the institutional effort as well as a vehicle for action planning at the unit, college/division, and institutional level. The model or framework can also provide the basis for an appropriate assessment program through which the institutional effort can be strengthened and evaluated.

The authors of this book, while acknowledging and respecting the varieties of roles and missions played out by universities, share a belief that the single most important day-to-day function on a college campus is human learning and development. That belief is reflected in the three models identified and described in this section.

Intellectual Work

The first of the three models discussed in this section is the only one expressly intended by for the purpose of application to campus student employment. Brian Pusser (2010), writing from a critical theoretical perspective, argues that, "at its best, the university is a place for intellectual work" (p. 134), but points out that, "as constrained as it may be, intellectual work in the academy stands in stark contrast to another type of labor in higher education, the efforts of undergraduate students as employees" (p. 135). Going further, Pusser (2010) observes, "Seen from this perspective [requirements of student intellectual development], certain types of student employment may not only be unproductive in the process of developing the capacity for student intellectual work, but they may also be counterproductive" (p. 135). Pusser (2010) later suggests that

> five key factors shape a conceptual model for understanding and trans-forming student employment: (1) enabling students to develop critical intellectual identities; (2) understanding student intellectual develop-ment as a public good; (3) recognizing the centrality of intellectual work in maximizing students' life chances; (4) understanding the impact of intellectual work as powerfully shaping the norms of authority and sub-ordination that characterizes work for wages; and (5) understanding the role of student intellectual and personal development in reducing stratification and inequality in higher education and the broader society. (p. 139)

Critical Intellectual Identity

Pusser comments that low-wage jobs, in which many students are engaged, do not by their very nature nurture critical thinking. He connects this cir-cumstance to the increasing focus in public policy on the exchange value of higher education and the increasing connection between the market and higher education. Transforming student employment to foster student intel-lectual work would require that institutions recognize these pressures and purposefully work against them by constructing student employment oppor-tunities that foster critical intellectual identity.

Public Good

Noting the rise over the last three decades of the neoliberal notion of higher education as largely a private good, Pusser suggests that public reinvestment will be necessary to provide the opportunity for colleges and universities to reposition their campus employment programs to have a focus on the public good. He identifies the conceptualization and implementation of this focus by student employment practitioners as an important challenge.

Maximizing Life Chances

Pusser draws on Ralf Dahrendorf's construct of *life chances* in which Dahrendorf (as cited in Pusser, 2010) defines them as

> the possibility of individual transformation through "patterns of social organization at once social and structural" (p. 29). Life chances are shaped by options (possibilities or choices) and constraints (bonds or obligations) that shape the ability to maximize opportunities. Both options and constraints are shaped by social structures and processes, history, culture, and social status. (p. 141)

Pusser contends that if higher education student employment programs were structured to maximize life chances, their focus would not be on the mere exchange of labor to support attendance. Rather, they would see a student's intellectual work as an opportunity to advance both student development and public good.

Norms of Authority Relations

Nodding to the extensive body of work on higher education as a site of reproduction of social norms, Pusser comments that little discussion has been given to student employment programs as a center of such activity. He identifies higher education as a place in which conflict plays out between social reproduction and social mobility and posits that "these analyses can be extended to argue that postsecondary student employment is also a site of contest between the reproduction of norms of the workplace and higher education as a site for emancipatory student intellectual work" (Pusser, 2010, p. 142).

Reducing Stratification and Inequality

Higher education is an engine for both reinforcing stratification and inequality and for challenging them. Hence, Pusser (2010) comments, "Depending on whether they raise or constrain consciousness, and the degree to which they empower students to make personal and collective choices about social justice, both student intellectual work and employment for wages have the potential to shape stratification and inequality" (p. 142).

Pusser lays out several necessary steps in order for the model of student intellectual work to move from theory to practice. These include student employment practitioners keeping in mind the difference between intellectual work and student employment, reimagining the role of student employment with regard to student development, and committing to funding student attendance in ways other than student employment. In discussing moving from theory to practice in pursuing transformational intellectual work programs for students, Pusser outlines the potential of such a program (see Table 8.1).

Principles of Good Practice

The second model highlighted is Chickering and Gamson's (1987) seven principles of good practice in undergraduate education. Supported by the American Association of Higher Education and the Education Commission for the States, Chickering and Gamson's (1987) work is intended as

TABLE 8.1
Potential for Pusser's Model of Transformative Student Intellectual Work

	On Campus for Wages[a]	On Campus, Volunteer[b]	Off-Campus for Wages[c]	Off-Campus Volunteer	Service-Learning[d]
Maximizes critical intellectual development	Some potential	High potential	Low potential	High potential	High potential
Promotes the public good characteristics of higher education	High potential	Some potential	Low potential	High potential	High potential
Maximizes the development of positive life chances	Some potential	Some potential	Low potential	High potential	High potential
Restructures authority relations	Low potential	Some potential	Low potential	High potential	Some potential
Contributes to the reduction of stratification and inequality	Some potential	Some potential	Low potential	Some potential	Some potential

[a]This category refers primarily to students covered by federal work-study funding or institutional work-study programs.
[b]Volunteer work may be institutionally mediated but is uncompensated and not for academic credit.
[c]This category refers primarily to employment other than that provided by federal work-study funding.
[d]Here service-learning is understood as off-campus student work that produces public benefits and provides students with academic credit.
Source. Pusser (2010, p. 150). Copyright © Stylus Publishing, LLC. Reprinted with permission.

"guidelines for faculty members, students, and administrators—with support from state agencies and trustees—to improve teaching and learning" (p. 3). Chickering and Gamson (1987) note, "An undergraduate education should prepare students to understand and deal intelligently with modern life. What better place to start but in the classroom and on our campuses?" (p. 3).

As the title of their work suggests, Chickering and Gamson (1987) identify seven principles of practice to foster undergraduate learning. Those principles are listed and briefly described in the following sections.

Encourage Contact Between Students and Faculty

Like Pusser, Chickering and Gamson identify the interaction between student and faculty member (both inside and outside the classroom) as important. They mention increased motivation, perseverance, commitment, and reflection as potential benefits to students of such interactions.

Develop Reciprocity and Cooperation Among Students

Among the benefits of reciprocity and cooperation in learning identified by Chickering and Gamson are increased involvement, sharpened thinking, and deepened understanding. Particularly interesting for the purposes of our discussion, Chickering and Gamson (1987) observe, "Good learning, like good work, is collaborative and social" (p. 3). Our point exactly.

Use Active Learning Techniques

Chickering and Gamson (1987) explain, "They [students] must talk about what they are learning, write about it, relate it to past experiences, apply it to their daily lives. They must make what they learn part of themselves" (p. 4). Here again, they point to the possibilities of learning outside the classroom, and they specifically mention cooperative job programs as one venue for active learning.

Give Prompt Feedback

Chickering and Gamson (1987) point out the importance of feedback to students in establishing baseline levels of knowledge and competency, formative feedback during learning, and summative feedback as evaluation and to foster further reflection. They stress, "Assessment without timely feedback contributes little to learning" (Chickering & Gamson, 1987, p. 4).

Emphasize Time on Task

According to Chickering and Gamson (1987), "There is no substitute for time on task" (p. 4). It may be arguable that there is no substitute, but it is nearly irrefutable that greater time on task has a positive impact on learning in college (Mayhew, Rockenbach, Bowman, Seifert, & Wolniak, 2016). They share that time management is an important skill for success in life, one that many students have yet to master.

Communicate High Expectations

High expectations are helpful for all learners. Chickering and Gamson (1987) posit that the benefit of high expectations is derived both when high expectations are communicated to students by faculty and institutions and when faculty and institutions are clear about holding high expectations of themselves.

Respect Diverse Talents and Ways of Learning

"People bring different talents and styles of learning to college. . . . Students need the opportunity to show their talents and learn in ways that work for them" (Chickering and Gamson, 1987, p. 5).

Although Chickering and Gamson focus their work on what takes place in the classroom and in the context of the formal curriculum, the authors of this book ask why not extend the principles to cocurricular learning? In particular in the case of our discussion, why not include student employment programs in the mix?

Effective Educational Practices

The third and final model highlighted in this chapter is premised on Kuh, Kinzie, Schuh, and Whitt's (2010) work on Documenting Effective Educational Practices (DEEP). Sponsored by the American Association for Higher Education, the DEEP project identified higher education institutions that exceeded expectations for student success based on projections using input variables from their student bodies. The DEEP team then studied these institutions to identify what environmental factors might help account for their strong performance. After analyzing the data from these studies, the DEEP team identified six features shared by the institutions in the study group. The features are identified and briefly discussed in the following paragraphs.

A Living Mission and Lived Educational Philosophy

The DEEP institutions all demonstrated a living mission and lived educational philosophy. Kuh and colleagues (2010) describe two characteristics that provided evidence of this feature: "(1) clearly articulated educational purposes and aspirations, (2) a coherent, relatively well understood philosophy that guides how we do things here" (p. 25).

An Unshakeable Focus on Student Learning

The DEEP institutions had a deep and sustained focus on learning. Four streams of practice characterizing these learning environments are: "(1) valuing undergraduate learning, (2) experimenting with engaging pedagogies, (3) demonstrating a cool passion for talent development, and (4) making time for students" (Kuh et al., 2010, p. 65).

Environments Adapted for Educational Enrichment
The settings, campus populations, and institutional characteristics varied among the DEEP schools. Yet they had in common that "students, faculty, and administrators at every one of the 20 DEEP schools believe their location and campus setting are advantages in terms of student learning" (Kuh et al., 2010, p. 91). These institutions both capitalize on their locations and create spaces, on campus and off, to foster learning and focus community members on learning.

Clearly Marked Pathways to Student Success
Kuh and colleagues (2010) noted that the colleges and universities in their study did two things particularly well with regard to guiding students to success, and they labeled these two qualities *acculturation* and *alignment*. They described the former as teaching students "what the institution values, what successful students do in their context, and how to take advantage of the institutional resources for their learning," and the latter as making available "what students need when they need it, and [having] responsive systems in place to support teaching, learning, and student success" (Kuh et al., 2010, p. 110).

An Improvement-Oriented Ethos
Likening the DEEP schools to the learning organizations described by Peter Senge (1990) or the institutions identified by Jim Collins (2011) as being on the good-to-great pathway, Kuh and colleagues (2010) observe that these institutions "seem to be in a perpetual learning mode—monitoring where they are, what they are doing, where they want to go, and how to maintain momentum toward positive change" (p. 133). They particularly point out a can-do commitment on these campuses marked by a willingness to take on big ideas, dedication of limited resources to such efforts, an internal motivation for improvement, and an openness to explore and adapt ideas from other institutions to their campus opportunities.

Shared Responsibility for Educational Quality and Student Success
In-contrast to Chickering and Gamson's (1987) nearly exclusive focus on students and faculty, Kuh and colleagues (2010) speak to a shared responsibility of students, staff, and faculty for assuring educational quality and student success. Kuh and colleagues (2010) speak to both the importance of engagement by those in key leadership positions and the importance of individuals making day-to-day "small gestures that create and sustain a caring community for students" (p. 157). They also point out "effective partnerships among those who have the most contact with students—faculty and student affairs professionals—fuel the collaborative spirit and positive attitude characterizing these campuses" (Kuh et al., 2010, p. 157).

The work of Kuh and colleagues (2010) on the DEEP project, like that of Chickering and Gamson (1987) on the principles of good practice in undergraduate learning, does not directly address itself to student employment. However, both models, along with Pusser's, have much to offer if we look to student employment programs as centers of student learning and success.

What Might Success Look Like?

Barr and McClellan (2011), in discussing models for budgeting, note that "hybrids are hot" (p. 77) when it comes to models that campuses typically employ. The authors of this book are working in that spirit when we suggest that an institution interested in establishing its student employment program as a high-impact practice (Watson et al., 2016) and hallmark of institutional excellence might do well to draw from all three models discussed in this chapter.

An institution might incorporate Pusser's thoughts on the institution and its student employment program as centers of conflict between social reproduction and social mobility. This conflict could be made explicit and drawn forward into the campus conversations about developing the student employment program, and the same could be done as part of the training program used for preparing students for campus employment opportunities. Similarly, the institution could adopt as integral to its efforts the notion of maximizing life chances through its student employment program. This includes reshaping student employment opportunities so as to promote intellectual work wherever possible rather than merely doing tasks for the convenience of the institution. Finally, and perhaps the most challenging, an institution could refashion its financial aid programs to deemphasize work as an element of affording attendance and instead commit itself to fund-raising for scholarship support, which would allow students to pursue student employment opportunities as a matter of intellectual work and public good.

Solidly grounding the institution's student employment program in Pusser's notion of transformative change for campus employment, the institution could then turn to the work of Chickering and Gamson's principles for matters of technical implementation and ongoing operation at the unit or program level. The authors of this book are more drawn to a broader notion of staff and faculty as playing important roles (e.g., the work of Kuh et al., 2010), but a high degree of personal engagement between supervisor and student employee is doubtlessly essential to fostering student learning, development, and success. This interaction ought to be focused on helping the students connect their student employment to their life experiences and goals, as well as to their ongoing learning in the formal curriculum. These conversations ought to also be encouraged among student employees, encouraging them to collectively bring forward ideas on how to better connect their work to unit and university success and empowering them as coleaders for institutional improvement. Student employment opportunities are active learning opportunities as long as they are shaped as teaching and learning experiences. If there is a high degree of engagement between supervisors and student employees, as well as among student employees as a group of the sort discussed here, and if student employment is constructed as an opportunity to advance intellectual work, then there ought to be ample opportunity to be aware of the strengths and interests of student employees and to find ways to bring those into the student employment experience.

The characteristics of the DEEP institutions as described by Kuh and colleagues (2010) offer a blueprint for institutional-level implementation and operation. Practical steps could include the following:

- development and adoption of a mission that is focused on human learning and development and education as a public good
- emphasis on opportunities for high-quality interactions between staff and faculty with students focused on learning and future success
- commitment to student employment as intellectual work and to work opportunities and work spaces designed to promote that goal
- development of student employment opportunities that serve the public good and connect students to the campus community
- clear linkage between student employment opportunities and student success, including connections with career and life aspiration development
- specific learning and success goals for student employment programs and a culture of assessment that assures collecting, analyzing, and sharing data and findings with a focus on continuous improvement
- fostering a shared sense of pride and ownership between students, staff, and faculty for student employment as a high-impact practice (Watson et al., 2016) and hallmark of individual and institutional achievement.

Imagine an institution having a student employment program developed with the hybrid model described and which incorporates the following characteristics:

- clear linkage to the institutional mission with its focus on learning and development and notion of higher education as a public good

- a financial aid program where support for student employment serves to foster learning experiences in addition to helping cover some part of cost of attendance
- donor support for student employment that fosters student learning and success as well as makes meaningful connections between students and community
- supervision of student employees viewed as an act of teaching and learning with development and reward programs commensurate with the role
- recruitment for student employment positions in which learning outcomes and opportunities for coleadership are highlighted
- explicit linkages between formal curriculum and cocurricular learning in student employment (e.g., communication, management, ethics, conflict studies, psychology, sociology, or others) with faculty engaged as partners in identifying linkages and helping develop student employment practitioners so that they can help students identify and reflect on those linkages
- assessment of learning, development, and impact on student success fully implemented and integrated into institutional assessment and reporting
- learning and development through student employment documented through cocurricular transcript
- student employees invited to participate as members of institutional planning efforts related to student employment and student success

It would be understandable if at this point a reader were wondering whether such a program is possible or feasible, given the investment of effort it would take to develop and implement a student employment program of the type described. Answering that question requires one to consider what the potential benefits might be of such an investment. It does not require much of a stretch to see that a student employment program with the characteristics here could promote student learning and retention; develop deeper relationships across campus among students, staff, and faculty; strengthen connections between campus and community; produce more graduates who are more satisfied with their student experience; develop graduates who employers or graduate and professional programs find more attractive; help recruit new students; and help attract greater support from legislators, donors, and other funding entities. We believe it would be fair to describe such a program as a high-impact practice (Watson et al., 2016) and hallmark of institutional excellence, and we argue that it could be well worth the time and effort of any institution to pursue such a program.

Qualities and Strategies

Three models or frameworks and a suggested hybrid of the three have been discussed here as a way of moving ahead, but institutions wishing to create a student employment program as a high-impact practice (Watson et al., 2016) and hallmark of institutional excellence have other models from which to select. For example, the list of high-impact practices identified by Watson and colleagues (2016), which was shared in chapter 3, might serve as a framework that is readily applicable in a variety of institutional settings. There are seven qualities, however, that the authors feel ought to be sought after as part of consideration of the model upon which to build institutional efforts.

First and foremost, any model ought to focus on students. This might include a focus on student learning and development, student success, student financial security, or some other aspect of the student experience. This approach may seem self-evident, but consider for a moment that far too many of our current student employment programs are focused on institutional convenience or necessity with relatively little attention to the student, other than an accumulation of policies and procedures related to hiring, payroll, and separation.

The second quality, closely related to the first, is that the focus on students ought to extend to incorporating the notion of student as cocreator of the experience with agency and responsibility. Simply treating students as the object of action or beneficence holds very little promise for powerful practice.

The third quality suggested as important in any potential model is its incorporation of high-quality and meaningful relationships between student employment practitioners and student employees. These relationships might be characterized as centering on teaching and learning. They might be thought of as mentor and protégé relationships. Some might characterize them as coaching relationships. Whatever the construct, the core of the matter will be the human interaction.

The fourth quality to be valued in any model is a focus on connecting the student employment experience to both the student's personal context and the broader institutional experience. Whatever the desired outcomes of the institutional effort represented in a student employment program, the likelihood of those outcomes being advanced is heightened when the program is connected in meaningful ways rather than being an isolated add-on in the likely already busy lives of student employees and student employment practitioners.

The fifth desirable quality of any model being considered as the basis for an institutional-level student employment program is that the model acknowledges and addresses higher education and the student experience as complex social phenomenon shaped at the individual level by personal circumstances. The model selected ought to be aligned with institutional beliefs regarding the role or roles of higher education in society and the nature of the student experience in higher education.

The sixth quality for a model is that it ought to be rooted thoughtfully in theories and models of practice that are purposefully and consistently applied throughout. These theories and models adopted should be aligned with the mission and other characteristics of the institution, appropriate for the students being served, and substantive enough to stand critical inquiry and the test of time.

The seventh quality of a desirable model is that it must have caring as an embedded and essential value. Knowledge of theory or adroitness of application are not solely sufficient. According to a recent study of 30,000 college graduates by the Gallup Organization (Gallup Organization, 2014), the simple act of caring matters a great deal. According to this study, the odds of being engaged at work after graduation more than doubled for graduates who were emotionally supported during college. These same graduates were close to three times as likely to be thriving in their well-being. Graduates who reported having an emotional attachment to their institution were 4.1 times as likely to report having a mentor who encouraged them, and 2.4 times as likely to have had a job or internship that enabled them to apply classroom learning in real-world environments.

A number of strategies could also be helpful to student employment practitioners and institutions in pursuing the development and implementation of a student employment program. Perhaps no single strategy is more important than that of purposefulness when considering institutional change (Barr et al., 2014). Purposefulness, or intentionality, ought to go hand in hand with consistency of effort. The work colleges discussed in chapter 1 serve as excellent models of purposefulness and consistency in higher education when it comes to student employment programs as a centerpiece of institutional effort.

Being explicit is also very important. Why are you engaged in bringing about this change? What are the assumptions at hand? How will the effort to develop student employment as a high-impact practice (Watson et al., 2016) and hallmark of institutional excellence support other institutional priorities? Will the effort conflict in any way with other priorities? What resources (financial, human, data, and facilities) will be required for the effort?

Closely related to being explicit is being specific. Exactly what are the goals for the program? How will the program be assessed? Who will be involved in evaluating the program's success? How will such evaluations be communicated to shareholders on campus and beyond?

Although this chapter is focused at the institutional level, it may not be possible, or even advisable, to try to move to an institution-wide program in one step. It might be helpful to take an incremental approach with a pilot program involving a few of the units on campus that are major centers for student employment. These are often administrative units, but the campus library is frequently one of the largest employers of students and is typically situated in academic affairs. Starting with a few partners may help in getting a program off the ground, and it is much easier to bring future partners into a proven success than a speculative venture. If the decision is made to pursue an incremental or pilot strategy, it is important to build a program that can be replicated across a variety of units on campus. Avoid tailoring the program too narrowly.

Finally, whether launching a pilot or an institution-wide program, be sure to engage key allies in the development and implementation process. Those allies include units with large numbers of student employees, career services, financial aid offices, human resources, faculty colleagues, student leaders, and student employees. It may also be helpful to include representatives from development and alumni affairs. Also, depending on the model adopted as the foundation, colleagues in student leadership development can be very helpful in the effort.

Conclusion

Throughout the chapters in this book, we have attempted to make the case that college student employment can and should be a central element in any higher education institution's efforts to support student learning, development, and success. We have focused our discussion on employment on campus, but this is not to say that higher education should not extend consideration of this question to also working to better connect employment off campus to these same institutional goals. We have also focused our discussion on undergraduates, but similar consideration can be given to student employment for graduate and professional students.

An additional point to consider when giving thought to ways in which to strengthen student employment programs is the potential of such programs to become tools for recruitment of students. "Recent surveys reinforce the notion that students are placing an increased emphasis on the employment-related benefits of post-secondary education" (Townsley, 2013, para. 1), with nearly 90% of incoming freshmen in a 2012 study saying being able to get a better job is an important reason for attending college. A robust student employment program that offers meaningful development and outcomes documented by the institution could be very attractive to students looking for a better pathway to future career success.

Whether focused on learning, development, retention, career development, or some other desirable outcome, it is important to note that students may understand the tangible benefits of campus employment as a convenient way to earn money. They may, however, miss the other, less tangible benefits. Student employment practitioners will need to make those benefits more transparent to students and highlight them in ways that students will notice (Educational Advisory Board, 2015).

Those of us in higher education know that significant numbers of students are working while enrolled in college. The authors also know that evidence regarding the relationship between student employment and important learning, development, and retention outcomes is mixed. Further, models are available that hold promise for strengthening those outcomes through changes in our student employment programs. As McGinniss (2014) wryly observes, "Students are not sea monkeys where they hit the water and start swimming and growing" (para. 12). Hopefully, as a result of reading this book and giving thought to the students and institutions you serve, we have encouraged you to consider the ways in which you might provide leadership in transforming student employment in your unit and on your campus.

REFERENCES

ACT. (2013). *National collegiate retention and persistence to degree rates.* Author. Retrieved from https://www.ruffalonl.com/documents/shared/Papers_and_Research/2013/ACT_persistence_2013.pdf

Albaneso, V. A. (2012). *An exploration of current practices in curricular design of resident assistant training programs* (Doctoral dissertation). Retrieved from http://ecommons.luc.edu/luc_diss/360

Albertine, S. (2011). Systemic change for student success: Goals and lessons of the LEAP states' initiative. *Peer Review, 13*(2). Retrieved from https://www.aacu.org/publications-research/periodicals/systemic-change-student-success-goals-and-lessons-leap-states

Allen, E., Hubain, B., Hunt, C., Lucero, S., & Stewart, S. (2012, May). Implementing racial identity development theories in the classroom. *Proceedings of the Race Matters: 2012 Diversity Summit.* Retrieved from http://www.racialequitytools.org/resourcefiles/Race%20Matters_%20Implementing%20Racial%20Identity%20Development%20Theories%20into%20the%20Classroom.pdf

American College Personnel Association. (n.d.). *History of ACPA.* Retrieved from http://www.myacpa.org/history

Anderson, L. W., & Krathwohl, D. (Eds.). (2001). *A taxonomy for learning, teaching, and assessing: A revision of Bloom's taxonomy of educational objectives.* Boston, MA: Allyn & Bacon.

Anderson, S. K., Wagoner, H. T., & Moore, K. G. (2005). Ethical choice: An outcome of being, becoming, and doing. In P. Williams & S. K. Anderson (Eds.), *Law and ethics of coaching* (pp. 41–61). Hoboken, NJ: John Wiley & Sons.

Arnett, J. J. (2000). Emerging adulthood: A theory of development from the late teens through the twenties. *American Psychologist, 55*(5), 469–480.

Arnett, J. J. (2006). Emerging adulthood: Understanding the new way of coming of age. In J. J. Arnett & J. L. Tanner (Eds.), *Emerging adults in America: Coming of age in the 21st century* (pp. 3–19). Washington, DC: American Psychological Association.

Arnett, J. J. (2010, September 21). *The agenda with Steve Paikin: Jeffrey Jensen Arnett, emerging adulthood.* Retrieved from https://www.youtube.com/watch?v=Y_f8DmU-gQQ

Arum, R., & Roksa, J. (2011). *Academically adrift: Limited learning on college campuses.* Chicago, IL: University of Chicago Press.

Association of American Colleges & Universities. (2011). *The LEAP vision for learning: Outcomes, practices, impact, and employers' views.* Washington, DC: Author.

Association of American Colleges & Universities. (2014). *About LEAP*. Retrieved from http://www.aacu.org/leap

Association of American Colleges & Universities. (n.d.). *VALUE*. Retrieved from https://www.aacu.org/value

Astin, A. W. (1975). *Preventing students from dropping out*. San Francisco, CA: Jossey-Bass.

Astin, A. W. (1984). Student involvement: A developmental theory for higher education. *Journal of College Student Personnel, 25*(4), 518–529.

Astin, A. W. (1993). *What matters in college? Four critical years revisited*. San Francisco, CA: Jossey-Bass.

Astin, A. W. (2011, February 14). In 'Academically Adrift', data don't back up sweeping claim. *The Chronicle of Higher Education*. Retrieved from http://www.chronicle.com/article/Academically-Adrift-a/126371/

Astin, H. S., & Antonio, A. L. (2000, November/December). Building character in college. *About Campus*, 3–7.

Bar-On, R. (1997). *The Emotional Quotient Inventory (EQ-i): A test of emotional intelligence*. Toronto, ON: Multi-Health Systems.

Barr, M. J., & McClellan, G. S. (2011). *Budgets and financial management in higher education*. San Francisco, CA: Jossey-Bass.

Barr, M. J., McClellan, G. S., & Sandeen, A. (2014). *Making change happen in student affairs: Challenges and strategies for professionals*. San Francisco, CA: Jossey-Bass.

Barrett, J. (2012, October). *The Internet of things: Where the web and the physical world meet* [Video]. Retrieved from http://tedxtalks.ted.com/video/The-Internet-of-Things-Dr-John

Bauer, T. N. (2010). *Onboarding new employees: Maximizing success*. SHRM Foundation's Effective Practice Guidelines Series. Retrieved from https://www.shrm.org/about/foundation/products/documents/onboarding%20epg-%20final.pdf

Baum, S. (2010). Student work and the financial aid system. In L. W. Perna (Ed.), *Understanding the working college student: New research and its implications for policy and practice* (pp. 3–20). Sterling, VA: Stylus.

Baxter Magolda, M. (1992). Co-curricular influences on college students' intellectual development. *Journal of College Student Development 33*(3), 203–213.

Baxter Magolda, M. (1999). Constructing adult identities. *Journal of College Student Development, 40*(6), 629–644.

Baxter Magolda, M. (2003). Identity and learning: Student affairs' role in transforming higher education. *Journal of College Student Development, 44*(1), 231–247.

Baxter Magolda, M. (2008). Three elements of self-authorship. *Journal of College Student Development, 49*(4), 269–284.

Baxter Magolda, M., & King, P. M. (2008). Toward reflective conversations: An advising approach that promotes self-authorship. *Peer Review, 10*(1). Retrieved from https://www.aacu.org/publications-research/periodicals/toward-reflective-conversations-advising-approach-promotes-self

Billett, S., & Choy, S. (2011). Cooperative and work-integrated education as a pedagogy for lifelong learning. In R. K. Coll & K. E. Zegwaard (Eds.), *International handbook for cooperative and work-integrated education: International perspectives of theory, research, and practice* (2nd ed., pp. 25–30). Lowell, MA: World Association for Cooperative Education.

Bilodeau, B. L., & Renn, K. A. (2005). Analysis of LGBT development models and implications for practice. In R. L. Sanlo (Ed.), *Sexual orientation and gender identity: Research, policy, and personal perspectives* (New Directions in Student Services, 11, pp. 25–39). San Francisco, CA: Jossey-Bass.

Blimling, G. S. (2010). *The resident assistant: Applications and strategies for working with college students in residence halls* (7th ed.). Dubuque, IA: Kendall/Hunt.

Blimling, G. S. (2013). Challenges of assessment and student affairs. In J. H. Schuh (Ed.), *Selected contemporary assessment issues* (New Directions for Student Services, 142, pp. 5–14). San Francisco, CA: Jossey-Bass.

Blustein, D. L. (2006). *The psychology of working: A new perspective for career development, counseling, and public policy.* New York, NY: Routledge.

Blustein, D. L. (2011). A relational theory of working. *Journal of Vocational Behavior, 79,* 1–17.

Borin, J. (2001). Training, supervising, and evaluating student information assistants. *Reference Librarian, 34*(72), 195–206.

Borrego, S. E. (2006). Mapping the learning environment. In R. P. Keeling (Ed.), *Learning Reconsidered 2: Implementing a campus-wide focus on the student experience* (pp. 11–16). Washington, DC: American College Personnel Association (ACPA), Association of College and University Housing Officers–International (ACUHO-I), Association of College Unions–International (ACU-I), National Academic Advising Association (NACADA), National Association of Campus Activities (NACA), National Association of Student Personnel Administrators (NASPA), and National Intramural–Recreational Sports Association (NIRSA).

Bourdieu, P. (1984). *Distinction: A social critique of the judgment of taste.* Cambridge, MA: Harvard University Press.

Boyatzis, R. E. (2006). An overview of intentional change from a complexity perspective. *Journal of Management Development, 25*(7), 607–623.

Bradberry, T., & Greaves, J. (2009). *Emotional intelligence 2.0.* San Diego, CA: TalentSmart.

Brainyquote. (2017). *Michael Jordan quotes.* Retrieved from https://www.brainyquote.com/quotes/quotes/m/michaeljor127660.html

Braxton, J. M. (Ed.). (2000). *Reworking the student departure puzzle.* Nashville, TN: Vanderbilt University Press.

Brigham Young University. (2014). *Student retention.* Retrieved from http://www.byu.edu/hr/?q=managers/hiring-students/student-retention

Bright, J. (2013). *Chaos theory of careers explained* [Video]. Retrieved from https://www.youtube.com/watch?v=BL2wTkgBEyk/

Bright, J., & Pryor, R. (2005). The chaos theory of careers: A user's guide. *Career Development Quarterly, 53*(4), 291–305.

Brint, S. (1994). *In an age of experts: The changing roles of professionals in politics and public life.* Princeton, NJ: Princeton University Press.

Brown, M. E., & Treviño, L. K. (2014). Do role models matter? An investigation of role modeling as an antecedent of perceived ethical leadership. *Journal of Business Ethics, 122*(4), 587–598.

Brown, S. D., & Gore, P. A., Jr. (1994). An evaluation of interest congruence indices: Distribution characteristics and measurement properties. *Journal of Vocational Behavior, 45*, 310–327.

Buchanan, L. (2007, November 1). The art of the huddle: How to run a prompt, painless, and productive morning meeting. *Inc.* Retrieved from http://www.inc.com/magazine/20071101/the-art-of-the-huddle.html

Busby, K., & Robinson, B. G. (2012). Developing the leadership team to establish and maintain a culture of evidence in student affairs. In M. M. Culp & G. J. Dungy (Eds.), *Building a culture of evidence in student affairs: A guide for leaders and practitioners* (pp. 35–39). Washington, DC: NASPA.

Business-Higher Education Forum. (2013). *Promoting effective dialogue between business and education around the need for deeper learning.* Washington, DC: Author.

Business-Higher Education Forum. (2014). *Educating the enabled professional: 2014 annual report.* Washington, DC: Author.

Busteed, B. (2014, September 25). The blown opportunity. *Inside Higher Education.* Retrieved from https://www.insidehighered.com/views/2014/09/25/essay-about-importance-mentors-college-students

Career (n.d.a). In *English Oxford Living Dictionaries.* Retrieved from http://en.oxforddictionaries.com/definition/career

Career (n.d.b). In *Merriam-Webster's Online Dictionary.* Retrieved from http://www.merriam-webster.com/dictionary/career

Careersnz. (2017). *Super's theory.* Author. Retrieved from https://www.careers.govt.nz/practitioners/career-practice/career-theory-models/supers-theory/

Carnegie Mellon University. (n.d.). *Information for on-campus employers.* Retrieved from http://www.cmu.edu/career/employers/on-campus_employers/

Cass, V. C. (1984). Homosexual identity formation: Testing a theoretical model. *Journal of Sex Research, 40*(2), 219–235.

Chickering, A. W. (2006, May–June). Every student can learn—if. . . . *About Campus 11*(2), 9.

Chickering, A. W. (2010, Summer). Our purposes: Personal reflections on character development and social responsibility in higher education. *Liberal Education, 96*(3), 54.

Chickering, A. W., & Gamson, Z. F. (1987, March). Seven principles for good practice in undergraduate education. *AAHE Bulletin, 39*(7), 3–7.

Chickering, A. W., & Reisser, L. (1993). *Education and identity* (2nd ed.). San Francisco, CA: Jossey-Bass.

Chickering, A. W., and Schlossberg, N. K. (1995). *Getting the most out of college.* Needham Heights, MA: Allyn and Bacon.

Chickering, A. W., & Stamm, L. (2002, May/June). Making our purposes clear. Getting beyond conflicting priorities and competing interests. *About Campus, 7*(2), pp. 30–32.

Chur-hansen, A., & McLean, S. (2006). On becoming a supervisor: The importance of feedback and how to give it. *Australasian Psychiatry, 14*(1), 67–71.

Clark, J. E., & Eynon, B. (2009). E-portfolios at 2.0: Surveying the field. *Peer Review, 11*(1), 18–23.

College of William & Mary. (n.d.). *About student employment and federal work study.* Retrieved from http://www.wm.edu/admission/financialaid/docs/SEWS/Confidentiality%20Agreement.pdf

Collegiate Employment Research Institute. (2016). *T-shaped professionals.* Retrieved from http://www.ceri.msu.edu/t-shaped-professionals/

Collins, J. (2011). *Good to great.* New York, NY: Harper Business.

Coomes, M. D., & Gerda, J. J. (2016). "A long and honorable history": Student affairs in the United States. In G. S. McClellan and J. Stringer (Eds.), *The handbook of student affairs administration*, 4th ed. (pp. 3–23). San Francisco, CA: Jossey-Bass.

Cote, J. E. (2014). The dangerous myth of emerging adulthood: An evidence-based critique of a flawed developmental theory. *Applied Developmental Science, 18*(4), 177–188.

Cross, W. E., Jr. (1995). The psychology of nigrescence: Revising the Cross model. In J. G. Ponterotto, J. M. Casas, L. A. Suzuki, & C. M. Alexander (Eds.), *Handbook of multicultural counseling.* Thousand Oaks, CA: Sage.

Croteau, J. M., Anderson, M. D., & Vanderwal, B. L. (2008). Models of workplace sexual identity disclosure and management: Reviewing and extending concepts. *Group and Organization Management, 33*(5), 532–565.

Cruzvergara, C., & Dey, F. (2014). *10 future trends in college career services.* LinkedIn Pulse. Retrieved from https://www.linkedin.com/pulse/20140715120812-11822737-10-future-trends-in-college-career-services

Culp, M. M., & Dungy, G. J. (Eds.). (2012). *Building a culture of evidence in student affairs: A guide for leaders and practitioners.* Washington, DC: NASPA.

D'Abate, C. P., & Eddy, E. R. (2008). Mentoring as a learning tool: Enhancing the effectiveness of an undergraduate business mentoring program. *Mentoring & Tutoring: Partnership in Learning, 16*(4), 363–378.

Dalton, J. C., Crosby, P. C., Valente, A., & Eberhardt, D. (2009). Maintaining and modeling everyday ethics in student affairs. In G. S. McClellan & J. Stringer (Eds.), *The handbook of student affairs administration* (3rd ed., pp. 166–186). San Francisco, CA: Jossey-Bass.

De Walt, P. S. (2011). In search of an authentic African American and/or Black identity: Perspectives of first-generation, U.S.-born Africans attending a predominantly White institution. *Journal of Black Studies, 42*(3), 479–503.

Denecke, D., Feaster, K., Okahana, H., Allum, J., & Stone, K. (2016). *Financial education: Developing high-impact programs for graduate and undergraduate students.* Washington, DC: Council of Graduate Schools.

Dezube, D. (2016). How to interview students and entry level candidates. *Monster. com.* Retrieved from http://hiring.monster.com/hr/hr-best-practices/recruiting-hiring-advice/interviewing-candidates/how-to-interview-entry-level.aspx

Dominiak-Kochanek, M. (2016). A preliminary examination of identity exploration and commitment among Polish adolescents with and without motor disability: Does disability constitute diversity in identity development? *International Journal of Disability, Development, and Education, 63*(3), 357–368.

Duhon, D. L., Bushardt, S. C., & Daniel, F. (2006). An experiential exercise in giving feedback to enhance student skills. *Decision Sciences Journal of Innovative Education, 4*(1), 141–146.

Educational Advisory Board. (2015). *Reimagining experiential learning: Skill-building opportunities outside the classroom.* Washington, DC: Author.

Ellinger, A. D. (2002). Mentoring in contexts: The workplace and educational institutions. In C. A. Hansman (Ed.), *Critical perspectives on mentoring: Trends and issues* (pp. 15–26). Columbus, OH: ERIC Clearinghouse on Adult, Career, and Vocation Education.

Ely, R. J. (1995). The power in demography: Women's social constructions of gender identity at work. *Academy of Management Journal, 30*(3), 589–634.

Ender, S. C. (1984). Student paraprofessionals within student affairs: The state of the art. In S. C. Ender & R. Winston (Eds.), *Using students as paraprofessional staff* (New Directions in Student Services 27, pp. 3–21). San Francisco, CA: Jossey-Bass.

Eraut, M. (2004). Informal learning in the workplace. *Studies in Continuing Education, 26*(2), 247–273.

Ernst & Young. (2015). *Mentoring: At the crossroads of education, business, and community: The power and promise of private sector engagement in youth mentoring.* New York, NY: Author.

Evans, N. J. (1987). A framework for assisting student affairs staff in fostering moral development. *Journal of Counseling and Development, 66*, 191–194.

Ewell, P. T. (1997, December). Organizing for learning: A new imperative. *AAHE Bulletin, 50*(4), 3–6.

Eynon, B. & Gambino, L. M. (2017). *High-impact ePortfolio practice: A catalyst for student, faculty, and institutional learning.* Sterling, VA: Stylus.

Fatum, B. (2013). *Health classrooms, emotional intelligence, and brain research. Six Seconds.* Retrieved from http://www.6seconds.org/2013/05/29/healthy-classrooms-emotional-intelligence-and-brain-research/

Federal Student Aid. (n.d.a). Federal work-study jobs help students earn money to pay for college or career school. Washington, DC: U.S. Department of Education. Retrieved from https://studentaid.ed.gov/sa/types/work-study

Federal Student Aid. (n.d.b). Job location and development. Washington, DC: U.S. Department of Education. Retrieved from https://ifap.ed.gov/sfahandbooks/attachments/Vol6Ch6.pdf

Feller, R. W., & Whichard, J. (2005). *Knowledge nomads and the nervously employed.* Austin, TX: Pro-Ed Publishers.

Finley, A., & McNair, T. (2013). *Assessing underserved students' engagement in high-impact practices.* Washington, DC: Association of American Colleges & Universities.

Foubert, J. D. (2013). *Lessons learned: How to avoid the biggest mistakes made by college resident assistants* (2nd ed.). Abingdon, UK: Taylor and Francis.

Foundation for Individual Rights in Education. (2016). *Private universities.* Retrieved from https://www.thefire.org/spotlight/public-and-private-universities/

Freeman, S. C. (1993). Donald Super: A perspective on career development. *Journal of Career Development, 19*(4), 261.

Freidson, E. (1990). Labors of love in theory and practice. In E. Erickson and S. P. Vallas (Eds.), *The nature of work: Sociological perspectives* (pp. 149–161). New Haven, CT: Yale University Press.

Gaff, J. (2002). The disconnect between graduate education and the realities of faculty work: A review of recent research. *Liberal Education, 88*(3), 6–12. Retrieved from https://www.aacu.org/publications-research/periodicals/disconnect-between-graduate-education-and-realities-faculty-work

Gallegos, P. V., & Ferdman, B. M. (2007). Identity orientation of Latinos in the United States: Implications for leaders and organizations. *Business Journal of Hispanic Research, 1*(1), 27–41.

Gallup Organization. (2014). *Great jobs, great lives: The 2014 Gallup-Purdue index report.* Washington, DC: Author.

Gardner, P. D., & Perry, A. L. (2011). The role of cooperative and work-integrated education in graduate transition into the workforce. In R. K. Coll & K. E. Zegwaard (Eds.), *International handbook for cooperative and work-integrated education: International perspectives of theory, research, and practice* (2nd ed., pp. 313–320). Lowell, MA: World Association for Cooperative Education.

Garringer, M., Kupersmidt, J., Rhodes, J., Stelter, R., & Tai, T. (2015). *Elements of effective practices for mentoring* (4th ed.). Boston, MA: MENTOR: The National Mentoring Partnership.

Gehman, J., Treviño, L. K., & Garud, R. (2013). Values work: A process study of the emergence and performance of organizational values practices. *Academy of Management Journal, 56*(1), 84–112.

Gelatt, H. B. (1989). Positive uncertainty: A new decision-making framework for counseling. *Journal of Counseling Psychology, 36,* 252–256.

Gewirtz, D. (2009, October 22). A short history of jobs. *CNN.com.* Retrieved from http://ac360.blogs.cnn.com/2009/10/22/a-short-history-of-jobs/

Gilligan, C. (1982). *In a different voice.* Cambridge, MA: Harvard University Press.

Gilligan, C. (1995). Hearing the difference: Theorizing connection. *Hypatia, 10*(2), 120–127.

Gleason, P. M. (1993). College student employment, academic progress, and post-college labor market success. *Journal of Student Financial Aid, 23*(2), 5–14.

Goleman, D. (1995). *Emotional intelligence: Why it can matter more than IQ.* New York, NY: Bantam Books.

Goodman, J., Schlossberg, N., & Anderson, M. (2006). *Counseling adults in transition.* New York, NY: Spring Publishing.

Gottfredson, G. D. (1999). John L. Holland's contributions to vocational psychology: A review and evaluation. *Journal of Vocational Behavior, 55,* 15–40.

Gottfredson, G. D., & Johnstun, M. L. (2009). John Holland's contributions: A theory-ridden approach to career assistance. *Career Development Quarterly, 58*(2), 99–107.

Grenny, J. (2015, August 6). The key to giving and receiving negative feedback. *Harvard Business Review.* Retrieved from https://hbr.org/2015/08/the-key-to-giving-and-receiving-negative-feedback

Hagedorn, L. S. (2005). How to define retention: A new look at an old problem. In A. Seidman (Ed.), *College student retention* (pp. 81–100). Westport, CT: Praeger.

Hall, K. (2002). *Free speech on public college campuses overview. First Amendment Center.* Retrieved from http://www.firstamendmentcenter.org/free-speech-on-public-college-campuses/

Handman, D. (2013, August 14). Social media policies in the workplace: It's all about respect. *Bloomberg BNA.* Retrieved from http://www.bna.com/social-media-policies-in-the-workplace-its-all-about-respect/

Hansen, M. T., & Oetinger, B. V. (2001, March 20). Introducing T-shaped managers: Knowledge management's next generation. *Harvard Business Review, 79*(3). Retrieved from https://hbr.org/2001/03/introducing-t-shaped-managers-knowledge-managements-next-generation.

Hansman, C. A. (2002). Diversity and power in mentoring relationships. In C. A. Hansman (Ed.), *Critical perspectives on mentoring: Trends and issues* (pp. 39–48). Columbus, OH: ERIC Clearinghouse on Adult, Career, and Vocation Education.

Harke, B. (June, 22, 2010). High school to college transition, part 1: The freshman myth. *Huffingtonpost.com.* Retrieved from http://www.huffingtonpost.com/brian-harke/high-school-to-college-tr_b_620043.html

Harms, P. L., & Roebuck, D. B. (2010). Teaching the art and craft of giving and receiving feedback. *Business Communications Quarterly, 73*(4), 413–431.

Hart Research Associates. (2006). *How should colleges prepare students to succeed in today's global economy?* Washington, DC: Association of American Colleges & Universities.

Hart Research Associates. (2013). *It takes more than a major: Employer priorities for college learning and student success.* Washington, DC: Association of American Colleges & Universities.

Hart Research Associates. (2015). *Falling short? College learning and career success.* Washington, DC: Association of American Colleges & Universities.

Hartung, P. J. (2013). Career construction. In R. W. Feller (Ed.), *Ten ideas that changed career development* (p. 11). Broken Arrow, OK: National Career Development Association.

Held, V. (2014). The ethics of care as normative guidance: Comment on Gilligan. *Journal of Social Philosophy, 45*(1), 107–115.

Henderson, E., Berlin, A., Freeman, G., & Fuller, J. (2002). Twelve tips for promoting significant event analysis in undergraduate medical students. *Medical Teacher, 24*(2), 121–124.

Hesser, G., & Gotlieb, P. (2014). Building experiential education into the mission and values of your institution: New contexts. In G. Hesser (Ed.), *Strengthening experiential education: A new era* (pp. 17–31). Mount Royal, NJ: National Society for Experiential Education.

Hodges, D. (2011). The assessment of student learning and cooperative and work-integrated education. In R. K Coll & K. E. Zegwaard (Eds.), *International handbook for cooperative and work-integrated education: International perspectives of theory, research, and practice* (2nd ed., pp. 53–62). Lowell, MA: World Association for Cooperative Education.

Holland, J. L. (1959). A theory of vocational choice. *Journal of Counseling Psychology, 6*(1), 35–44.

Holland, J. L. (1968). Explorations of a theory of vocational choice: Longitudinal study using a sample of typical college students. *Journal of Applied Psychology Monograph Supplement, 52,* 1 (Part Two).

Holland, J. L. (1985). *Making vocational choices: A theory of vocational personalities and work environments* (2nd ed.). Englewood Cliffs, NJ: Prentice Hall.

Holland, J. L. (1996). Exploring careers with a typology: What we have learned and some new directions. *American Psychologist, 51*(4), 397–407.

Holland, J. L. (1997). *Making vocational choices: A theory of vocational personalities and work environments* (3rd ed.). Lutz, FL: PAR, Inc.

Holliday, W., & Nordgren, C. (2005). Extending the reach of librarians: Library peer mentor program at Utah State University. *College Research Librarian News, 66*(4), 282–284.

Hossler, D., & Bean, J. P. (1990). *The strategic management of college enrollments.* San Francisco, CA: Jossey-Bass.

Igo, S. E. (2011, September/October). *Academics adrift?* American Association of University Professors. Retrieved from https://www.aaup.org/article/academics-adrift#.WBSl7-ErKRs

Indiana University–Purdue University Fort Wayne. (2016). *FERPA information—tutorial & quiz.* Retrieved from https://www.ipfw.edu/offices/registrar/faculty/ferpa.html

Inkster, R. P., & Ross, R. G. (1995). *The internship as partnership: A handbook for campus-based coordinators and supervisors.* Raleigh, NC: National Society for Experiential Education.

Inkster, R. P., & Ross, R. G. (1998). *The internship as partnership: A handbook for business, nonprofits, and government agencies.* National Society for Experiential Education. Retrieved from www.nsee.org

Iowa State University Center for Learning and Teaching. (n.d.). *Revised Bloom's taxonomy.* Retrieved from http://www.celt.iastate.edu/teaching/effective-teaching-practices/revised-blooms-taxonomy

Iqbal, N. (2016, November 7). Delhi metro gears up for driverless trains. *Indian Express.* Retrieved from http://indianexpress.com/article/india/india-news-india/dmrc-delhi-driverless-metro-trains-3740621/

IUPUI Office of Student Employment. (2015). Home page. Retrieved from https://employment.iupui.edu/

Jackson, M. L., Moneta, L., & Nelson, K. A. (2009). Effective management of human capital in student affairs. In G. S. McClellan & J. Stringer (Eds.), *The Handbook of Student Affairs Administration* (3rd ed., pp. 357–380). San Francisco, CA: John Wiley & Sons.

Jacoby, D. (1998). *Laboring for freedom: A new look at the history of labor in America.* Armonk, NY: Sharpe.

Jaffe, E. J. (2015, April 13). *The case for driverless trains, by the numbers.* CityLab. com. Retrieved from http://www.citylab.com/tech/2015/04/the-case-for-driverless-trains-by-the-numbers/390408/.

Jensen, U. (2011). *Factors influencing student retention in higher education: Summary of influential factors in degree attainment and persistence to career or further education for at-risk / high educational need students.* Pacific Policy Research Center. Honolulu, HI: Kamehameha Schools–Research & Evaluation Division.

Johnson, C. E. (2006). *Ethics in the workplace: Tools and tactics for organizational transformation.* Thousand Oaks, CA: Sage.

Johnstone, D. B. (1999). Financing higher education: Who should pay? In P. G. Altbach, R. O. Berdahl, & P. J. Gumport (Eds.), *American higher education in the twenty-first century* (pp. 347–369). Baltimore, MD: Johns Hopkins University Press.

Jones, S. R. (1997). Voices of identity and difference: A qualitative exploration of the multiple dimensions of identity development in women college students. *Journal of College Student Development, 38*(4), 376–386.

Jones, S. R. (2009). Constructing identities at the intersections: An autoethnographic exploration of multiple dimensions of identity. *Journal of College Student Development, 50*(3), 287–304.

Jones, S. R., & McEwen, M. K. (2000). A conceptual model of multiple dimensions of identity. *Journal of College Student Development, 41*(4), 405–414.

Josselson, R. (1996). *Revising herself: The story of women's identity from college to midlife.* New York, NY: Oxford University Press.

Kanoy, K. (2011). *Emotional intelligence and graduation four years later.* (Unpublished manuscript.) Raleigh, NC: William Peace University.

Kansas State University Office of Assessment. (2016). *Action verb list.* Retrieved from http://www.k-state.edu/assessment/toolkit/outcomes/action.html

Kasworm, C. (2010). Adult workers as undergraduates: Significant challenges for higher education policy and practice. In L. W. Perna (Ed.), *Understanding the working college student: New research and its implications for policy and practice* (pp. 23–42). Sterling, VA: Stylus.

Kaufman, C. (n.d.). *The history of higher education in the United States.* WorldWideLearn. Retrieved from http://www.worldwidelearn.com/education-advisor/indepth/history-higher-education.php

Kaufman, P., & Feldman, K. A. (2004). Forming identities in college: A sociological approach. *Research in Higher Education, 45*(5), 463–496.

Keeling, R. P. (Ed). (2004). *Learning reconsidered: A campus-wide focus on the student experience*. Washington, DC: National Association of Student Personnel Administrators and American College Personnel Association.

Keeling, R. P. (Ed). (2006). *Learning reconsidered 2: Implementing a campus-wide focus on the student experience*. Washington, DC: American College Personnel Association (ACPA), Association of College and University Housing Officers–International (ACUHO-I), Association of College Unions–International (ACU-I), National Academic Advising Association (NACADA), National Association of Campus Activities (NACA), National Association of Student Personnel Administrators (NASPA), and National Intramural–Recreational Sports Association (NIRSA).

Keeling, R. P., & Underhile, R. (2007, June). *Putting learning reconsidered into practice: Developing and assessing student learning outcomes*. Presented at the Learning Reconsidered Institute, St. Louis, MO. Retrieved from http://assessment.uncg .edu/academic/docs/learning_reconsidered_institute_workshop.pdf

Keith, P. M. (2007). Barriers and nontraditional students' use of academic and social services. *College Student Journal, 41*(4), 1123–1127.

Kim, J. (2001). Asian American identity development theory. In C. L. Wijeyesinghe & B. W. Jackson, III (Eds.), *New perspectives on racial identity development: A theoretical and practical anthology* (pp. 67–90). New York, NY: New York University Press.

Kincaid, R. (n.d.). *An informal history of student employment*. Supervisor's Manual Unpublished. Retrieved from https://www.brockport.edu/academics/career/ supervisors/informal.html

Kincaid, R. (Ed). (1996). *Student employment: Linking college and the workplace*. Retrieved from http://digitalcommons.brockport.edu/cgi/viewcontent.cgi?articl e=1000&context=bookshelf

King, J. E. (2003). Nontraditional attendance and persistence: The cost of students' choices. In J. E. King, E. L. Anderson, & M. E. Corrigan (Eds.), *Changing student attendance patterns: Challenges for policy and practice* (New Directions for Higher Education, 121; pp. 69–83). San Francisco, CA: Jossey-Bass.

King, M. A. (2014). Ensuring quality in experiential education. In G. Hesser (Ed.), *Strengthening experiential education: A new era* (pp. 103–163). Mount Royal, NJ: National Society for Experiential Education.

King, M. A., & Sweitzer, H. F. (2014). Towards a pedagogy of internships. *Journal of Applied Learning in Higher Education, 6*, 37–60.

King, P. M., & Kitchener, K. S. (2004). Reflective judgment: Theory and research on the development of epistemic assumptions through adulthood. *Educational Psychologist, 39*(1), 5–18.

Kish-Gephart, J., Detert, J., Treviño, L. K., Baker, V., & Martin, S. (2014). Situational moral disengagement: Can the effects of self interest be mitigated? *Journal of Business Ethics, 125*(2), 267–285.

Kohlberg, L. (1973). The claim to moral adequacy of a highest stage of moral judgment. *Journal of Philosophy, 70*(18), 50–66.

Kohlberg, L. (1975). Moral education for a society in moral transition. *Educational Leadership, 33*, 46–54.

Kolb, D.-A. (1976). Management and the learning process. *California Management Review, 18*(3), 27–42.

Kolb, D.-A. (1984). *Experiential learning: Experience as the source of learning and development.* Englewood Cliffs, NJ: Prentice Hall.

Komives, S. R., & Carpenter, S. (2009). Professional development as lifelong learning. In G. S. McClellan & J. Stringer (Eds.), *The Handbook of Student Affairs Administration* (3rd ed.; pp. 371–387). San Francisco, CA: John Wiley & Sons.

Krathwohl, D. R. (2007). A revision of Bloom's taxonomy: An overview. *Theory Into Practice, 41*(4), 212–218.

Kroger, J., & Marcia, J. E. (2011). The identity statuses: Origins, meanings, and interpretations. In S. J. Schwartz, K. Luyckx, & V. L. Vignoles (Eds.), *Handbook of identity theory and research* (pp. 31–53). New York, NY: Springer.

Krumboltz, J. D. (2009). The happenstance learning theory. *Journal of Career Assessment, 17*(2), 135–154.

Kruse, K. (2014, August 12). How to receive feedback and criticism. *Forbes.com.* Retrieved from http://www.forbes.com/sites/kevinkruse/2014/08/12/how-to-receive-feedback-and-criticism/#63268409400b

Kuh, G. D. (1995). The other curriculum: Out-of-class experiences associated with student learning and personal development. *Journal of Higher Education, 6*(2), 123–155.

Kuh, G. D. (2003, March/April). What we're learning about student engagement from NSSE. *Change,* 25–32.

Kuh, G. D. (2008). *High-impact educational practices: What they are, who has access to them, and why they matter.* Washington, DC: Association of American Colleges & Universities.

Kuh, G. D. (2016). Making learning meaningful: Engaging students in ways that matter to them. In M. M. Watts (Ed.), *Finding the why: Personalizing learning in higher education* (New Directions for Teaching and Learning, 145, pp. 49–56) San Francisco, CA: Jossey-Bass.

Kuh, G. D., Kinzie, J., Buckley, J. A., Bridges, B. K., & Hayek, J. C. (2006). What matters to student success: A review of the literature. National Postsecondary Education Cooperative. Retrieved from nces.ed.gov/npec/pdf/kuh_team_report.pdf

Kuh, G. D., Kinzie, J., Buckley, J. A., Bridges, B. K., & Hayek, J. C. (2007). Piecing together the student success puzzle: Research, propositions, and recommendations. *ASHE Higher Education Report, 32*(5).

Kuh, G. D., Kinzie, J., Schuh, J. H., & Whitt, E. J. (2010). *Student success in college: Creating conditions that matter.* San Francisco, CA: Jossey-Bass.

Kuh, G., & Love, P. (2004). A cultural perspective on student departure. In J. M. Braxton (Ed.), *Reworking the student departure puzzle* (pp. 196–212). Nashville, TN: Vanderbilt University Press.

Kuh, G. D., O'Donnell, K., & Reed, S. (2013). *Ensuring quality and taking high-impact practices to scale.* Washington, DC: Association of American Colleges & Universities.

Kuk, L. (2009). The dynamics of organizational models within student affairs. In G. S. McClellan & J. Stringer (Eds.), *The Handbook of Student Affairs Administration* (3rd ed.; pp. 313–332). San Francisco, CA: John Wiley & Sons.

LaGuardia Community College. (n.d.). *What makes a good e-portfolio?* Retrieved from www.eportfolio.lagcc.cuny.edu/scholars/documents/Rubric.doc

Landrum, R. E. (2012, May 17). *Perry's scheme of intellectual development* [Video]. Retrieved from https://www.youtube.com/watch?v=qpAZMK3Pct0

Larkin, I., & Beatson, A. (2014). Blended delivery and online assessment: Scaffolding student reflections in work-integrated learning. *Marketing Education Review, 24*(1), 9–14.

Lederman, D. (2013, May 20). Less academically adrift? *Inside Higher Education.* Retrieved from https://www.insidehighered.com/news/2013/05/20/studies-challenge-findings-academically-adrift

Letzring, T. D., & Wolff, L. A. (2009). Student worker free speech on the public campus: A new twist to a constant issue. *College Student Affairs Journal, 28*(1), 5–21.

LeVan, K. S., & King, M. E. (2016, November 14). Teaching students how to manage feedback. *Faculty Focus.* Retrieved from https://www.facultyfocus.com/articles/teaching-and-learning/teaching-students-manage-feedback/

Levine, M. (2005, February 18). College graduates aren't ready for the real world. *The Chronicle of Higher Education, 51*(24), B11.

Lewis, J. S. (2008, June 20). Student workers can learn more on the job. *Chronicle of Higher Education,* A56.

Linn, R. (2001). The insights of Kohlberg and Gilligan into moral development and counseling. *Social Behavior and Personality, 29*(6), 593–600.

Lipsky, S. A. (2008). *A training guide for college tutors and peer educators.* London, UK: Pearson.

Luzzo, D. A. (1995). The relationship between career aspiration–current occupation congruence and the career maturity of undergraduates. *Journal of Employment Counseling, 32,* 132–140.

Luzzo, D. A., & Ward, B. E. (1995). The relative contributions of self-efficacy and locus of control to the prediction of vocational congruence. *Journal of Career Development, 21,* 307–317.

Mackes, M. (2017). *Principle for professional practice.* NACE Center for Career Development and Talent Acquisition. Retrieved from https://www.naceweb.org/career-development/organizational-structure/principles-for-professional-practice/

Makela, J. P., & Rooney, G. S. (2012). *Learning outcomes assessment step-by-step: Enhancing evidence–based practice in career services.* Broken Arrow, OK: National Career Development Association.

Manley, L., & Holley, R. P. (2014). Hiring and training work-study students: A case study. *College & Undergraduate Libraries, 21*(7), 76–89.

Marquardt, M. (2005). *Leading with questions: How leaders find the right solutions by knowing what to ask.* San Francisco, CA: John Wiley & Sons.

Matthews, D., Zanville, H., & Duncan, A. G. (2016). *The emerging learning system: Report on the recent convening and new directions for action.* Indianapolis, IN: Lumina Foundation.

Maslow, A. H. (1943). A theory of human motivation. *Psychological Review, 50(4)*, 370–396.

Mayhew, M. J., Rockenbach, A. N., Bowman, N. A., Seifert, T. A., & Wolniak, G. C. (2016). *How college affects students: 21st-century evidence that higher education works.* San Francisco, CA: Jossey-Bass.

McCormick, A. C., Moore, J. V., III, & Kuh, G. D. (2010). Working during college: Its relationship to student engagement and educational outcomes. In L. W. Perna (Ed.), *Understanding the working college student: New research and its implications for policy and practice* (pp. 179–212). Sterling, VA: Stylus.

McDaniel, M. A., & Snell, A. F. (1999). Holland's theory and occupational information. *Journal of Vocational Behavior, 55*, 74–85.

McGinniss, J. (2014, April 9). *Working at learning: Developing an integrated approach to student development.* In The Library With The Lead Pipe. Retrieved from http://www.inthelibrarywiththeleadpipe.org/2014/working-at-learning-developing-an-integrated-approach-to-student-staff-development/

McGlone, C. A., and Rey, S. (2012). Managing, leading, and supervising student employees and staff. In G. S. McClellan, C. King, & D. L. Rockey Jr. (Eds.), *The handbook of college athletics and recreation administration* (pp. 159–174). San Francisco, CA: Jossey-Bass.

McKee, A. (2015, April 24). How to help someone develop emotional intelligence. *Harvard Business Review.* Retrieved from https://hbr.org/2015/04/how-to-help-someone-develop-emotional-intelligence.

McNair, T. B. (2016). *Making excellence inclusive through experiential learning: Intentionality, innovation, and implementation.* Keynote presentation at the annual conference of the National Society for Experiential Education, San Antonio, TX.

Mentoring Partnership. (2016). *Peer mentor handbook.* Pittsburgh, PA: The Mentoring Partnership of Southwestern Pennsylvania. Retrieved from http://www.mentoringpittsburgh.org/

Merriam, S. B., Caffarella, R. S., & Baumgartner, L. M. (2007). *Learning in adulthood: A comprehensive guide* (3rd ed.). San Francisco, CA: John Wiley & Sons.

Miller, R., & Morgaine, W. (2009). The benefits of using e-portfolios for students and faculty in their own words. *Peer Review, 11*(1), 8–12.

Mind Tools. (n.d.). *SMART goals: How to make your goals achievable.* Retrieved from https://www.mindtools.com/pages/article/smart-goals.htm

Mitchell, K. E., Levin, A. L., & Krumboltz, J. D. (1999). Planned happenstance: Constructing unexpected career opportunities. *Journal of Counseling and Development, 77*(2), 115–124.

Moll, L. C. (2005, May 12). *Funds of knowledge.* Retrieved from https://www.youtube.com/watch?v=aWS0YBpGkkE.

Moll, L. C., Amanti, C., Neff, D., & Gonzalez, N. (1992). Funds of knowledge for teaching: Using a qualitative approach to connect homes and classrooms. *Theory Into Practice, 21*(2), 132–141.

Morrish, J. (2015, February 24). Where does the word career come from? *Management Today*. Retrieved from http://www.managementtoday.co.uk/article/133408/does-word-come-from

Mueller, C. W. (2000). Work motivation. In E. Borgatta & R. Montgomery (Eds.), *Encyclopedia of sociology* (2nd ed.; pp. 3261–3279). New York, NY: Macmillan.

Nasir, M., & Masrur, R. (2010). An exploration of emotional intelligence of the students of IIUI in relation to gender, age, and academic achievement. *Bulletin of Education and Research, 32*, 37–51.

National Association of Colleges and Employers. (2015a). *Career readiness defined*. Retrieved from http://www.naceweb.org/knowledge/career-readiness-competencies.aspx

National Association of Colleges and Employers. (2015b). *Job Outlook 2016: The attributes employers want to see on new college graduates' resumes*. Retrieved from http://www.naceweb.org/career-development/trends-and-predictions/job-outlook-2016-attributes-employers-want-to-see-on-new-college-graduates-resumes/

National Association of Colleges and Employers. (2016). *Job Outlook 2016 Spring Update*. Retrieved from https://www.odu.edu/content/dam/odu/offices/cmc/docs/nace/2016-spring-update.pdf

National Association of Colleges and Employers. (2010). *Job Outlook 2010*. Bethlehem, PA: Author. Retrieved from www.naceweb.org

National Center for Education Statistics. (2008). *Digest of Education Statistics*. Washington, DC: U.S. Department of Education.

National Center for Education Statistics. (2016). *Digest of Education Statistics, 2015*. Washington, DC: U.S. Department of Education.

National Center for O'NET Development. (n.d.). *Home page*. Retrieved from https://www.onetonline.org/

National Institute for Learning Outcomes Assessment. (n.d.). *NILOA Resources*. Retrieved from http://www.learningoutcomeassessment.org/NILOAResources.html

National Society for Experiential Education. (1998). *8 principles of good practice for all experiential learning activities*. Retrieved from http://www.nsee.org/8-principles

National Survey of Student Engagement. (2014). *About NSSE*. Retrieved from http://nsse.iub.edu/html/about.cfm

Nauta, M. M. (2010). The development, evolution, and status of Holland's theory of vocational personalities: Reflections and future directions for counseling psychology. *Journal of Counseling Psychology, 57*(1), 11–22.

Newton, F. B., & Enders, S. C. (2010). *Students helping students: A guide for peer educators on college campuses*. Hoboken, NJ: John Wiley & Sons.

Ni, P. (2014). 8 simple ways to avoid being manipulated. *Bright Side*. Retrieved from https://brightside.me/article/eight-simple-ways-to-avoidbeing-manipulated-11405/

Noel, L. (1996). The student employment professional: An emerging partner in student success. In R. Kincaid (Ed.), *Student employment: Linking college and the workplace* (pp. 31–36). Columbia, SC: National Resource Center for the Freshmen Year Experience and Students in Transition, University of South Carolina.

Noel-Levitz. (2010). *Enhancing student success by treating "student jobs" as "real jobs."* Coralville, IA: Author.

Northern Michigan University. (2016). *Student employment handbook.* Retrieved from https://www.nmu.edu/careerservices/student-employment-handbook-1

O'Neill, N. (2010). Internships as a high-impact practice: Some reflections on quality. *Peer Review, 12*(4). Retrieved from https://www.aacu.org/publications-research/periodicals/internships-high-impact-practice-some-reflections-quality

Ortiz, A. M., & Waterman, S. J. (2016). The changing student population. In G. S. McClellan & J. Stringer (Eds.), *The handbook for student affairs administration* (4th ed.; pp. 267–286). San Francisco, CA: Jossey-Bass.

Pascarella, E. T., & Terenzini, P. T. (2015). *How college affects students* (2nd ed.). San Francisco, CA: Jossey-Bass.

Patton, W., & Creed, P. A. (2001). Developmental issues in career maturity and career decision. *Career Development Quarterly, 49,* 336–351.

Pauken, P. D. (2015). Due process, substantive and procedural. *Law and Higher Education.* Retrieved from http://lawhigheredu.com/47-due-process-substantive-and-procedural.html.

Peña, E. V., Stapleton, L. D., & Schaffer, L. M. (2016). Critical perspectives on disability identity. In E. S. Abes (Ed.), *Critical perspectives on student development theory* (New Directions for Student Services, 154, pp. 85–96). San Francisco, CA: Jossey-Bass.

Perna, L. W. (2010). Introduction. In L. W. Perna (Ed.), *Understanding the working college student: New research and its implications for policy and practice* (pp. xiii–xxvi). Sterling, VA: Stylus.

Perna, L. W., Cooper, M., & Li, C. (2007). Improving educational opportunities for students who work. In E. P. St. John (Ed.), *Confronting education inequality: Reframing, building understanding, and making change. Readings on equal education* (Vol. 22, pp. 11–12). New York: AMS Press.

Perozzi, B. (2009). Introduction. In B. Perozzi (Ed.), *Enhancing student learning through college employment* (pp. vii–xiv). Bloomington, IN: Association of College Unions International.

Perry, W. G., Jr. (1970). *Forms of intellectual and ethical development in the college years.* New York, NY: Holt, Rinehart & Winston.

Phillips, P. (2016). The power of giving feedback: Outcomes from implementing an online peer assessment system. *Issues in Accounting Education, 31*(1), 1–15.

Phinney, J. S., & Ong, A. D. (2007). Conceptualization and measurement of ethnic identity: Current status and future directions. *Journal of Counseling Psychology, 54*(3), 271–281.

Pidgeon, M. (2008). Pushing against the margins: Indigenous theorizing of "success" and retention in higher education. *Journal of College Student Retention: Research, Theory & Practice, 10*(3), 339–360.

Pink, D. H. (2001). *Free agent nation: The future of working for yourself.* New York, NY: Warner Business Books.

Pistilli, M. D., & Gardner, J. N. (2015). Theories of retention and student success. John N. Gardner Institute for Excellence in Undergraduate Education Symposium on Student Retention, January 14, Costa Mesa, CA.

Pokorny, B. (2011, November 17). When are student assistants "employees" under the FLSA? *Wage & Hour Insights*. Retrieved from http://www.wagehourinsights .com/2011/11/when-are-student-assistants-employees-under-the-flsa/

Pope, M., & Sveinsdotir, M. (2005). Frank, we hardly knew ye: The very personal side of Frank Parsons. *Journal of Counseling and Development, 83*(1), 105–115.

Porter, C. J., & Dean, L. A. (2015). Meaning making: Identity development of Black undergraduate women. *NASPA Journal About Women in Higher Education, 82*(2), 125–139.

Pusser, B. (2010). Of a mind to labor: Reconceptualizing student work and higher education. In L. W. Perna (Ed.), *Understanding the working college student: New research and its implications for policy and practice* (pp. 134–154). Sterling, VA: Stylus.

Reese, M., & Levy, R. (2009). Assessing the future: E-portfolio trends, usage, and options. *EDUCAUSE Center for Applied Research Bulletin, 2009*(4), 1–12.

Reilly, K. (2014, April 8). Job descriptions that win: Three outstanding examples. LinkedIn. Retrieved from https://business.linkedin.com/talent-solutions/blog/2014/ 04/job-descriptions-that-win-3-outstanding-examples#!

Renn, K. A. (2008). Research on biracial and multiracial identity development: Overview and synthesis. In K. A. Renn and P. Shang (Eds.), *Biracial and multiracial students* (New Directions in Student Services, 123, pp. 13–21). San Francisco, CA: Jossey-Bass.

Renn, R., Steinbauer, R., Taylor, R., & Detwiler, D. (2014). School-to-work transition: Mentor career support and student career planning, job search intentions, and self-defeating job search behavior. *Journal of Vocational Behavior, 85*, 422–432.

Rentz, A. L. (Ed.) (1994). *Student affairs: A profession's heritage*. Washington, DC: American College Personnel Association.

Rest, J. (1984). Research on moral development: Implications for training psychologists. *Counseling Psychologist, 12*(3), 19–29.

Reznowski, G., & McManus, B. (2009). You *can* take it with you? Student library employees, e-portfolios, and "edentity" construction. *Electronic Journal of Academic and Special Librarianship, 10*(3). Retrieved from http://southernlibrarianship .icaap.org/content/v10n03/reznowski_g01.html

Ribeiro, F. M., & Lubbers, M. (2015). Funds of knowledge and epistemic authority in higher education. In F. M. Ribeiro, Y. Politis, & B. Culum, *New voices in higher education research and scholarship* (pp. 38–69). Hershey, PA: IGI Global.

Rieske, L. J., & Benjamin, M. (2015). Utilizing peer mentor roles in learning communities. In M. Benjamin (Ed.), *Learning communities from start to finish* (New Directions for Student Services, 149, pp. 67–78). San Francisco, CA: Jossey-Bass.

Rockey, D. L., & Barcelona, R. J. (2012). An overview of fitness and recreation in collegiate settings. In G. S. McClellan, C. King, & D. L., Rockey Jr. (Eds.), *The handbook of college athletics and recreation administration* (pp. 21–43). San Francisco, CA: Jossey-Bass.

Rosenberg, M., & McCullough, B. C. (1981). Mattering: Inferred significance and mental health. *Research in Community and Mental Health, 2,* 163–182.

Ross, R., & Sheehan, B. J. (2014). Integrating experiential education into the curriculum. In G. Hesser (Ed.), *Strengthening experiential education: A new era* (pp. 34–64). Mount Royal, NJ: National Society for Experiential Education.

Rowh, M. (2014, May). 8 simple rules for managing student workers. *University Business, 16*(5), 40–43.

Ryan, M., & Ryan, M. (2013). Theorising a model for teaching and assessing reflective learning in higher education. *Higher Education Research and Development, 32*(2), 244–257.

Saginaw Valley State University. (2016). *Student employee due process/appeals.* Retrieved from http://www.svsu.edu/careerservices/oncampusstudentemployment/studentinfo/

Salovey, P., & Mayer, J. D. (1990). Emotional intelligence. *Imagination, Cognition, and Personality, 9*(3), 185–211.

Samuels, A. (2015, March 6). Know your rights: What students can do about sexual harassment in the workplace. *USA Today College.* Retrieved from http://college .usatoday.com/2015/03/06/know-your-rights-what-students-can-do-about-sexual-harassment-in-the-workplace/

Sanders Thompson, V. L. (2001). The complexity of African-American racial identification. *Journal of Black Studies, 32*(2), 155–165.

Savickas, M. L. (1997). Career adaptability: An integrative construct for life-span, life-space theory. *Career Development Quarterly, 45*(3), 247–259.

Savickas, M. L. (2013). Constructing careers: Actors, agents, and authors. *Counseling Psychologist, 41*(4), 179.

Savickas, M. L., Nota, L., Rossier, J., Dauwalder, J. P., Duarte, M. E., Guichard, J., Soresi, S., Van Esbroeck, R., & van Vianen, A. E. M. (2009). Life-designing: A paradigm for career construction theory. *Journal of Vocational Behavior, 75,* 239–250.

Savoca, M. (2016). *Campus employment as a high-impact practice: Relationship to academic success and persistence of first-generation college students* (Doctoral dissertation). Retrieved from https://dspace.library.colostate.edu/bitstream/handle/10217/173353/Savoca_colostate_0053A_13463.pdf?sequence=1&isAllowed=y

Savoca, M., & Zalewski, U. (2016). The campus as a learning laboratory: Transforming student employment. *Journal of Student Employment, 15*(1), 3–11.

Schlee, R. P. (2000). Mentoring and the professional development of business students. *Journal of Management Education, 24*(3), 322–337.

Schlossberg, N. K. (1989). Marginality and mattering: Key issues in building community. In D. C. Roberts (Ed.), *Designing campus activities to foster a sense of community* (New Directions for Student Services, 48, pp. 5–15). San Francisco, CA: Jossey-Bass.

Schuh, J. H. (2016). Fiscal pressures on higher education and student affairs. In G. S. McClellan & J. Stringer (Eds.), *The handbook for student affairs administration* (4th ed.; pp. 73–94). San Francisco, CA: Jossey-Bass.

Schuh, J. H. (Ed.). (2013). Developing a culture of assessment in student affairs. In J. H. Schuh (Ed.), *Selected contemporary assessment issues* (New Directions for Student Services, 142, pp. 89–98). San Francisco, CA: Jossey-Bass.

Scrogham, E., & McGuire, S. P. (2009). Orientation, training, and development. In B. Perozzi (Ed.), *Enhancing student learning through college employment* (pp. 199–220). Indianapolis, IN: Association of College Unions International.

Seidman, A. (2005). *College student retention.* Westport, CT: American Council on Education and Praeger.

Senge, P. M. *The fifth discipline: The art and practice of the learning organization.* New York, NY: Knopf Doubleday, 1990.

Shapiro, D. N., Rios, D., & Stewart, A. J. (2010). Conceptualizing lesbian sexual identity development: Narrative accounts of socializing structures and individual decisions and actions. *Feminism and Psychology, 20*(4), 491–510.

Society for Human Resource Management. (2016, January 19). *Managing and leveraging workplace use of social media.* Retrieved from https://www.shrm.org/resourcesandtools/tools-and-samples/toolkits/pages/managingsocialmedia.aspx

Slagell, J., & Langendorfer, J. M. (2003). Don't tread on me: The art of supervising student assistants. *Serials Librarian, 44,* 279–284.

Spohrer, J. (2015, August 23). Systems thinking and T-shaped professionals [Web log]. *Service Science.* Retrieved from http://service-science.info/archives/3841

Spohrer, J., Gardner, P., & Gross, L. (2015). *A T primer: Understanding components of the T.* Retrieved from https://docs.google.com/viewer?a=v&pid=sites&srcid=b-XN1LmVkdXx0LXN1bW1pdC0yMDE1LXByZXNlbnRhdGlvbnN8Z3g6Z WNiNDRlMjk5NTkzZmFl

Spokane, A. R., & Cruza-Guet, M. C. (2005). Holland's theory of vocational personalities in work environments. In S. D. Brown & R. W. Lent (Eds.), *Career development and counseling: Putting theory and research to work* (pp. 42–70). Hoboken, NJ: John Wiley & Sons.

Stein, S. J., Book, H. E., & Kanoy, K. (2013). *The student EQ edge: Emotional intelligence and your academic and personal success.* New York, NY: Wiley.

Stony Brook University. (n.d.a). *Student employee learning outcomes.* Retrieved from http://studentaffairs.stonybrook.edu/assessment/selo/index.html

Stony Brook University. (n.d.b). *On campus employment.* Retrieved from https://career.stonybrook.edu/on-campus-employment

Stony Brook University. (2016, October 5). ESPN3 Production/Camera Operation (Basketball games). [Web post]. Retrieved from https://stonybrook.joinhand-shake.com/jobs/518062

Su, A. J. (2015, August 13). Giving feedback when you're conflict averse. *Harvard Business Review.* Retrieved from https://hbr.org/2015/08/giving-feedback-when-youre-conflict-averse

Super, D. E. (1953). A theory of vocational development. *American Psychologist, 8*(5), 185–190.

Super, D. E. (1975). Career education and career guidance for the life span and for life roles. *Journal of Career Education, 2*(2), 27–42.

Super, D. E., Savickas, M. L., & Super, C. M. (1996). The life-span, life-space approach to careers. In D. Brown & L. Brown (Eds.), *Career choice and development* (3rd ed.; pp. 121–178). San Francisco, CA: Jossey-Bass.

Swail, W. S. (2002). Higher education and the new demographics: Questions for policy. *Change, 34,* 15–23.

Swail, W. S. (2004). *The art of student retention: A handbook for practitioners and administrators.* Austin, TX: Texas State Higher Education Coordinating Board.

Sykes, C., & Dean, B. A. (2012) A practice-based approach to student reflection in the workplace during a work integrated learning placement. *Studies in Continuing Education, 35*(2), 179–192.

Tanner, J. L. (2006). Recentering during emerging adulthood: A critical turning point in life-span human development. In J. J. Arnett & J. L. Tanner (Eds.), *Emerging adults in America: Coming of age in the 21st century.* Washington, DC: American Psychological Association.

Tatum, B. (1992). Talking about race, learning about racism: The application of racial identity development theory in the classroom. *Harvard Educational Review, 62*(1), 1–24.

Thelin, J. R., Edwards, J. R., & Moyen. E. (n.d.). Higher education in the United States. *StateUniversity.com.* Retrieved from http://education.stateuniversity.com/pages/2044/Higher-Education-in-United-States.html

Thompson, M. D., & Epstein, I. I. (2013). Examining student character development within the liberal arts. *Education, 3*(1), 91-97.

Tierney, W. G. (1999). Models of minority college-going and retention: Cultural integrity versus cultural suicide. *Journal of Negro Education, 68*(1), 80–91.

Tierney, W. G. (2004). Power, identity, and the dilemma of college student departure. In J. M. Braxton (Ed.), *Reworking the student departure puzzle* (pp. 213–234). Nashville, TN: Vanderbilt University Press.

Tinsley, H. E. A. (2000). The congruence myth: An analysis of the efficacy of the person-environment fit model. *Journal of Vocational Behavior, 56,* 405–423.

Tinto, V. (1975). Dropouts from higher education: A theoretical synthesis of recent research. *Review of Educational Research, 45,* 89–125.

Tinto, V. (1993). *Leaving college: Rethinking the causes and cures of student attrition* (2nd ed.). Chicago, IL: University of Chicago Press.

Tinto, V. (1999). Taking retention seriously: Rethinking the first year of college. *NACADA Journal 19*(2), 5–9.

Towle, M., & Olsen, D. (2009). Partnering with outsourced service-providers to create learning opportunities for students. In B. Perozzi (Ed.), *Enhancing student learning through college employment* (pp. 179–198). Bloomington, IN: Association of College Unions International.

Townsley, D. (2013, July 10). Why colleges are teaching professional readiness. *Huffington Post.* Retrieved from http://www.huffingtonpost.com/debra-townsley/why-colleges-are-teaching_b_3572585.html

Trinity University. (2016, October 5). Trinity University Work Study Program 2016–2017. [Web post]. Retrieved from http://www.trinitydc.edu/hr/2016/08/16/admissions-assistant-work-study/

T-Summit. (2016). What is the T? Retrieved from http://tsummit.org/t

Tucker, B. (2014). Student evaluation surveys: Anonymous comments that offend or are unprofessional. *International Journal of Higher Education and Education Planning, 68*(3), 347–358.

Tuttle, T., McKinney, J., & Rago, M. (2005). *College students working: The choice nexus.* Bloomington, IN: Indiana Project on Academic Success (IPAS), Indiana University. Retrieved from www.indiana.edu/~ipas1/workingstudentbrief.pdf

United States Department of Labor. (2016a). *Questions and answers about the minimum wage.* Retrieved from https://www.dol.gov/whd/minwage/q-a.htm

United States Department of Labor. (2016b). *Fair Labor Standards Act Advisor.* Retrieved from http://webapps.dol.gov/elaws/whd/flsa/docs/ftsplink.asp.

United States Department of Labor. (n.d.). *My next move.* Retrieved from https://blog.dol.gov/tag/my-next-move/.

University of Oregon. (2016). *Policies and procedures: Student workers.* Retrieved from https://hr.uoregon.edu/recruit/student-employment/policy-and-procedures#Student

Ulin, D. L. (2015). "It ain't over till it's over" and other lessons from chairman Yogi Berra. *Los Angeles Times*, September 23.

University of Iowa. (2016). *Division of Student Life student employee survey summary.* Retrieved from https://vp.studentlife.uiowa.edu/initiatives/grow/how-we-grow/

University of North Carolina–Charlotte (n.d.). *Writing objectives using Bloom's taxonomy.* Retrieved from http://teaching.uncc.edu/learning-resources/articles-books/best-practice/goals-objectives/writing-objectives

Vanderbilt University Center for Teaching. (2017). *Bloom's taxonomy.* Retrieved from https://cft.vanderbilt.edu/guides-sub-pages/blooms-taxonomy/

Van Gennep, A. (1960). *The rites of passage.* Chicago, IL: University of Chicago Press.

Voss, D. (2016, August). Problem-solving module. Presented at the Stony Brook University Division of Information Technology Student Consultant Training, Stony Brook, NY.

Vrable, A. (2014, May 15). Why the morning huddle is the best meeting you'll ever have. *Sandglaz.* Retrieved from http://blog.sandglaz.com/how-to-run-a-morning-huddle-with-your-team/

Vroom, V. (1964). *Work and motivation.* New York, NY: Wiley.

Washington, M. (1996). The minority student in college: A historical analysis. In C. Turner, M. Garcia, A. Nora, & L. I. Rendón (Eds.), *Racial & ethnic diversity in higher education* (pp. 69–82). Boston, MA: Pearson.

Watson, C. E., Kuh, G. D., Rhodes, T., Penny Light, T., & Chen, H. (2016). E-portfolios: The eleventh high-impact practice. *International Journal of ePortfolio, 6*(2), 65–69.

Wenger, L. (2016, January 2). The nine commandments for supervisors. *Healthier Workplaces.* Retrieved from http://www.workforceperformancegroup.net/

Wijeysesinghe, C. L. (2001). Racial identity in multiracial people: An alternative paradigm. In C. L. Wijeysesinghe & B. W. Jackson III (Eds.), *New perspectives on racial identity development: A theoretical and practical anthology* (pp. 129–152). New York, NY: New York University Press.

Wilensky, H. L. (1964). The professionalization of everyone? *American Journal of Sociology, 70*(2), 137–158.

Wilson, L. O. (2016). Anderson and Krathwohl: Understanding the new version of Bloom's taxonomy. *The Second Principle*. Retrieved from http://thesecondprinciple .com/teaching-essentials/beyond-bloom-cognitive-taxonomy-revised/

Winston-Salem State University. (2017). *Job description bank*. Retrieved from https:// www.wssu.edu/student-life/career-development-services/student-employment/ work-study-employers/job-description-bank/index.html

Work. (2015). In *Merriam-Webster.com*. Retrieved from https://www.merriam-webster.com/dictionary/work

Work Colleges Consortium. (2014a). *About work colleges*. Retrieved from http:// www.workcolleges.org/about-work-colleges

Work Colleges Consortium. (2014b). *Meet the work colleges*. Retrieved from http:// www.workcolleges.org/node/30

Work Colleges Consortium. (2015). Retrieved from http://www.workcolleges.org/

Zegwaard, K. E., & Coll, R. K. (2011). Using cooperative education and work-integrated education to provide career clarification. *Science Education International, 22*(4), 282–291.

Zhang, L., & Haller, B. (2013). Consuming image: How mass media impact the identity of people with disabilities. *Communication Quarterly, 61*(3), 319–334.

Zhu, W., Treviño, L. K., & Zheng, X. (2016). Ethical leaders and their followers: The transmission of moral identity and moral attentiveness. *Business Ethics Quarterly, 26*(1), 95–115.

Zirkel, S., & Johnson, T. (2016). Mirror, mirror on the wall: A critical examination of the conceptualization of the study of black racial identity in education. *Educational Researcher, 45*(5), 301–311.

Ziskin, M., Torres, V., Hossler, D., & Gross, J. D. K. (2010). Mobile working students: A delicate balance of college, family, and work. In L. W. Perna (Ed.), *Understanding the working college student: New research and its implications for policy and practice* (pp. 67–92). Sterling, VA: Stylus.

ABOUT THE AUTHORS

George S. McClellan is associate professor of higher education at the University of Mississippi. He previously served as the vice chancellor for student affairs at Indiana University–Purdue University Fort Wayne (IPFW) for 10 years. Prior to joining the IPFW community, McClellan served as vice president for student development at Dickinson State University, interim director of assessment and research for campus life at the University of Arizona, and director of graduate and off-campus housing at Northwestern University. McClellan is coeditor of *The Handbook for Student Affairs Administration* (Jossey-Bass, 2009, 2016); *The Handbook for College Athletics and Recreation Management* (Jossey-Bass, 2012); *Stepping Up to Stepping Out: Preparing Students for Life After College* (Jossey-Bass, 2012); *Ahead of the Game: Understanding and Addressing Campus Gambling* (Jossey-Bass, 2006); and *Serving Native American Students in Higher Education* (Jossey-Bass, 2005). He is coauthor of *Making Change Happen in Student Affairs: Challenges and Strategies for Professionals* (Jossey-Bass, 2014); *Budgets and Financial Management in Higher Education* (Jossey-Bass, 2011, in press) and *In Search of Safer Communities: Emerging Practices for Student Affairs in Addressing Campus Violence* (Jossey-Bass, 2008). In addition, he has authored or coauthored numerous other articles and chapters on subjects related to student affairs. McClellan is active in both the National Association of Student Personnel Administrators (NASPA) and the American College Personnel Association (ACPA), having served as a member of the editorial boards for NASPA's *Journal of College and Character* and ACPA's *Journal of College Student Development*. He was a founding member of both the Administrators in Graduate and Professional Student Services and Indigenous Peoples Knowledge Communities in NASPA and past chair of the NASPA Excellence Awards program. McClellan was a member of the NASPA Foundation board during that group's successful campaign to increase its endowment to $1 million, was named in 2010 as a Pillar of the Profession by the NASPA Foundation, and received the Outstanding Contribution to Higher Education Award from NASPA Region IV-East in 2012. In addition, McClellan was named an Annuit Coeptis Senior Scholar by ACPA in 2017 and is a past recipient of that association's Outstanding Contribution to Research in American Indian Higher Education award. McClellan received his PhD in higher education from the University of Arizona (2003). Both his MSEd in higher education (1998) and BA in English and American literature (1982) were earned from Northwestern University.

Kristina (Krissy) Creager serves as the associate vice chancellor for enrollment management and student success at Indiana University–Purdue University Fort Wayne, where she has worked since July 2009. A first-generation college student, Creager found her calling to higher education during her sophomore year of undergrad and has not looked back. She has had the privilege to serve at three distinctly different institutions—large, public residential; small, private Jesuit; and mid-size, public regional. Beginning her career in academic advising and student life, and now working primarily to serve university-wide beginning students and at-risk populations, she is dedicated to the holistic development and personal success of all students. She remains involved with NASPA–Student Affairs Professionals in Higher Education, attending and presenting at annual conferences around the country and serving as a program reviewer for many years. She is also a proud member of the Alice Manicur Symposium class of 2016. Creager holds a PhD in global leadership in higher education from the Indiana Institute of Technology (2016), an MEd in student development administration from Seattle University (2009), and a BS in journalism from Northern Arizona University (2007).

Marianna Savoca is the director of career services at Stony Brook University, the flagship research campus of the State University of New York (SUNY), where she oversees a centralized comprehensive career service, including a large experiential program of internships, co-op, and community engagement, as well as on-campus student employment. Savoca is also an adjunct faculty member in the higher education administration program at Stony Brook, where she teaches courses on career counseling and external relations in higher education. Her research interests include first-generation college student success, experiential education, and career development. She has been recognized for her work with the SUNY Chancellor's Award for Excellence in Professional Service, a Fulbright Award for Administrators in International Education, the National Society for Experiential Education's (NSEE) Rising Leader Award, and the Outstanding Service Award from the Eastern Association of Colleges and Employers. Savoca serves on the board of directors of NSEE. She earned a PhD in higher education from Colorado State University (2016), an MS in higher education from Indiana University–Bloomington (1995), and a BS in liberal studies from the State University of New York, Binghamton (1989).

INDEX

AAC&U. *See* Association of
    American Colleges &
    Universities
ACPA. *See* American College
    Personnel Association
adult learners, 68
    Chickering 3*R* framework and,
        69–70
    enrollment growing for, 114
    student employment
        orientations for, 71
ALOI. *See* Assessment of Learning
    Outcomes Interventions
Alvin Community College, 161
Amanti, C., 69
American Association for Higher
    Education, 191
American College Personnel
    Association (ACPA), 6, 45,
    72–73, 87
American Council on Education
    Student Personnel Point of
    View (SPPV), 185
American Society of Training and
    Development. *See* Association
    of Talent Development
Anderson, L. W., 62
Anderson, S. K., 35–37
Antonio, A. L., 31
apprenticeships, history of, 44–45
Arendt, Hannah, 8
Arnett, Jeffrey, 15–18, 56
assessment
    ePortfolios for, 166–70

of learning outcomes, 163–66
positive restlessness for, 162
student evaluations in, 165
Assessment of Learning Outcomes
    Interventions (ALOI),
    160–61, 163–66
Association of American Colleges
    & Universities (AAC&U)
    on ePortfolios, 167
    VALUE project of, 78
    Value Rubrics of, 166
    workplace ethic rubric of, 161
Association of Talent Development
    (ATD), 144
Astin, A. W.
    I-E-O model of, 104, 108–9,
        115
    on retention, impact of, 103
    student involvement theory of,
        104, 106–7
Astin, H. S., 31
ATD. *See* Association of Talent
    Development

Barcelona, R. J., 11
Barr, M. J., 193
Baumgartner, L. M.,
    68, 82–83
Baxter Magolda, Marcia
    EI and, 117
    self-authorship and, 26–28, 56
    study by, 26–28
    three-phase conversation of, 29
Bean, J. P., 103

and work within an environment they cannot expect to mold solely through their execution of skills and strategies. Kuk and Banning offer readers a new lens for viewing leadership, one that goes beyond a focus on the behavior and values of leaders as individuals to examine how positional leaders interact with their environments to engage in leadership "in context."

Sty/us

22883 Quicksilver Drive
Sterling, VA 20166-2102

Subscribe to our e-mail alerts: www.Styluspub.com

Also available from Stylus

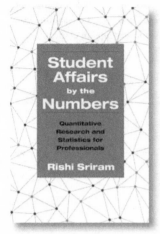

Student Affairs by the Numbers

Quantitative Research and Statistics for Professionals

Rishi Sriram

"*Student Affairs by the Numbers* couldn't arrive at a better time. The pressure from state-based performance-based funding, increased rigor from regional accrediting agencies, and an increase in a 'return-on-investment' approach to funding and program review underscores the critical importance of developing a core competence in quantitative statistics and assessment. This book is a valuable resource for student affairs professionals and graduate students who are developing research and evaluation efforts on core student affairs programs and services." —*Kevin Kruger, President of NASPA – Student Affairs Administrators in Higher Education*

Student affairs professionals need to know how to design a study, collect data, analyze data, interpret results, and present the results in an understandable manner. This book establishes the need for these skills in student affairs and then quickly moves to how to develop a research culture, how to conduct research, how to understand statistics, and concludes with how to change our research/assessment behaviors in order to make higher education better for students.

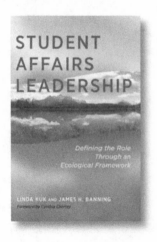

Student Affairs Leadership

Defining the Role Through an Ecological Framework

Linda Kuk and James H. Banning

Foreword by Cynthia Cherrey

"This work opens new doors into the study of leadership for the student affairs profession. 'Contextual leadership' is a developing area to be applied differently than the governmental and corporate settings. This concept, researched and aided by the theory of the ecological perspective, will help future administrators prepare and execute their leadership roles well for years to come. Kuk and Banning's research will impact and strengthen the student affairs profession." —*John R. Laws, EdD, Vice Chancellor Student Affairs, Ivy Tech Community College*

This book is addressed to aspiring and senior student affairs officers and offers a new "ecological" framework that recognizes that today's leaders are affected by factors they may not control

(Continued on preceding page)